Microservices Deployment Cookbook

Master over 60 recipes to help you deliver complete, scalable, microservice-based solutions and see the improved business results immediately

Vikram Murugesan

BIRMINGHAM - MUMBAI

Microservices Deployment Cookbook

First published: January 2017

Production reference: 1240117

Published by Packt Publishing Ltd.
Livery Place
35 Livery Street
Birmingham
B3 2PB, UK.
ISBN 978-1-78646-943-4

www.packtpub.com

Credits

Author

Vikram Murugesan

Reviewer

Kishore Kumar Yekkanti

Commissioning Editor

Kartikey Pandey

Acquisition Editor

Vijin Boricha

Content Development Editor

Amedh Gemraram Pohad

Technical Editors

Prashant Chaudhari
Vishal Kamal Mewada

Copy Editor

Madhusudan Uchil

Project Coordinator

Judie Jose

Proofreader

Safis Editing

Indexer

Pratik Shirodkar

Graphics

Kirk D'Penha

Production Coordinator

Melwyn Dsa

About the Author

Vikram Murugesan is a software architect who has over 10 years of experience building distributed systems and products. He currently works as a principal architect with Egen Solutions Inc. In his current job, he focuses on building platforms based on JVM (Java, Scala, and Groovy), big data, and cloud technologies. He is a passionate programmer and is interested in learning new technologies. He is also interested in coaching, mentoring, and building scalable teams that build great software.

I would like to take a moment to thank everyone that has been a huge support during the course of writing this book. Firstly, thanks to Mr. Raghu Potini, who motivated me to write this book and has been supportive throughout the writing process. Without his support and motivation, this book would have not been possible. Secondly, I would like to thank Mr. Andrew Leasck, who has been my inspiration since the beginning of my career. When I started writing the book, I did not know much about the publishing process or the amount of team work it needs. While working with the Packt Publishing team, they made me realize that it requires enormous amount of team effort, coordination and patience. The Packt Publishing team made it look so simple, but behind the scenes, they put so much effort and thoughts into giving life to this book. Without them, this would have not been possible. Hats off to the Packt team members that helped me during this process. Everyone has a role model in life. My father has always been my role model and an inspiration. Thanks to my father, Mr. Murugesan, who would have been really proud about this book. Special thanks to my mother, Vijayarani, wife, Subamalar, and daughther, Sreesha, who have been very patient and supportive during the course of writing this book.

About the Reviewer

Kishore Kumar Yekkanti is an seasoned developer who worked across various domains and technologies over the past 10 years. He played key roles in various product and agile consulting companies such as Stayzilla, Thoughtworks, and, currently at CurrencyFair. His domain expertise spans the finance, supply chain, e-commerce, cloud, infrastructure management, health, retail, ICT4D, and entertainment industries. He is passionate about open source software and is a core contributor to many humanitarian open source projects. His current focus is on scaling microservices in highly distributed applications that are deployed using container-based systems in the cloud. Kishore is also a core reviewer for another microservices book called *Developing Microservices with Node.js*.

I would like thank my wife, Jyothsna, and my daughter, Dhruti, who put up with me all along irrespective of my crazy schedules.

www.PacktPub.com

For support files and downloads related to your book, please visit www.PacktPub.com.

Did you know that Packt offers eBook versions of every book published, with PDF and ePub files available? You can upgrade to the eBook version at www.PacktPub.com and as a print book customer, you are entitled to a discount on the eBook copy. Get in touch with us at service@packtpub.com for more details.

At www.PacktPub.com, you can also read a collection of free technical articles, sign up for a range of free newsletters and receive exclusive discounts and offers on Packt books and eBooks.

https://www.packtpub.com/mapt

Get the most in-demand software skills with Mapt. Mapt gives you full access to all Packt books and video courses, as well as industry-leading tools to help you plan your personal development and advance your career.

Why subscribe?

- Fully searchable across every book published by Packt
- Copy and paste, print, and bookmark content
- On demand and accessible via a web browser

Customer Feedback

Thank you for purchasing this Packt book. We take our commitment to improving our content and products to meet your needs seriously—that's why your feedback is so valuable. Whatever your feelings about your purchase, please consider leaving a review on this book's Amazon page. Not only will this help us, more importantly it will also help others in the community to make an informed decision about the resources that they invest in to learn.

You can also review for us on a regular basis by joining our reviewers' club. **If you're interested in joining, or would like to learn more about the benefits we offer, please contact us**: customerreviews@packtpub.com.

Table of Contents

Preface

The goal of this book is to introduce you to some of the most popular and newest technologies and frameworks that will help you build and deploy microservices at scale. With the current evolution in this space, it is really difficult to keep up with all the new frameworks and tools. If you are an open source fan like me, you would already know that you have to spend a lot of time in trying out these new frameworks and libraries in order to understand their potential and the exact problem that they are trying to solve. Of course, each framework would have been built for a specific purpose, and you will often end up in a situation where you don't have a silver bullet for all your microservice concerns. In this book, you will learn some of the most commonly used frameworks and technologies that help you build and deploy microservices at scale.

Throughout this book, we will be sticking to a specific application and will try to build upon that application. For example, we will be using the same application to configure service discovery, monitoring, streaming, log management, and load balancing. So by the end of this book, you will have a fully loaded microservice that demonstrates every aspect of a microservice.

This book covers several libraries and frameworks that help you build and deploy microservices. After reading this book, you will not be an expert on all of them, but you will know where to start and how to proceed. That's the whole intention of this book. I hope you'll like it. Good luck microservicing!

What this book covers

Chapter 1, *Building Microservices with Java*, shows you how to build Java-based RESTful microservices using frameworks such as Spring Boot, Wildfly Swarm, Dropwizard, and Spark Java . This chapter will also show you how to write RESTful APIs using Spring MVC and Spark Java.

Chapter 2, *Containerizing Microservices with Docker*, shows you how to package your application using Maven plugins such as the Maven Shade plugin and Spring Boot Maven plugin. This chapter will also show you how to install Docker on your local computer. You will also learn how to containerize your application using Docker and later push your microservice's Docker image to the public Docker Hub.

`Chapter 3`, *Deploying Microservices on Mesos*, shows you how to orchestrate a Dockerized Mesos cluster with Marathon on your local machine. You will also learn how to deploy your Dockerized microservice to a Mesos cluster using Marathon. Later, you will learn how to scale your microservice; configure ports, volumes, and environment variables; and view container logs in Marathon. Finally you will learn how to use Marathon's REST API for managing your microservice.

`Chapter 4`, *Deploying Microservices on Kubernetes*, shows you how to orchestrate a Dockerized Kubernetes cluster using Minikube on your local machine. You will also learn how to deploy your Dockerized microservice to a Kubernetes cluster using the Kubernetes dashboard as well as kubectl. Later, you will learn how to scale your microservice; configure ports, volumes, and environment variables; and view container logs in Kubernetes using the dashboard as well as kubectl.

`Chapter 5`, *Service Discovery and Load Balancing Microservices*, shows you how you to run a Dockerized Zookeeper instance on your local machine. You will learn how to implement service discovery and load balancing using Zookeeper. This chapter also introduces you to Consul, where you will be running a Dockerized Consul instance on your local machine. Later, you will learn how to implement service discovery and load balancing using Consul and Spring Cloud. You will also learn how to implement service discovery and load balancing using Consul and Nginx.

`Chapter 6`, *Monitoring Microservices*, shows you how to configure Spring Boot Actuator and gives you an overview of all the metrics that are exposed by Spring Boot Actuator. You will also learn how to create your own metrics using the Dropwizard metrics library and later expose them via Spring Boot Actuator. Later, you will learn how to run a Dockerized Graphite instance on your local machine. The metrics that you created using Dropwizard will then be published to Graphite. Finally, you will learn how to run a Dockerized Grafana instance on your local machine and then use it to expose your metrics in the form of dashboards.

`Chapter 7`, *Building Asynchronous Streaming Systems with Kafka and Spark*, shows you how to set up and run a Dockerized Kafka broker on your local machine. You will learn how to create topics in Kafka and build Kafka Streams application in our microservice that will stream data asynchronously. You will build a similar Spark Streaming job that will have the ability to stream data asynchronously. You will get an overview of improving the performance of your streaming application. Later, you will learn how to aggregate your application logs into a Kafka topic and then explore the possibilities of integrating it with popular log-management systems.

Chapter 8, *More Clustering Frameworks - DC/OS, Docker Swarm, and YARN*, will give you an overview of other popular clustering frameworks in the market. You will get a high-level idea of Mesosphere's DC/OS, Docker Swarm, and Apache YARN. You will also get to see how DC/OS and Docker Swarm can be used to deploy microservices on a larger scale.

What you need for this book

You will need the following software and hardware to execute the recipes on this book.

Hardware:

- Desktop or laptop with at least 16 GB memory and a 4-core CPU

Software:

- Java Development Kit
- Apache Maven
- Spring Tool Suite

Who this book is for

This book is for Java developers that would like to learn how to build microservices, deploy them on a clustered environment, monitor them, and manage them at scale. Familiarity with Java is a plus, as most of the recipes in this book are based on Java.

Sections

In this book, you will find several headings that appear frequently (*Getting ready, How to do it..., How it works..., There's more...,* and *See also*).

To give clear instructions on how to complete a recipe, we use these sections as follows:

Getting ready

This section tells you what to expect in the recipe, and describes how to set up any software or any preliminary settings required for the recipe.

How to do it...

This section contains the steps required to follow the recipe.

How it works...

This section usually consists of a detailed explanation of what happened in the previous section.

There's more...

This section consists of additional information about the recipe in order to make the reader more knowledgeable about the recipe.

See also

This section provides helpful links to other useful information for the recipe.

Conventions

In this book, you will find a number of text styles that distinguish between different kinds of information. Here are some examples of these styles and an explanation of their meaning.

Code words in text, database table names, folder names, filenames, file extensions, pathnames, dummy URLs, user input, and Twitter handles are shown as follows: "Start the `GeoLocationApplication.java` class as a Spring Boot application from your STS IDE."

A block of code is set as follows:

```
<!-- <dependency>
  <groupId>org.springframework.cloud</groupId>
  <artifactId>spring-cloud-starter-consul-all</artifactId>
  <version>1.1.2.RELEASE</version>
</dependency> -->
```

Any command-line input or output is written as follows:

```
curl -H "Content-Type: application/json" -X GET
http://localhost:8080/geolocation
```

New terms and **important words** are shown in bold. Words that you see on the screen, for example, in menus or dialog boxes, appear in the text like this: "The next button that we would want to use most of the time is the **Short URL** button."

Warnings or important notes appear in a box like this.

 Tips and tricks appear like this.

Reader feedback

Feedback from our readers is always welcome. Let us know what you think about this book—what you liked or disliked. Reader feedback is important for us as it helps us develop titles that you will really get the most out of.

To send us general feedback, simply e-mail feedback@packtpub.com, and mention the book's title in the subject of your message.

If there is a topic that you have expertise in and you are interested in either writing or contributing to a book, see our author guide at www.packtpub.com/authors.

Customer support

Now that you are the proud owner of a Packt book, we have a number of things to help you to get the most from your purchase.

Downloading the example code

You can download the example code files for this book from your account at http://www.packtpub.com. If you purchased this book elsewhere, you can visit http://www.packtpub.com/support and register to have the files e-mailed directly to you.

You can download the code files by following these steps:

1. Log in or register to our website using your e-mail address and password.
2. Hover the mouse pointer on the **SUPPORT** tab at the top.
3. Click on **Code Downloads & Errata**.
4. Enter the name of the book in the **Search** box.
5. Select the book for which you're looking to download the code files.

6. Choose from the drop-down menu where you purchased this book from.
7. Click on **Code Download**.

You can also download the code files by clicking on the **Code Files** button on the book's webpage at the Packt Publishing website. This page can be accessed by entering the book's name in the **Search** box. Please note that you need to be logged in to your Packt account.

Once the file is downloaded, please make sure that you unzip or extract the folder using the latest version of:

- WinRAR / 7-Zip for Windows
- Zipeg / iZip / UnRarX for Mac
- 7-Zip / PeaZip for Linux

The code bundle for the book is also hosted on GitHub at `https://github.com/PacktPubl ishing/Microservices-Deployment-Cookbook`. We also have other code bundles from our rich catalog of books and videos available at `https://github.com/PacktPublishing/`. Check them out!

Errata

Although we have taken every care to ensure the accuracy of our content, mistakes do happen. If you find a mistake in one of our books—maybe a mistake in the text or the code—we would be grateful if you could report this to us. By doing so, you can save other readers from frustration and help us improve subsequent versions of this book. If you find any errata, please report them by visiting `http://www.packtpub.com/submit-errata`, selecting your book, clicking on the **Errata Submission Form** link, and entering the details of your errata. Once your errata are verified, your submission will be accepted and the errata will be uploaded to our website or added to any list of existing errata under the Errata section of that title.

To view the previously submitted errata, go to `https://www.packtpub.com/books/conten t/support`and enter the name of the book in the search field. The required information will appear under the **Errata** section.

Piracy

Piracy of copyrighted material on the Internet is an ongoing problem across all media. At Packt, we take the protection of our copyright and licenses very seriously. If you come across any illegal copies of our works in any form on the Internet, please provide us with the location address or website name immediately so that we can pursue a remedy.

Please contact us at `copyright@packtpub.com` with a link to the suspected pirated material.

We appreciate your help in protecting our authors and our ability to bring you valuable content.

Questions

If you have a problem with any aspect of this book, you can contact us at `questions@packtpub.com`, and we will do our best to address the problem.

1

Building Microservices with Java

In this chapter, we will cover the following recipes:

- Creating a project template using STS and Maven
- Writing microservices with Spring Boot
- Writing REST APIs with Spring MVC
- Writing microservices with WildFly Swarm
- Writing microservices with Dropwizard
- Writing REST APIs with SparkJava

Microservices have gained a lot of traction recently. A microservice-based architecture is one way of designing your software. In such an architecture, applications are broken down into smaller services so that they can be deployed and managed separately. This takes away a lot of pain points that occur in traditional monolithic applications. With that being said, microservices can be built using any programming language. In fact, there are many libraries and frameworks that help programmers build microservices using Java, Scala, C#, JavaScript, Python, Ruby, and so on. In this book, we will focus more on building and deploying microservices with Java.

Introduction

In a traditional microservice-based design, monolithic applications will be broken down into smaller services that can talk to other services either in a synchronous or asynchronous model, based on the need and use case. The first question that anyone would have when breaking down monolithic applications is "what are the potential services that my application can be broken down into?" There is no rule of thumb or straight-forward answer to this. But usually, one looks for independent functionalities. Each and every functionality can be considered to be built as its own service.

To illustrate this, let's take a look at an example application and see how it could be broken down into smaller, manageable and deployable microservices. The sample application we will be looking at is a biker tracking application. This application will have the following functionalities:

- Web interface to monitor the user's progress on a map
- REST API to consume the user's geolocation data constantly
- Analytics code to perform calculations for biking route suggestions, weather predictions, biking gear suggestions, calories burnt, water intake, and so on

Let's take a look at how this application might have been designed as a monolithic application:

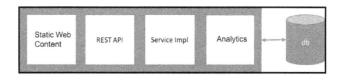

As you can see, the whole application is bundled as one artifact and therefore promotes a **single point of failure** (**SPOF**). If for some reason the analytics code crashes your JVM, we will lose the web interface, REST APIs, and analytics as a whole. Now, let's take a look at how this might be broken down into manageable microservices:

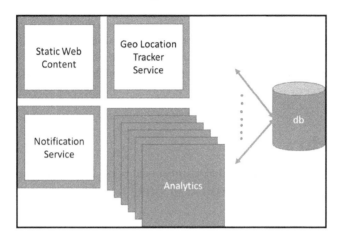

In this architecture diagram, you can see that each and every functionality is deployed as its own microservice. The service implementations have been broken down into a **Notification Service**, which will take care of sending notifications to the users, and the **Geo Location Tracker Service**, which keeps track of the geolocation (latitude and longitude) information of all the users. The **Analytics** code has been broken down into its own microservices. So if one type of analytics microservice goes down, the other microservices will keep functioning properly. You might have noticed that the REST APIs are missing. They are actually not missing, but integrated into their respective microservices.

Now let's not waste any more time and jump directly into building one part of this application. To be able to illustrate the extensive concepts that this book offers, I have chosen the geolocation tracker service as our example microservice. This service will be responsible for collecting the geolocation of all users of this application and then storing them in a data store.

Creating a project template using STS and Maven

Creating a project for your microservice is no different than creating a simple Java project. We will use Maven as our build framework as it is considered to be one of the most popular build frameworks. If you are comfortable using other frameworks, such as Gradle, SBT, or Ivy, feel free to use them. But keep in mind that the recipes throughout this book will use Maven extensively. Unless you are an expert in your preferred framework, I strongly recommend using Maven.

Getting ready

In order to create your microservice project, you will need the following software. Follow the instructions on their respective websites to install them:

- JDK 1.8+
- Maven 3.3.9+
- Spring Tool Suite (STS) 3.8.0+

Make sure both Java and Maven are in your PATH variable so that you can use the `java` and `mvn` commands on every terminal shell without having to set PATH each time. **Spring Tool Suite** is a sophisticated version of Eclipse that has lot of Spring plugins and extensions. If you are familiar with other IDEs, feel free to use them. But for familiarity, this book will use STS for all recipes.

How to do it...

After you have installed the above-mentioned software, open Spring Tool Suite. The first time you open it, you will be requested to choose a workspace. Go ahead and enter your workspace location. In this recipe, we will learn how to create a template Maven project using STS and Maven. STS comes with Maven Integration out of the box. So we don't have to configure it any further. After your STS IDE has completed startup, follow the below instructions to create a new Maven project:

1. In your STS window, right-click anywhere on the **Package Explorer**, select **New**, and then select **Maven Project**, as shown in the following screenshot:

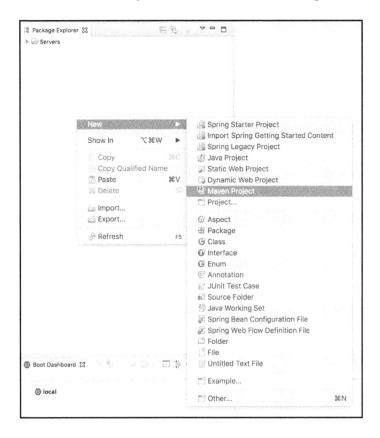

2. This will open a popup that will let you chose the type of Maven project you would like to create. We will skip the archetype selection by checking the box that says **Create a simple project (skip archetype selection)** and then hit **Next**:

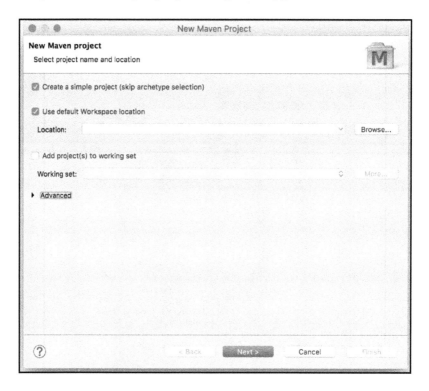

3. In the next window, enter the following details to create your project:

   - **Group Id**: com.packt.microservices
   - **Artifact Id**: geolocation
   - **Name**: geolocation

4. After you have entered the details, hit **Finish**:

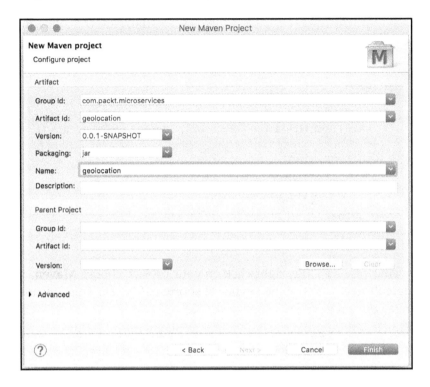

5. This will create a simple Maven JAR module with all the required directories in place. Depending on your IDE settings, STS configures your new project with the default Java version. If you have not set any defaults, it will configure your project with Java 1.5. You can verify this by checking your project structure in STS. The following screenshot shows that STS uses Java 1.5 for your project:

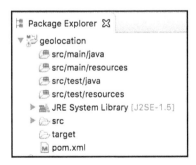

6. We will use Java 8's **lambda expressions** in other chapters. So let's change the Java version from 1.5 to 1.8. In order to change the Java version, we will configure the `maven-compiler-plugin` in the `pom.xml` file. Add the following section of code to your `pom.xml` file's `project` section:

```
<build>
  <plugins>
   <plugin>
      <groupId>org.apache.maven.plugins</groupId>
      <artifactId>maven-compiler-plugin</artifactId>
    <version>3.5.1</version>
    <configuration>
      <source>1.8</source>
      <target>1.8</target>
    </configuration>
    </plugin>
  </plugins>
  </build>
```

7. Save your `pom.xml` file, right-click on your project, choose **Maven**, and then hit **Update Project...** or use the keyboard shortcut *Alt + F5*. This will automatically change your project's Java version to 1.8.

8. Our microservice project is now ready to play with.

There's more...

If you are more comfortable using the command line to create Maven projects, issue the following command in your terminal to create the new project:

```
mvn -B archetype:generate -DarchetypeGroupId=org.apache.maven.archetypes \
-DgroupId=com.packt.microservices -DartifactId=geolocation \
-Dname=geolocation
```

After Maven creates the project, you should be able to import your project into your IDE. As this is something out of the scope of this book, we will not be looking at how to import an existing Maven project into your IDE.

Writing microservices with Spring Boot

Now that our project is ready, let's look at how to write our microservice. There are several Java-based frameworks that let you create microservices. One of the most popular frameworks from the Spring ecosystem is the Spring Boot framework. In this recipe, we will look at how to create a simple microservice application using Spring Boot.

Getting ready

Any application requires an entry point to start the application. For Java-based applications, you can write a class that has the `main` method and run that class as a Java application. Similarly, Spring Boot requires a simple Java class with the `main` method to run it as a Spring Boot application (microservice). Before you start writing your Spring Boot microservice, you will also require some Maven dependencies in your `pom.xml` file.

How to do it...

1. Create a Java class called `com.packt.microservices.geolocation.GeoLocationApplication.java` and give it an empty `main` method:

```
package com.packt.microservices.geolocation;
  public class GeoLocationApplication {
    public static void main(String[] args) {
    // left empty intentionally
   }
  }
```

2. Now that we have our basic template project, let's make our project a child project of Spring Boot's `spring-boot-starter-parent pom` module. This module has a lot of prerequisite configurations in its `pom.xml` file, thereby reducing the amount of boilerplate code in our `pom.xml` file. At the time of writing this, `1.3.6.RELEASE` was the most recent version:

```
<parent>
  <groupId>org.springframework.boot</groupId>
  <artifactId>spring-boot-starter-parent</artifactId>
  <version>1.3.6.RELEASE</version>
</parent>
```

3. After this step, you might want to run a Maven update on your project as you have added a new parent module. If you see any warnings about the version of the `maven-compiler` plugin, you can either ignore it or just remove the `<version>3.5.1</version>` element. If you remove the version element, please perform a Maven update afterward.

4. Spring Boot has the ability to enable or disable Spring modules such as Spring MVC, Spring Data, and Spring Caching. In our use case, we will be creating some REST APIs to consume the geolocation information of the users. So we will need Spring MVC. Add the following dependencies to your `pom.xml` file:

```
<dependencies>
  <dependency>
    <groupId>org.springframework.boot</groupId>
    <artifactId>spring-boot-starter-web</artifactId>
  </dependency>
</dependencies>
```

5. We also need to expose the APIs using web servers such as Tomcat, Jetty, or Undertow. Spring Boot has an in-memory Tomcat server that starts up as soon as you start your Spring Boot application. So we already have an in-memory Tomcat server that we could utilize.

6. Now let's modify the `GeoLocationApplication.java` class to make it a Spring Boot application:

```
package com.packt.microservices.geolocation;
import org.springframework.boot.SpringApplication;
import org.springframework.boot.autoconfigure
 .SpringBootApplication;
 @SpringBootApplication
 public class GeoLocationApplication {
   public static void main(String[] args) {
   SpringApplication.run(GeoLocationApplication.class, args);
  }
 }
```

As you can see, we have added an annotation, `@SpringBootApplication`, to our class. The `@SpringBootApplication` annotation reduces the number of lines of code written by adding the following three annotations implicitly:

- `@Configuration`
- `@ComponentScan`
- `@EnableAutoConfiguration`

If you are familiar with Spring, you will already know what the first two annotations do. `@EnableAutoConfiguration` is the only annotation that is part of Spring Boot. The `AutoConfiguration` package has an intelligent mechanism that guesses the configuration of your application and automatically configures the beans that you will likely need in your code.

You can also see that we have added one more line to the `main` method, which actually tells Spring Boot the class that will be used to start this application. In our case, it is `GeoLocationApplication.class`. If you would like to add more initialization logic to your application, such as setting up the database or setting up your cache, feel free to add it here.

1. Now that our Spring Boot application is all set to run, let's see how to run our microservice. Right-click on `GeoLocationApplication.java` from **Package Explorer**, select **Run As**, and then select **Spring Boot App**. You can also choose **Java Application** instead of **Spring Boot App**. Both the options ultimately do the same thing. You should see something like this on your STS console:

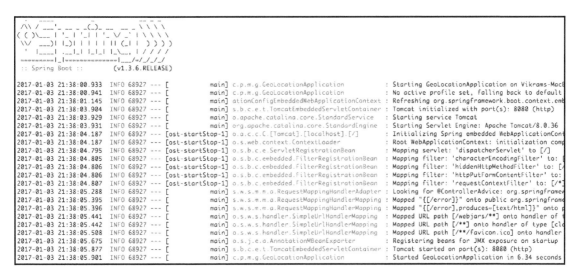

2. If you look closely at the console logs, you will notice that Tomcat is being started on port number 8080. In order to make sure our Tomcat server is listening, let's run a simple `curl` command. cURL is a command-line utility available on most Unix and Mac systems. For Windows, use tools such as Cygwin or even Postman. Postman is a Google Chrome extension that gives you the ability to send and receive HTTP requests. For simplicity, we will use cURL. Execute the following command on your terminal:

```
curl http://localhost:8080
```

3. This should give us an output like this:

```
{"timestamp":1467420963000,"status":404,"error":"Not
Found","message":"No message available","path":"/"}
```

This error message is being produced by Spring. This verifies that our Spring Boot microservice is ready to start building on with more features. There are more configurations that are needed for Spring Boot, which we will perform later in this chapter along with Spring MVC.

Writing REST APIs with Spring MVC

There are two types of communication models. One of them is **synchronous**, where the client waits for the server to respond to its request. The other is **asynchronous**, where the client fires a request and forgets. Though Servlet 3.0 and above let you create asynchronous servlets, in our recipes, we will focus on traditional servlet-based HTTP APIs for simplicity. We will also be looking at asynchronous communication in later chapters.

Getting ready

When it comes to building REST APIs, there are several frameworks to choose from. As we already set up the Spring ecosystem in our previous recipe, it would make more sense and be much easier to use Spring MVC to expose REST APIs.

How to do it...

The true advantage of Spring Boot is that you do not have to add any new dependencies to enable web support for your application. Spring Boot's parent `pom` file (`spring-boot-starter-parent`) takes care of that for you. Now let's take a look at how to write our first API. If you are familiar with Spring MVC, this should be really straight-forward for you:

1. Create a `Controller` class called `com.packt.microservices.geolocation.GeoLocationController.java`, which will be responsible for basic CRUD operations for the geolocation of all users:

```
package com.packt.microservices.geolocation;

import org.springframework.web.bind.annotation.RequestMapping;
import org.springframework.web.bind.annotation.RestController;

@RestController
@RequestMapping("/geolocation")
public class GeoLocationController {

}
```

> There are two things to note here. The `@RestController` annotation indicates that we are going to use this controller to expose our REST APIs. It implicitly adds the `@ResponseBody` annotation to all controller methods as that is something you would want to do when exposing your REST APIs using Spring MVC. The `@RequestMapping` annotation specifies where your HTTP resource is located. We are setting `@RequestMapping` on the controller level to apply it to all controller methods.

 Using `@RequestMapping` on the `Controller` class level to define a root resource path is considered to be one of the best practices. Instead of having to create API paths such as `/getGeolocation` or `/createGeolocation`, it is always a better practice to use the same path, `/geolocation`, with the `GET` method to get geolocation data and the `POST` method to create geolocation data.

2. Before we jump into creating our APIs, we will need some classes for the domain object and service. Let's start with creating our domain object. Assume that our GeoLocation consists latitude and longitude. We will be defining both latitude and longitude as double to provide better precision. Now we will have to say which user's geolocation it is. So we might want to add a userId. We also need to say at what time the user was at the geolocation. So we might want to add a timestamp in EPOCH time format. The timestamp will be of type long. This is how your **plain old java object (POJO)** class will look:

```java
package com.packt.microservices.geolocation;

import java.io.Serializable;
import java.util.UUID;

  public class GeoLocation implements Serializable {

    private static final long serialVersionUID = 1L;
   private double latitude;
   private double longitude;
   private UUID userId;
   private long timestamp;
  public double getLatitude() {
    return latitude;
  }
  public void setLatitude(double latitude) {
    this.latitude = latitude;
  }
  public double getLongitude() {
   return longitude;
  }
  public void setLongitude(double longitude) {
    this.longitude = longitude;
  }
  public UUID getUserId() {
   return userId;
  }
  public void setUserId(UUID userId) {
    this.userId = userId;
  }
 public long getTimestamp() {
  return timestamp;
  }
  public void setTimestamp(long timestamp) {
   this.timestamp = timestamp;
  }
 }
```

As you can see, we have used the `java.util.UUID` class to represent the `userId`, assuming that this UUID uniquely identifies a user. We will not be creating the user `POJO` as it is out of scope for this recipe.

In an ideal scenario, one would be using a NoSQL or relational database to store the geolocations. In this case, NoSQL sounds more suitable due to several reasons, including the fact that our data is time series data, in JSON format, unstructured but will change over time and we will have a humongous amount of data.

3. For simplicity purposes, we will be storing our geolocations in an in-memory `java.util.List<GeoLocation>` collection. Let's create our repository that holds all our geolocation objects, `com.packt.microservices.geolocation.GeoLocationRepository.java`:

```
package com.packt.microservices.geolocation;

import java.util.ArrayList;
import java.util.Collections;
import java.util.List;

import org.springframework.stereotype.Repository;

@Repository
public class GeoLocationRepository {

  private List<GeoLocation> geolocations = new
  ArrayList<GeoLocation>();
    public void addGeoLocation(GeoLocation geolocation) {
      geolocations.add(geolocation);
    }
    public List<GeoLocation> getGeoLocations() {
      return Collections.unmodifiableList(geolocations);
    }
}
```

4. Now let's take a look at how your `Service` interface will look:

```
package com.packt.microservices.geolocation;

import java.util.List;

public interface GeoLocationService {

   public GeoLocation create(GeoLocation geolocation);
   public List<GeoLocation> findAll();
}
```

5. Both our repository and service have a very simple interface. Ideally in real-time applications, you might want to add more complicated methods that not only perform CRUD operations but also sort, filter, select only specific fields, and so on. Now let's take a look at our `com.packt.microservices.geolocation.GeoLocationServiceImpl.java` class:

```
package com.packt.microservices.geolocation;

import java.util.List;

import org.springframework.beans.factory.annotation.Autowired;

import org.springframework.stereotype.Service;

@Service
public class GeoLocationServiceImpl implements
GeoLocationService {
   @Autowired
   private GeoLocationRepository repository;

   @Override
   public GeoLocation create(GeoLocation geolocation) {
    repository.addGeoLocation(geolocation);
    return geolocation;
   }

   @Override
   public List<GeoLocation> findAll() {
     return repository.getGeoLocations();
   }
}
```

It is always strongly recommended that you write unit test cases for any new code. But as that is a little out of scope for this book, we will not be writing unit test cases for any of the previous code. To learn more about unit testing Spring Boot applications, please take a look at Spring Boot's documentation at https://docs.spring.io/spring-boot/docs/current/reference/html/boot-features-testing.html.

6. Now that our domain and service classes are all set to go, let's modify our `Controller` class to save and find geolocations. Add the following snippet into your `Controller` class body:

```
@Autowired
private GeoLocationService service;

@RequestMapping(method = RequestMethod.POST, produces =
"application/json", consumes = "application/json")
    public GeoLocation create(@RequestBody GeoLocation geolocation) {
      return service.create(geolocation);
    }

@RequestMapping(method = RequestMethod.GET, produces =
"application/json")
    public List<GeoLocation> findAll() {
      return service.findAll();
    }
```

In this implementation, there are a few things to notice. The `@RequestMapping` annotation does not have a `path` defined as it is already derived from the class-level annotation. For both the `create` and `findAll` methods, we are using the same path but different HTTP methods as per best practice. Since we are dealing only with JSON here, we have set the `produces` and `consumes` values to `application/json`. The return types of the `create` and `findAll` methods are `GeoLocation` and `List<GeoLocation>` respectively. Spring MVC internally uses Jackson to convert them to their equivalent JSON strings.

That's it! We are now ready to test our application:

1. Let's try to create two geolocations using the POST API and later try to retrieve them using the GET method. Execute the following cURL commands in your terminal one by one:

```
curl -H "Content-Type: application/json" -X POST -d'{"timestamp":
1468203975, "userId": "f1196aac-470e-11e6-beb8-9e71128cae77", "latitude":
41.803488, "longitude": -88.144040}' http://localhost:8080/geolocation
```

2. This should give you an output similar to the following (pretty-printed for readability):

```
{
  "latitude": 41.803488,
  "longitude": -88.14404,
  "userId": "f1196aac-470e-11e6-beb8-9e71128cae77",
  "timestamp": 1468203975
}
```

```
curl -H "Content-Type: application/json" -X POST -d '{"timestamp":
1468203975, "userId": "f1196aac-470e-11e6-beb8-9e71128cae77", "latitude":
9.568012, "longitude": 77.962444}' http://localhost:8080/geolocation
```

3. This should give you an output similar to the following (pretty-printed for readability):

```
{
  "latitude": 9.568012,
  "longitude": 77.962444,
  "userId": "f1196aac-470e-11e6-beb8-9e71128cae77",
  "timestamp": 1468203975
}
```

4. To verify whether your entities were stored correctly, execute the following cURL command:

```
curl http://localhost:8080/geolocation
```

5. This should give you an output similar to the following (pretty-printed for readability):

```
[
{
  "latitude": 41.803488,
  "longitude": -88.14404,
  "userId": "f1196aac-470e-11e6-beb8-9e71128cae77",
  "timestamp": 1468203975
},
{
  "latitude": 9.568012,
  "longitude": 77.962444,
  "userId": "f1196aac-470e-11e6-beb8-9e71128cae77",
  "timestamp": 1468203975
}
]
```

You now have a fully working version of your microservice. The remaining recipes in this chapter try to achieve the same logic with different frameworks, such as WildFly Swarm and Dropwizard. Later in this chapter, we will also look at another framework that helps you build REST APIs quickly called SparkJava (different from Apache Spark). If you will be using Spring Boot for your microservices, you can jump to the next chapter. If you are interested in any of the frameworks that were mentioned, jump to the appropriate recipe in this chapter.

Writing microservices with WildFly Swarm

WildFly Swarm is a J2EE application packaging framework from RedHat that utilizes the in-memory Undertow server to deploy microservices. In this recipe, we will create the same `GeoLocation` API using WildFly Swarm and JAX-RS.

To avoid confusion and dependency conflicts in our project, we will create the WildFly Swarm microservice as its own Maven project. This recipe is just here to help you get started on WildFly Swarm. When you are building your production-level application, it is your choice to either use Spring Boot, WildFly Swarm, Dropwizard, or SparkJava based on your needs.

Getting ready

Similar to how we created the Spring Boot Maven project, create a Maven WAR module with the **groupId** `com.packt.microservices` and **name/artifactId** `geolocation-wildfly`. Feel free to use either your IDE or the command line. Be aware that some IDEs complain about a missing `web.xml` file. We will see how to fix that in the next section.

How to do it…

1. Before we set up the WildFly Swarm project, we have to fix the missing `web.xml` error. The error message says that Maven expects to see a `web.xml` file in your project as it is a WAR module, but this file is missing in your project. In order to fix this, we have to add and configure `maven-war-plugin`. Add the following code snippet to your `pom.xml` file's `project` section:

```
<build>
  <plugins>
    <plugin>
```

```
<groupId>org.apache.maven.plugins</groupId>
<artifactId>maven-war-plugin</artifactId>
<version>2.6</version>
<configuration>
  <failOnMissingWebXml>false</failOnMissingWebXml>
</configuration>
    </plugin>
    </plugins>
  </build>
```

2. After adding the snippet, save your `pom.xml` file and perform a Maven update. Also, if you see that your project is using a Java version other than 1.8, follow the *Creating a project template using STS and Maven* recipe to change the Java version to 1.8. Again, perform a Maven update for the changes to take effect.

3. Now, let's add the dependencies required for this project. As we know that we will be exposing our APIs, we have to add the JAX-RS library. JAX-RS is the standard JSR-compliant API for creating RESTful web services. JBoss has its own version of JAX-RS. So let's add that dependency to the `pom.xml` file:

```
<dependencies>
  <dependency>
    <groupId>org.jboss.spec.javax.ws.rs</groupId>
      <artifactId>jboss-jaxrs-api_2.0_spec</artifactId>
      <version>1.0.0.Final</version>
      <scope>provided</scope>
  </dependency>
</dependencies>
```

The one thing that you have to note here is the **provided** scope. The provided scope in general means that this JAR need not be bundled with the final artifact when it is built. Usually, the dependencies with provided scope will be available to your application either via your web server or application server. In this case, when Wildfly Swarm bundles your app and runs it on the in-memory Undertow server, your server will already have this dependency.

4. The next step toward creating the `GeoLocation` API using Wildfly Swarm is creating the domain object. Use the `com.packt.microservices.geolocation.GeoLocation.java` file from the previous recipe.

5. Now that we have the domain object, there are two classes that you need to create in order to write your first JAX-RS web service. The first of those is the `Application` class. The `Application` class in JAX-RS is used to define the various components that you will be using in your application. It can also hold some metadata about your application, such as your `basePath` (or `ApplicationPath`) to all resources listed in this `Application` class. In this case, we are going to use `/geolocation` as our `basePath`. Let's see how that looks:

```
package com.packt.microservices.geolocation;

import javax.ws.rs.ApplicationPath;
import javax.ws.rs.core.Application;

@ApplicationPath("/geolocation")
  public class GeoLocationApplication extends Application {

  public GeoLocationApplication() {}
  }
```

> There are two things to note in this class; one is the `Application` class and the other is the `@ApplicationPath` annotation-both of which we've already talked about.

6. Now let's move on to the `resource` class, which is responsible for exposing the APIs. If you are familiar with Spring MVC, you can compare Resource classes to Controllers. They are responsible for defining the API for any specific resource. The annotations are slightly different from that of Spring MVC. Let's create a new resource class called `com.packt.microservices.geolocation.GeoLocationResource.java` that exposes a simple GET API:

```
package com.packt.microservices.geolocation;

import java.util.ArrayList;
import java.util.List;

import javax.ws.rs.GET;
import javax.ws.rs.Path;
import javax.ws.rs.Produces;

@Path("/")
public class GeoLocationResource {

  @GET
  @Produces("application/json")
```

```
public List<GeoLocation> findAll() {
  return new ArrayList<>();
}
}
```

All the three annotations, @GET, @Path, and @Produces, are pretty self explanatory.

Before we start writing the APIs and the service class, let's test the application from the command line to make sure it works as expected. With the current implementation, any GET request sent to the /geolocation URL should return an empty JSON array.

So far, we have created the RESTful APIs using JAX-RS. It's just another JAX-RS project:

1. In order to make it a microservice using Wildfly Swarm, all you have to do is add the wildfly-swarm-plugin to the Maven pom.xml file. This plugin will be tied to the package phase of the build so that whenever the package goal is triggered, the plugin will create an uber JAR with all required dependencies. An uber JAR is just a fat JAR that has all dependencies bundled inside itself. It also deploys our application in an in-memory Undertow server. Add the following snippet to the plugins section of the pom.xml file:

```xml
<plugin>
  <groupId>org.wildfly.swarm</groupId>
  <artifactId>wildfly-swarm-plugin</artifactId>
  <version>1.0.0.Final</version>
  <executions>
    <execution>
      <id>package</id>
      <goals>
        <goal>package</goal>
      </goals>
    </execution>
  </executions>
</plugin>
```

2. Now execute the mvn clean package command from the project's root directory, and wait for the Maven build to be successful. If you look at the logs, you can see that wildfly-swarm-plugin will create the uber JAR, which has all its dependencies. You should see something like this in your console logs:

```
[INFO] --- wildfly-swarm-plugin:1.0.0.Final:package (package) @ geolocation-wildfly ---
[INFO] Scanning for needed WildFly Swarm fractions with mode: when_missing
[INFO] Detected fractions: jaxrs:1.0.2.Final
[INFO] Adding fractions: container:1.0.2.Final, ee:1.0.2.Final, io:1.0.2.Final, jaxrs:1.0.2.Final, naming:1.0.2.Final, security:1.0.2.Final, undertow:1.0.2.Final
```

3. After the build is successful, you will find two artifacts in the target directory of your project. The `geolocation-wildfly-0.0.1-SNAPSHOT.war` file is the final WAR created by the `maven-war-plugin`. The `geolocation-wildfly-0.0.1-SNAPSHOT-swarm.jar` file is the uber JAR created by the `wildfly-swarm-plugin`. Execute the following command in the same terminal to start your microservice:

```
java -jar target/geolocation-wildfly-0.0.1-SNAPSHOT-swarm.jar
```

4. After executing this command, you will see that Undertow has started on port number 8080, exposing the geolocation resource we created. You will see something like this:

5. Execute the following cURL command in a separate terminal window to make sure our API is exposed. The response of the command should be `[]`, indicating there are no geolocations:

```
curl http://localhost:8080/geolocation
```

6. Now let's build the service class and finish the APIs that we started. For simplicity purposes, we are going to store the geolocations in a collection in the service class itself. In a real-time scenario, you will be writing repository classes or DAOs that talk to the database that holds your geolocations. Get the `com.packt.microservices.geolocation.GeoLocationService.java` interface from the previous recipe. We'll use the same interface here.

7. Create a new class called `com.packt.microservices.geolocation.GeoLocationServiceImpl.java` that extends the `GeoLocationService` interface:

```
package com.packt.microservices.geolocation;

import java.util.ArrayList;
import java.util.Collections;
```

```
import java.util.List;

public class GeoLocationServiceImpl implements
GeoLocationService {
  private static List<GeoLocation> geolocations = new
  ArrayList<>
  ();

 @Override
  public GeoLocation create(GeoLocation geolocation) {
    geolocations.add(geolocation);
    return geolocation;
  }

 @Override
  public List<GeoLocation> findAll() {
    return Collections.unmodifiableList(geolocations);
  }
}
```

8. Now that our service classes are implemented, let's finish building the APIs. We already have a very basic stubbed-out GET API. Let's just introduce the service class to the resource class and call the findAll method. Similarly, let's use the service's create method for POST API calls. Add the following snippet to GeoLocationResource.java:

```
private GeoLocationService service = new
GeoLocationServiceImpl();

@GET
@Produces("application/json")
public List<GeoLocation> findAll() {
  return service.findAll();
}
@POST
@Produces("application/json")
@Consumes("application/json")
public GeoLocation create(GeoLocation geolocation) {
  return service.create(geolocation);
}
```

9. We are now ready to test our application. Go ahead and build your application. After the build is successful, run your microservice: let's try to create two geolocations using the POST API and later try to retrieve them using the GET method. Execute the following cURL commands in your terminal one by one:

```
        curl -H "Content-Type: application/json" -X POST -d
'{"timestamp": 1468203975, "userId": "f1196aac-470e-11e6-
beb8-9e71128cae77", "latitude": 41.803488, "longitude": -88.144040}'
http://localhost:8080/geolocation
```

10. This should give you something like the following output (pretty-printed for readability):

```
{
    "latitude": 41.803488,
    "longitude": -88.14404,
    "userId": "f1196aac-470e-11e6-beb8-9e71128cae77",
    "timestamp": 1468203975
}
```

```
        curl -H "Content-Type: application/json" -X POST -d '{"timestamp":
1468203975, "userId": "f1196aac-470e-11e6-beb8-9e71128cae77", "latitude":
9.568012, "longitude": 77.962444}' http://localhost:8080/geolocation
```

11. This command should give you an output similar to the following (pretty-printed for readability):

```
{
    "latitude": 9.568012,
    "longitude": 77.962444,
    "userId": "f1196aac-470e-11e6-beb8-9e71128cae77",
    "timestamp": 1468203975
}
```

12. To verify whether your entities were stored correctly, execute the following cURL command:

```
curl http://localhost:8080/geolocation
```

13. This should give you an output like this (pretty-printed for readability):

```
[
  {
    "latitude": 41.803488,
    "longitude": -88.14404,
    "userId": "f1196aac-470e-11e6-beb8-9e71128cae77",
    "timestamp": 1468203975
  },
  {
    "latitude": 9.568012,
    "longitude": 77.962444,
    "userId": "f1196aac-470e-11e6-beb8-9e71128cae77",
```

```
        "timestamp": 1468203975
   }
]
```

Whatever we have seen so far will give you a head start in building microservices with WildFly Swarm. Of course, there are tons of features that WildFly Swarm offers. Feel free to try them out based on your application needs. I strongly recommend going through the WildFly Swarm documentation for any advanced usages. If you already know that you are going to be using WildFly Swarm for your microservices, you can skip the rest of the recipes in this chapter and jump to next chapter. The final two recipes in this chapter will show you how to create microservices using Dropwizard and how to create RESTful APIs with SparkJava.

Writing microservices with Dropwizard

Dropwizard is a collection of libraries that help you build powerful applications quickly and easily. The libraries vary from Jackson, Jersey, Jetty, and so on. You can take a look at the full list of libraries on their website. This ecosystem of libraries that help you build powerful applications could be utilized to create microservices as well. As we saw earlier, it utilizes Jetty to expose its services. In this recipe, we will create the same GeoLocation API using Dropwizard and Jersey.

To avoid confusion and dependency conflicts in our project, we will create the Dropwizard microservice as its own Maven project. This recipe is just here to help you get started with Dropwizard. When you are building your production-level application, it is your choice to either use Spring Boot, WildFly Swarm, Dropwizard, or SparkJava based on your needs.

Getting ready

Similar to how we created other Maven projects, create a Maven JAR module with the **groupId** com.packt.microservices and **name/artifactId** geolocation-dropwizard. Feel free to use either your IDE or the command line. After the project is created, if you see that your project is using a Java version other than 1.8, follow the *Creating a project template using STS and Maven* recipe to change the Java version to 1.8. Perform a Maven update for the change to take effect.

How to do it…

The first thing that you will need is the `dropwizard-core` Maven dependency. Add the following snippet to your project's `pom.xml` file:

```
<dependencies>
  <dependency>
    <groupId>io.dropwizard</groupId>
    <artifactId>dropwizard-core</artifactId>
    <version>0.9.3</version>
  </dependency>
</dependencies>
```

Guess what? This is the only dependency you will need to spin up a simple Jersey-based Dropwizard microservice.

Before we start configuring Dropwizard, we have to create the `domain` object, `service` class, and `resource` class. Follow the steps from the previous recipe to create the following four files:

- `com.packt.microservices.geolocation.GeoLocation.java`
- `com.packt.microservices.geolocation.GeoLocationService.java`
- `com.packt.microservices.geolocation.GeoLocationServiceImpl.java`
- `com.packt.microservices.geolocation. GeoLocationResource.java`

Let's see what each of these classes does. The `GeoLocation.java` class is our domain object that holds the geolocation information. The `GeoLocationService.java` class defines our interface, which is then implemented by the `GeoLocationServiceImpl.java` class. If you take a look at the `GeoLocationServiceImpl.java` class, we are using a simple collection to store the `GeoLocation` domain objects. In a real-time scenario, you will be persisting these objects in a database. But to keep it simple, we will not go that far.

To be consistent with the previous recipe, let's change the path of `GeoLocationResource` to `/geolocation`. To do so, replace `@Path("/")` with `@Path("/geolocation")` on line number 11 of the `GeoLocationResource.java` class.

We have now created the `service` classes, `domain` object, and `resource` class. Let's configure Dropwizard.

In order to make your project a microservice, you have to do two things:

1. Create a Dropwizard configuration class. This is used to store any meta-information or resource information that your application will need during runtime, such as DB connection, Jetty server, logging, and metrics configurations. These configurations are ideally stored in a YAML file, which will then be mapped to your `Configuration` class using Jackson. In this application, we are not going to use the YAML configuration as it is out of scope for this book.

If you would like to know more about configuring Dropwizard, refer to their **Getting Started** documentation page at `http://www.dropwizard.io/0.7.1/docs/getting-started.html`.

2. Let's create an empty `Configuration` class called `GeoLocationConfiguration.java`:

```
package com.packt.microservices.geolocation;

import io.dropwizard.Configuration;

public class GeoLocationConfiguration extends Configuration {

}
```

3. The YAML configuration file has a lot to offer. Take a look at a sample YAML file from Dropwizard's *Getting Started* documentation page to learn more. The name of the YAML file is usually derived from the name of your microservice. The microservice name is usually identified by the return value of the overridden method `public String getName()` in your `Application` class. Now let's create the `GeoLocationApplication.java` application class:

```
package com.packt.microservices.geolocation;

import io.dropwizard.Application;
import io.dropwizard.setup.Environment;
public class GeoLocationApplication extends
Application<GeoLocationConfiguration> {
  public static void main(String[] args) throws Exception {
    new GeoLocationApplication().run(args);
  }

  @Override
  public void run(GeoLocationConfiguration config, Environment
    env) throws Exception {
```

```
        env.jersey().register(new GeoLocationResource());
    }
}
```

There are a lot of things going on here. Let's look at them one by one. Firstly, this class extends `Application` with the `GeoLocationConfiguration` generic. This clearly makes an instance of your `GeoLocationConfiguraiton.java` class available so that you have access to all the properties you have defined in your YAML file at the same time mapped in the `Configuration` class. The next one is the `run` method. The `run` method takes two arguments: your `configuration` and `environment`. The `Environment` instance is a wrapper to other library-specific objects such as `MetricsRegistry`, `HealthCheckRegistry`, and `JerseyEnvironment`. For example, we could register our Jersey resources using the `JerseyEnvironment` instance. The `env.jersey().register(new GeoLocationResource())` line does exactly that. The `main` method is pretty straight-forward. All it does is call the `run` method.

4. Before we can start the microservice, we have to configure this project to create a runnable uber JAR. Uber JARs are just fat JARs that bundle their dependencies in themselves. For this purpose, we will be using the `maven-shade-plugin`. Add the following snippet to the `build` section of the `pom.xml` file. If this is your first plugin, you might want to wrap it in a `<plugins>` element under `<build>`:

```xml
<plugin>
  <groupId>org.apache.maven.plugins</groupId>
  <artifactId>maven-shade-plugin</artifactId>
  <version>2.3</version>
  <configuration>
    <createDependencyReducedPom>true</createDependencyReducedPom>
    <filters>
      <filter>
        <artifact>*:*</artifact>
        <excludes>
          <exclude>META-INF/*.SF</exclude>
          <exclude>META-INF/*.DSA</exclude>
          <exclude>META-INF/*.RSA</exclude>
        </excludes>
      </filter>
    </filters>
  </configuration>
  <executions>
    <execution>
```

```
                <phase>package</phase>
                <goals>
                  <goal>shade</goal>
                </goals>
                <configuration>
                  <transformers>
                    <transformer
implementation="org.apache.maven.plugins.shade.resource.ServicesResourceTra
nsformer" />
                    <transformer
implementation="org.apache.maven.plugins.shade.resource.ManifestResourceTra
nsformer">
<mainClass>com.packt.microservices.geolocation.GeoLocationApplication</main
Class>
                  </transformer>
                </transformers>
              </configuration>
            </execution>
          </executions>
        </plugin>
```

5. The previous snippet does the following:

> It creates a runnable uber JAR that has a reduced `pom.xml` file that does not include the dependencies that are added to the uber JAR. To learn more about this property, take a look at the documentation of `maven-shade-plugin`.

> It utilizes `com.packt.microservices.geolocation.GeoLocationApplication` as the class whose `main` method will be invoked when this JAR is executed. This is done by updating the `MANIFEST` file.

> It excludes all signatures from signed JARs. This is required to avoid security errors.

6. Now that our project is properly configured, let's try to build and run it from the command line. To build the project, execute `mvn clean package` from the project's root directory in your terminal. This will create your final JAR in the target directory. Execute the following command to start your microservice:

```
java -jar target/geolocation-dropwizard-0.0.1-SNAPSHOT.jar server
```

7. The `server` argument instructs Dropwizard to start the Jetty server. After you issue the command, you should be able to see that Dropwizard has started the in-memory Jetty server on port 8080. If you see any warnings about health checks, ignore them. Your console logs should look something like this:

```
INFO   [2016-07-12 02:52:36,651] org.eclipse.jetty.util.log: Logging initialized @761ms
INFO   [2016-07-12 02:52:36,705] io.dropwizard.server.ServerFactory: Starting GeoLocationApplication
INFO   [2016-07-12 02:52:36,725] io.dropwizard.server.DefaultServerFactory: Registering jersey handler with root path prefix: /
INFO   [2016-07-12 02:52:36,741] io.dropwizard.server.DefaultServerFactory: Registering admin handler with root path prefix: /
INFO   [2016-07-12 02:52:36,784] org.eclipse.jetty.setuid.SetUIDListener: Opened application@57ac5227{HTTP/1.1}{0.0.0.0:8080}
INFO   [2016-07-12 02:52:36,784] org.eclipse.jetty.setuid.SetUIDListener: Opened admin@4ba302e0{HTTP/1.1}{0.0.0.0:8081}
INFO   [2016-07-12 02:52:36,786] org.eclipse.jetty.server.Server: jetty-9.2.z-SNAPSHOT
INFO   [2016-07-12 02:52:37,134] io.dropwizard.jersey.DropwizardResourceConfig: The following paths were found for the configured resources:

    GET     / (com.packt.microservices.geolocation.GeoLocationResource)
    POST    / (com.packt.microservices.geolocation.GeoLocationResource)

INFO   [2016-07-12 02:52:37,135] org.eclipse.jetty.server.handler.ContextHandler: Started i.d.j.MutableServletContextHandler@76911385{/,null,AVAILABLE}
INFO   [2016-07-12 02:52:37,138] io.dropwizard.setup.AdminEnvironment: tasks =

    POST    /tasks/log-level (io.dropwizard.servlets.tasks.LogConfigurationTask)
    POST    /tasks/gc (io.dropwizard.servlets.tasks.GarbageCollectionTask)

WARN   [2016-07-12 02:52:37,138] io.dropwizard.setup.AdminEnvironment:
!!!!!!!!!!!!!!!!!!!!!!!!!!!!!!!!!!!!!!!!!!!!!!!!!!!!!!!!!!!!!!!!!!!!!!!!!!!!!!!!!!
!!!!!!!!!!!!!!!!!!!!!!!!!!!!!!!!!!!!!!!!!!!!!!!!!!!!!!!!!!!!!!!!!!!!!!!!!!!!!!!!!!
!    THIS APPLICATION HAS NO HEALTHCHECKS. THIS MEANS YOU WILL NEVER KNOW      !
!    IF IT DIES IN PRODUCTION, WHICH MEANS YOU WILL NEVER KNOW IF YOU'RE       !
!    LETTING YOUR USERS DOWN. YOU SHOULD ADD A HEALTHCHECK FOR EACH OF YOUR    !
!    APPLICATION'S DEPENDENCIES WHICH FULLY (BUT LIGHTLY) TESTS IT.            !
!!!!!!!!!!!!!!!!!!!!!!!!!!!!!!!!!!!!!!!!!!!!!!!!!!!!!!!!!!!!!!!!!!!!!!!!!!!!!!!!!!
!!!!!!!!!!!!!!!!!!!!!!!!!!!!!!!!!!!!!!!!!!!!!!!!!!!!!!!!!!!!!!!!!!!!!!!!!!!!!!!!!!
INFO   [2016-07-12 02:52:37,140] org.eclipse.jetty.server.handler.ContextHandler: Started i.d.j.MutableServletContextHandler@7e46d648{/,null,AVAILABLE}
INFO   [2016-07-12 02:52:37,146] org.eclipse.jetty.server.ServerConnector: Started application@57ac5227{HTTP/1.1}{0.0.0.0:8080}
INFO   [2016-07-12 02:52:37,146] org.eclipse.jetty.server.ServerConnector: Started admin@4ba302e0{HTTP/1.1}{0.0.0.0:8081}
INFO   [2016-07-12 02:52:37,147] org.eclipse.jetty.server.Server: Started @1258ms
0:0:0:0:0:0:0:1 - - [12/Jul/2016:02:53:04 +0000] "GET / HTTP/1.1" 200 2 "-" "curl/7.43.0" 41
0:0:0:0:0:0:0:1 - - [12/Jul/2016:02:53:12 +0000] "POST / HTTP/1.1" 200 114 "-" "curl/7.43.0" 30
0:0:0:0:0:0:0:1 - - [12/Jul/2016:02:53:24 +0000] "POST / HTTP/1.1" 200 115 "-" "curl/7.43.0" 3
0:0:0:0:0:0:0:1 - - [12/Jul/2016:02:53:34 +0000] "GET / HTTP/1.1" 200 232 "-" "curl/7.43.0" 2
0:0:0:0:0:0:0:1 - - [12/Jul/2016:02:53:41 +0000] "POST /geolocation HTTP/1.1" 404 43 "-" "curl/7.43.0" 7
```

8. We are now ready to test our application. Let's try to create two geolocations using the `POST` API and later try to retrieve them using the `GET` method. Execute the following cURL commands in your terminal one by one:

```
curl -H "Content-Type: application/json" -X POST -d '{"timestamp":
1468203975, "userId": "f1196aac-470e-11e6-beb8-9e71128cae77", "latitude":
41.803488, "longitude": -88.144040}' http://localhost:8080/geolocation
```

9. This should give you an output similar to the following (pretty-printed for readability):

```
{
    "latitude": 41.803488,
    "longitude": -88.14404,
    "userId": "f1196aac-470e-11e6-beb8-9e71128cae77",
    "timestamp": 1468203975
}
```

```
curl -H "Content-Type: application/json" -X POST -d '{"timestamp":
1468203975, "userId": "f1196aac-470e-11e6-beb8-9e71128cae77", "latitude":
9.568012, "longitude": 77.962444}' http://localhost:8080/geolocation
```

10. This should give you an output like this (pretty-printed for readability):

```
{
    "latitude": 9.568012,
    "longitude": 77.962444,
    "userId": "f1196aac-470e-11e6-beb8-9e71128cae77",
    "timestamp": 1468203975
}
```

11. To verify whether your entities were stored correctly, execute the following cURL command:

```
curl http://localhost:8080/geolocation
```

12. It should give you an output similar to the following (pretty-printed for readability):

```
[
    {
        "latitude": 41.803488,
        "longitude": -88.14404,
        "userId": "f1196aac-470e-11e6-beb8-9e71128cae77",
        "timestamp": 1468203975
    },
    {
        "latitude": 9.568012,
        "longitude": 77.962444,
        "userId": "f1196aac-470e-11e6-beb8-9e71128cae77",
        "timestamp": 1468203975
    }
]
```

Excellent! You have created your first microservice with Dropwizard. Dropwizard offers more than what we have seen so far. Some of it is out of scope for this book. I believe the metrics API that Dropwizard uses could be used in any type of application. Therefore, we will look at how to use it in later chapters.

Writing REST APIs with SparkJava

In the previous recipes, we saw how to create a microservice using various frameworks such as Spring Boot, WildFly Swarm, and Dropwizard. This recipe is going to be a little different for the fact that we are going to see how to create a self-managed RESTful API using a framework called **SparkJava**. Not to be confused with Apache Spark, the SparkJava framework claims to be a micro-framework for building web applications. Their HTTP API was inspired by Ruby's Sinatra framework. It is so simple that bringing up an HTTP GET API requires fewer than ten lines of code. Owing to this, SparkJava is something that could be considered when you would like to quickly build HTTP-based microservices.

To avoid confusion and dependency conflicts in our project, we will create the SparkJava microservice as its own Maven project. This recipe is just here to help you get started with SparkJava. When you are building your production-level application, it is your choice to either use Spring Boot, WildFly Swarm, Dropwizard, or SparkJava based on your needs.

Getting ready

Similar to how we created other Maven projects, create a Maven JAR module with the **groupId** com.packt.microservices and **name/artifactId** geolocation-sparkjava. Feel free to use either your IDE or the command line. After the project is created, if you see that your project is using a Java version other than 1.8, follow the *Creating a project template using STS and Maven* recipe to change the Java version to 1.8. Perform a Maven update for the change to take effect.

How to do it…

The first thing that you will need is the SparkJava dependency. Add the following snippet to your project's pom.xml file:

```
<dependencies>
  <dependency>
    <groupId>com.sparkjava</groupId>
    <artifactId>spark-core</artifactId>
    <version>2.5</version>
  </dependency>
</dependencies>
```

We now have to create the domain object and service class. Follow the *Writing microservices with WildFly Swarm* recipe to create the following three files:

- com.packt.microservices.geolocation.GeoLocation.java
- com.packt.microservices.geolocation.GeoLocationService.java
- com.packt.microservices.geolocation.GeoLocationServiceImpl.java

Let's see what each of these classes does. The GeoLocation.java class is our domain object that holds the geolocation information. The GeoLocationService.java interface defines our interface, which is then implemented by the GeoLocationServiceImpl.java class. If you take a look at the GeoLocationServiceImpl.java class, we are using a simple collection to store the GeoLocation domain objects. In a real-time scenario, you will be persisting these objects in a database. But to keep it simple, we will not go that far.

The next thing that SparkJava needs is a controller. If you are familiar with Spring MVC, you can relate this controller to that of Spring MVC's. The controller has a collection of routes defined for each URL pattern in your API. Follow these steps:

1. Let's create our controller com.packt.microservices.geolocation.GeoLocationController.java with a stubbed-out GET API:

```
package com.packt.microservices.geolocation;

import static spark.Spark.*;

public class GeoLocationController {

  public static void main(String[] args) {
    get("/geolocation", (req, resp) -> "[]");
  }
}
```

2. The quickest way to test this is by running this class as a Java application. If you get SLF4J errors in your console after you start the application, add the following Maven dependency to your pom.xml file and restart your application:

```
<dependency>
  <groupId>org.slf4j</groupId>
  <artifactId>slf4j-simple</artifactId>
  <version>1.7.21</version>
</dependency>
```

The `slf4j-simple` dependency routes all the SLF4J log messages to the `System.err` stream.

3. Your console logs should look something like this after the restart:

```
[Thread-0] INFO org.eclipse.jetty.util.log - Logging initialized @152ms
[Thread-0] INFO spark.embeddedserver.jetty.EmbeddedJettyServer - == Spark has ignited ...
[Thread-0] INFO spark.embeddedserver.jetty.EmbeddedJettyServer - >> Listening on 0.0.0.0:4567
[Thread-0] INFO org.eclipse.jetty.server.Server - jetty-9.3.6.v20151106
[Thread-0] INFO org.eclipse.jetty.server.ServerConnector - Started ServerConnector@6f97ac6c{HTTP/1.1,[http/1.1]}{0.0.0.0:4567}
[Thread-0] INFO org.eclipse.jetty.server.Server - Started @238ms
```

From the logs, we can clearly see that the service is running on port 4567.

4. Execute the following `curl` command in a terminal window to make sure our API is exposed. The response of the following command should be [], indicating there are no geolocations:

`curl http://localhost:4567/geolocation`

5. Now let's finish building the APIs. We already have a very basic stubbed-out GET API. Let's just introduce the service class to the controller and call the `findAll` method. Similarly, let's use the service's `create` method for POST API calls. Before we do that, we need to do one more thing. By default, SparkJava does not perform JSON serialization and deserialization. We will be using a library called `gson` to do that. So add the following dependency to your `pom.xml` file:

```xml
<dependency>
    <groupId>com.google.code.gson</groupId>
    <artifactId>gson</artifactId>
    <version>2.7</version>
</dependency>
```

6. Now let's replace the `main` method of `GeoLocationController.java` with this:

```java
public static void main(String[] args) {
  GeoLocationService service = new GeoLocationServiceImpl();
  Gson gson = new Gson();

  get("/geolocation", (req, resp) -> {
    return service.findAll();
  }, gson::toJson);

  post("/geolocation", (req, resp) -> {
    return service.create(gson.fromJson(req.body(),
```

```
GeoLocation.class));
    }, gson::toJson);
  }
```

Yes, there are too many things happening here. Let's try to understand them one by one:

- The `get` method now uses the service's `findAll` method
- The third argument to the `get` method is the `ResponseTransformer`, which says how your response should be transformed before being sent to the client
- Since the `ResponseTransformer` is a `FunctionalInterface` with just one method `render` that takes in the rendering logic as an object, we are passing the method reference to Gson's `toJson` method as the rendering logic here.

- The `post` method, which uses the service's `create` method, uses Gson to transform the request body to a `GeoLocation` value.

We are now ready to test our application. Restart the application. Let's try to create two geolocations using the POST API and later try to retrieve them using the GET method:

1. Execute the following cURL commands in your terminal one by one:

```
curl -H "Content-Type: application/json" -X POST -d '{"timestamp":
1468203975, "userId": "f1196aac-470e-11e6-beb8-9e71128cae77", "latitude":
41.803488, "longitude": -88.144040}' http://localhost:4567/geolocation
```

2. This should give you an output similar to the following (pretty-printed for readability):

```
{
  "latitude": 41.803488,
  "longitude": -88.14404,
  "userId": "f1196aac-470e-11e6-beb8-9e71128cae77",
  "timestamp": 1468203975
}
```

```
curl -H "Content-Type: application/json" -X POST -d '{"timestamp":
1468203975, "userId": "f1196aac-470e-11e6-beb8-9e71128cae77", "latitude":
9.568012, "longitude": 77.962444}' http://localhost:4567/geolocation
```

3. This should give you an output like this (pretty-printed for readability):

```
{
  "latitude": 9.568012,
  "longitude": 77.962444,
  "userId": "f1196aac-470e-11e6-beb8-9e71128cae77",
```

```
    "timestamp": 1468203975
}
```

4. To verify whether your entities were stored correctly, execute the following cURL command:

```
curl http://localhost:4567/geolocation
```

5. It should give you output similar to the following (pretty-printed for readability):

```
[
  {
    "latitude": 41.803488,
    "longitude": -88.14404,
    "userId": "f1196aac-470e-11e6-beb8-9e71128cae77",
    "timestamp": 1468203975
  },
  {
    "latitude": 9.568012,
    "longitude": 77.962444,
    "userId": "f1196aac-470e-11e6-beb8-9e71128cae77",
    "timestamp": 1468203975
  }
]
```

There are several other configurations that you can make to SparkJava, such as changing the default port, using query parameters, and using path parameters. I'll leave that to you to experiment.

Conclusion

At the beginning of this chapter, we quickly saw an overview of what microservices are and how they benefit organizations by making it easier to manage and deploy independent services. We looked at an example of a geolocation tracker application to see how it can be broken down into smaller and manageable services. Next, we saw how to create the GeoLocationTracker service using the Spring Boot framework. We also learned how to expose our APIs that consume and read geolocations using Spring MVC. Next, we saw how to build the same application using WildFly Swarm, and JAX-RS. Later, we built the same application using Dropwizard. Finally, we saw how to implement the same service using the SparkJava framework.

I hope you now have a good understanding of what microservices are and how to create them using your favorite framework. The choice of framework completely depends on your needs and your current ecosystem. We strongly recommend you evaluate them before picking one. In the next chapter, we will learn how to package this microservice and later containerize it using Docker.

2
Containerizing Microservices with Docker

In this chapter, we will focus more on how to package and ship our microservice. We will learn the following recipes:

- Building an executable JAR using the Maven Shade plugin
- Building an executable JAR using the Spring Boot Maven plugin
- Installing and setting up Docker
- Writing your Dockerfile
- Building your Docker image
- Running your microservice inside a Docker container
- Pushing your image to Docker Hub

Building an executable JAR using Maven Shade plugin

Before we jump into this recipe, let's talk about why we are doing this. Our goal is to construct a shippable artifact that can be executed from any platform or machine. In order to do that, we have to make sure our final artifact has all dependencies packaged in it. All we are trying to do here is build a fat JAR with all dependencies, called the uber JAR, which we talked about in the previous chapter. Almost all frameworks that help build microservices, such as Spring Boot and WildFly Swarm, have their own Maven plugins that help you build an executable JAR.

But if you use frameworks such as SparkJava and RatPack that are not really microservice frameworks but help in building HTTP APIs, you will have to make sure you use the right Maven or Gradle plugin to create an executable JAR.

Ratpack is a framework that lets you build high-performance HTTP services. Internally, it uses Netty as its HTTP engine. It utilizes Netty's event-based non-blocking mechanism to expose HTTP services, so your APIs will be asynchronous. Also, the way you write APIs in Ratpack is a little different from how you write them in other libraries. For more information about Ratpack, look at their documentation at `https://ratpack.io/manual/current/`.

Getting ready

If you are already using Spring Boot or WildFly Swarm, you can skip this recipe as it already takes care of packaging your application. In order to enforce the packaging of your executable JAR, we will be using the `maven-shade-plugin`. This plugin is especially built for this purpose. Let's take a look at how to do this in our SparkJava project. All this time, we have been running our `geolocation-sparkjava` project from the IDE. Now let's see how we can create an executable JAR for this project and run it from the command-line.

How to do it…

1. Add this snippet to the **Build | Plugins** section of your project's `pom.xml` file:

```
<plugin>
<groupId>org.apache.maven.plugins</groupId>
  <artifactId>maven-shade-plugin</artifactId>
   <version>2.4.3</version>
    <executions>
    <execution>
      <phase>package</phase>
      <goals>
      <goal>shade</goal>
      </goals>
      <configuration>
        <transformers>
          <transformer
            implementation="org.apache.maven.plugins.shade.
            resource.ManifestResourceTransformer">
            <mainClass>com.packt.microservices.
```

```
                geolocation.GeoLocationController</mainClass>
              </transformer>
            </transformers>
          </configuration>
        </execution>
      </executions>
    </plugin>
```

2. Let's try to understand the snippet. The plugin makes sure that whenever the package phase of your Maven build is triggered, it uses the `ManifestResourceTransformer` to add the given `mainClass` name to your `META-INF/MANIFEST.MF` file's `Main-Class` property. This property specifies the entry point to your JAR file. With that said, let's go ahead and run the Maven package goal. Issue the following command from the project's root directory in your terminal:

   `mvn clean package`

3. The previous Maven command packages your project into an executable JAR using the `maven-shade-plugin`. Before it packages, it also runs other Maven goals, including `clean, validate, compile,` and `test`. We will not be discussing these Maven goals in depth as they are out of the scope of this book. The previous command should give you something like this on your console:

```
[INFO] --- maven-shade-plugin:2.4.3:shade (default) @ geolocation-sparkjava ---
[INFO] Including com.sparkjava:spark-core:jar:2.5 in the shaded jar.
[INFO] Including org.slf4j:slf4j-api:jar:1.7.13 in the shaded jar.
[INFO] Including org.eclipse.jetty:jetty-server:jar:9.3.6.v20151106 in the shaded jar.
[INFO] Including javax.servlet:javax.servlet-api:jar:3.1.0 in the shaded jar.
[INFO] Including org.eclipse.jetty:jetty-http:jar:9.3.6.v20151106 in the shaded jar.
[INFO] Including org.eclipse.jetty:jetty-util:jar:9.3.6.v20151106 in the shaded jar.
[INFO] Including org.eclipse.jetty:jetty-io:jar:9.3.6.v20151106 in the shaded jar.
[INFO] Including org.eclipse.jetty:jetty-webapp:jar:9.3.6.v20151106 in the shaded jar.
[INFO] Including org.eclipse.jetty:jetty-xml:jar:9.3.6.v20151106 in the shaded jar.
[INFO] Including org.eclipse.jetty:jetty-servlet:jar:9.3.6.v20151106 in the shaded jar.
[INFO] Including org.eclipse.jetty:jetty-security:jar:9.3.6.v20151106 in the shaded jar.
[INFO] Including org.eclipse.jetty.websocket:websocket-server:jar:9.3.6.v20151106 in the shaded jar.
[INFO] Including org.eclipse.jetty.websocket:websocket-common:jar:9.3.6.v20151106 in the shaded jar.
[INFO] Including org.eclipse.jetty.websocket:websocket-client:jar:9.3.6.v20151106 in the shaded jar.
[INFO] Including org.eclipse.jetty.websocket:websocket-servlet:jar:9.3.6.v20151106 in the shaded jar.
[INFO] Including org.eclipse.jetty.websocket:websocket-api:jar:9.3.6.v20151106 in the shaded jar.
[INFO] Including org.slf4j:slf4j-simple:jar:1.7.21 in the shaded jar.
[INFO] Including com.google.code.gson:gson:jar:2.7 in the shaded jar.
[INFO] Replacing original artifact with shaded artifact.
[INFO] Replacing /Users/vmurugesan/Work/sts-4.8/workspace/geolocation-sparkjava/target/geolocation-sparkjava-0.0.1-SNAPSHOT.jar with /Users/
T-shaded.jar
[INFO] Dependency-reduced POM written at: /Users/vmurugesan/Work/sts-4.8/workspace/geolocation-sparkjava/dependency-reduced-pom.xml
[INFO] ------------------------------------------------------------------------
[INFO] BUILD SUCCESS
[INFO] ------------------------------------------------------------------------
[INFO] Total time: 1.838 s
[INFO] Finished at: 2016-07-24T16:09:35-05:00
[INFO] Final Memory: 20M/218M
[INFO] ------------------------------------------------------------------------
```

4. If you watch closely, you can see that towards the end of the build, the `maven-shade-plugin` is creating a shaded artifact with dependencies such as `sparkjava`, `slf4j`, `jetty`, and `gson`. These JARs are required during the run time of this application. The final artifact will be available in the `target` directory of the project. The `maven-shade-plugin` will replace the original `geolocation-sparkjava-0.0.1-SNAPSHOT.jar` artifact with the shaded artifact.

5. Now let's go ahead and run the application; issue the following Java command:

```
java -jar target/geolocation-sparkjava-0.0.1-SNAPSHOT.jar
```

6. With this command, you can see that your application has started and is listening for new requests on port `4567`:

```
[Thread-0] INFO org.eclipse.jetty.util.log - Logging initialized @192ms
[Thread-0] INFO spark.embeddedserver.jetty.EmbeddedJettyServer - == Spark has ignited ...
[Thread-0] INFO spark.embeddedserver.jetty.EmbeddedJettyServer - >> Listening on 0.0.0.0:4567
[Thread-0] INFO org.eclipse.jetty.server.Server - jetty-9.3.z-SNAPSHOT
[Thread-0] INFO org.eclipse.jetty.server.ServerConnector - Started ServerConnector@331208e6{HTTP/1.1,[http/1.1]}{0.0.0.0:4567}
[Thread-0] INFO org.eclipse.jetty.server.Server - Started @299ms
```

7. Now that our service is ready, let's go ahead and test it by posting a geolocation. Execute the following cURL commands in your terminal:

```
curl -H "Content-Type: application/json" -X POST -d '{"timestamp":
1468203975, "userId": "f1196aac-470e-11e6-beb8-9e71128cae77", "latitude":
41.803488, "longitude": -88.144040}' http://localhost:4567/geolocation
```

8. This should give you an output similar to the following (pretty-printed for readability):

```
{
  "latitude": 41.803488,
  "longitude": -88.14404,
  "userId": "f1196aac-470e-11e6-beb8-9e71128cae77",
  "timestamp": 1468203975
}
```

9. The previous Maven plugin can be used with any type of project. If you are planning to use other frameworks and want to make an executable JAR, you can use the `maven-shade-plugin` to do so.

Building an executable JAR using the Spring Boot Maven plugin

This recipe is intended for Spring Boot users only. If you are using a different framework that does not support building executable JARS, please refer to previous recipe.

Getting ready

The `spring-boot-maven-plugin` is a Maven plugin built by the Spring Boot team to make packaging your Spring Boot applications easier. It not only allows you to package your project, but also helps with running and debugging your application. It introduces a new goal called `repackage`, which pretty much repackages your original artifact (JAR or WAR) with an executable uber JAR that has all dependencies in it. If you are familiar with the `maven-shade-plugin`, the `repackage` goal in Spring Boot does shading.

How to do it...

In order to illustrate this recipe, we will be using the geolocation project that we built in `Chapter 1`, *Building Microservices with Java* using Spring Boot:

1. Open the `pom.xml` file of the geolocation project and look at the parent section. You will see that we have specified spring-boot-starter-parent as the parent Maven module. This module does a few things: it is responsible for declaring the basic spring-core dependency in the `dependencyManagement` section of its `pom.xml` file. It also defines the `pluginManagement` section of the `pom.xml` file with all the Maven plugins that you will need. One of those plugins is spring-boot-maven-plugin. If you are using STS IDE, please go ahead and click on its parent section in the `pom.xml` file by holding the *Ctrl* button (*Command* in Mac).

2. This will take you to the `pom.xml` file of the spring-boot-starter-parent project. You will see something like this in the `pluginManagement` section:

```
<plugin>
  <groupId>org.springframework.boot</groupId>
  <artifactId>spring-boot-maven-plugin</artifactId>
  <executions>
    <execution>
      <goals>
      <goal>repackage</goal>
      </goals>
```

```
      </execution>
    </executions>
    <configuration>
      <mainClass>${start-class}</mainClass>
    </configuration>
  </plugin>
```

3. Go ahead and add the above plugin to the pom file of geolocation project. As you can see, the plugin uses the `repackage` goal to create the executable JAR file. The other thing that you have to notice is the `mainClass` configuration. It holds the `${start-class}` value. This indicates that we have to define a property in our `pom.xml` file with the name `start-class`.

4. Let's go ahead and define the `start-class` property in the `pom.xml` file of our geolocation project. Use the following snippet to add the `start-class` property to your POM file's `project` section:

```
<properties>
<start-class>com.packt.microservices.geolocation.
   GeoLocationApplication</start-class>
</properties>
```

5. After adding the property, if you see any errors in your project, perform a Maven update. Now, we are ready to test our application from the command line.

6. Open a terminal and issue the following command from the project's root directory:

```
mvn clean package spring-boot:run
```

7. As you can see, we are using the `run` goal of `spring-boot-maven` plugin. This will first build your project and then give you something like this on the console:

8. The package goal in the previous command should have created the uber JAR in the `target` directory for us. If you wish, you could try running the JAR using the `java -jar` command as well. Now that our service is ready, let's go ahead and test it by posting a geolocation. Execute the following `curl` commands in your terminal:

```
curl -H "Content-Type: application/json" -X POST -d
'{"timestamp": 1468203975, "userId": "f1196aac-470e-11e6-
beb8-9e71128cae77", "latitude": 41.803488,"longitude": -88.144040}'
http://localhost:8080/geolocation
```

9. This should give you an output similar to the following (pretty-printed for readability):

```
{
    "latitude": 41.803488,
    "longitude": -88.14404,
    "userId": "f1196aac-470e-11e6-beb8-9e71128cae77",
    "timestamp": 1468203975
}
```

The previous method showed you how to package your application using the `spring-boot-maven-plugin`. But if you would like to use the `maven-shade-plugin`, you can do that too. The support for using `maven-shade-plugin` is available in the spring-boot-starter-parent project. If you look at the POM file of the parent project, you can see the `maven-shade-plugin` defined. The choice of using either `spring-boot-maven-plugin` or `maven-shade-plugin` is left to you and purely depends on your need.

There are other goals that `spring-boot-maven-plugin` provides. Some of them are the `start` and `stop` goals. The start goal is very similar to `run`, except it does not block the operation. It is usually used when you would like to run integration tests on your microservice. The `stop` goal is used to stop the application that was started using the `start` goal. To learn more about this plugin, visit the documentation page at `http://docs.spring.io/spring-boot/docs/1.3.6.RELEASE/maven-plugin/index.html`.

Installing and setting up Docker

Before we look at the recipe, let's quickly talk about why we will need Docker installed. Docker has been one of the most popular container frameworks and has picked up traction in the past few years. In fact, there are a lot many organizations that completely depend on Docker for shipping and deploying their applications. Gone are the days when Developers, Build Meisters, Infrastructure Engineers, and Deployment Coordinators would deploy any new code and infrastructure every release in the middle of the night, making sure the deployment of the new code or infrastructure does not affect existing users. With frameworks such as Docker, Mesos, and Kubernetes, deployments have become so much easier than how they were a few years back.

Let's say you would like to deploy a web application to Tomcat. There are definitely some prerequisites; for instance, you will need at least a four-core machine with 16 GB memory and 100 GB disk space. And after that, you have to install an operating system on it. After you have your OS installed, you need many other tools, such as Java, Tomcat, Nginx, and perhaps other monitoring and log management tools. Now you need someone to maintain this machine–upgrades, installations, deployments, and so on. It becomes even harder if you want a horizontal and vertical cluster.

Now you need more resources, plus you will need more administrators to manage your machines. What if you could run your application inside a container that has all these prerequisites already set up? What if you could create images that already have your prerequisites and your application? That's exactly what Docker helps you with. Docker helps you build images with whatever you need and also helps you run containers for your images on machines that have Docker installed. Machines that have Docker installed are called **Docker hosts**. You will see this term being used a lot throughout the book.

Getting ready

At the time of writing this, native Docker installations for both Mac and Windows are still in beta. So we will be using Docker Machine in this recipe and the rest of the book. Moreover, we will be using the Mac version of Docker Machine. If you are a Windows user, most of the instructions are still going to be the same.

If you are a Linux user, you can skip the steps where we work with Docker Machine. Installing Docker on Linux is so much easier compared to Mac and Windows. Please follow the installation instructions on Docker's website to install it on your Linux machine. You can find the documentation here: `https://docs.docker.com/engine/installation/#/on-linux`.

Docker Machine for Mac or Windows utilizes Oracle VirtualBox to spin off virtual machines that act as Docker hosts. Docker Machine will communicate with the VirtualBox VM instances for any commands you issue in your command line. For more information on how Docker Machine works, take a look at this link: `https://docs.docker.com/machine/concepts`. As this is a little out of scope for this book, it is strongly recommended that you read and understand how Docker and Docker Machine work before moving to the next section.

How to do it...

1. Let's go to the homepage of Docker Toolbox at `https://www.docker.com/products/docker-toolbox`. Docker Toolbox is currently supported for Windows and Mac. It is just a package of four different products from Docker: Docker Engine, Docker Machine, Docker Compose, and Docker Kitematic.

 Docker Kitematic is Docker's attempt at a UI-driven management console for Docker on your machine. We will be looking at Docker Compose in the next chapter.

2. From the home page, choose your operating system type and download the DMG (for Mac) or EXE (for Windows) file. At the time of writing this, the following is how the Docker Toolbox homepage looked like. Over time, there could be changes but the idea is to download the DMG or EXE file from the home page.

3. Once the download is complete, go ahead and open the downloaded installer file. You should see something like this. Go ahead and click on **Continue**.

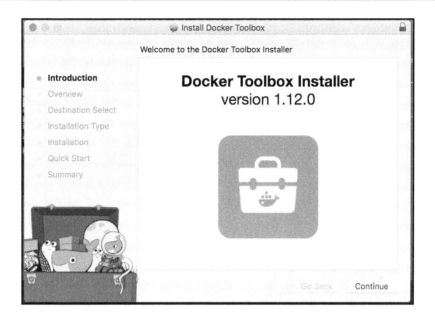

4. In the Overview section, you will have the option to let Docker collect anonymous data for their purposes. Either check or uncheck that option and hit **Continue**:

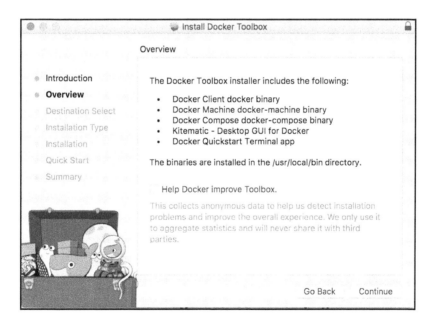

5. The next two sections, **Destination Select** and **Installation Type**, are pretty straight-forward. You will be prompted to choose where you would like to install Docker Toolbox. Choose the directory of your choice and hit **Install**:

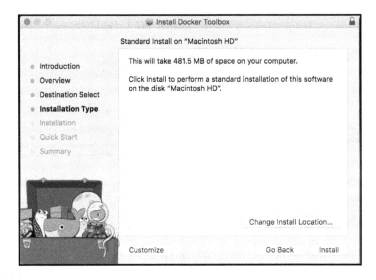

6. You will be shown the progress of your installation, and when it is complete, you will see something like this:

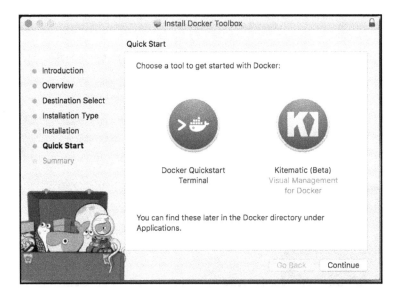

7. You will be prompted to either open **Docker Quickstart Terminal** or **Kitematic**. Skip them both and hit **Continue** to complete the installation.

8. Now let's test our installation. As we are using Mac in our recipes, you will see Unix commands used throughout the book. For Windows users, it might be a good idea to install Cygwin if you are familiar with it. Either way, the commands should be the same on both operating systems. Issue the following command on your terminal:

```
docker-machine ls
```

9. This command is used to list the VirtualBox VMs created in your machine. By default, you will see one VM created, with the name `default`. You will see something like this:

10. By default, this VM might not have sufficient resources to run the frameworks we would want to use. So let's recreate this VM with 4 CPUs and 4096 MB memory. Execute the following command to recreate your VM (if it asks for delete confirmation, choose **Yes**):

```
docker-machine rm default && docker-machine create -d virtualbox --
virtualbox-memory=4096 --virtualbox-cpu-count=4 default
```

11. We are doing two things in the preceding command: removing the existing VM and recreating the VM with more resources. As you can see, we are passing VirtualBox specific arguments `--virtualbox-memory` and `--virtualbox-cpu-count` to increase the memory and CPU count respectively. In our case, we have provided 4 CPUs and 4096 MB memory to our VM. This should be sufficient to run the frameworks that we will be using in this book.

After you run the command you should have seen something like this:

```
About to remove default
Are you sure? (y/n): y
Successfully removed default
Running pre-create checks...
Creating machine...
(default) Copying /Users/mvikramramesh/.docker/machine/cache/boot2docker.iso to /Users/mvikramramesh/.docker/machine/machines/default/boot2docker.iso...
(default) Creating VirtualBox VM...
(default) Creating SSH key...
(default) Starting the VM...
(default) Check network to re-create if needed...
(default) Waiting for an IP...
Waiting for machine to be running, this may take a few minutes...
Detecting operating system of created instance...
Waiting for SSH to be available...
Detecting the provisioner...
Provisioning with boot2docker...
Copying certs to the local machine directory...
Copying certs to the remote machine...
Setting Docker configuration on the remote daemon...
Checking connection to Docker...
Docker is up and running!
To see how to connect your Docker Client to the Docker Engine running on this virtual machine, run: docker-machine env default
```

12. If you see that your VM is stopped, issue the following command to start it:

    docker-machine start default

13. After you issue the previous command, you will see this:

```
Starting "default"...
(default) Check network to re-create if needed...
(default) Waiting for an IP...
Machine "default" was started.
Waiting for SSH to be available...
Detecting the provisioner...
Started machines may have new IP addresses. You may need to re-run the `docker-machine env` command.
```

14. As you can see, you will have to run the `env` command to make your shell ready to use this `docker-machine` instance. In order to do that, issue the following command on your console:

    eval $(docker-machine env default)

15. This makes your shell ready to use your newly created Docker Machine instance called `default`. If you would like to see your VirtualBox VM, open VirtualBox, and you will see that your Docker host has been created and is running. Now let's try to spin off our first Docker container:

    docker run hello-world

16. You should see something like this:

```
Unable to find image 'hello-world:latest' locally
latest: Pulling from library/hello-world

c04b14da8d14: Pull complete
Digest: sha256:0256e8a36e2070f7bf2d0b0763dbabdd67798512411de4cdcf9431a1feb60fd9
Status: Downloaded newer image for hello-world:latest

Hello from Docker!
This message shows that your installation appears to be working correctly.

To generate this message, Docker took the following steps:
 1. The Docker client contacted the Docker daemon.
 2. The Docker daemon pulled the "hello-world" image from the Docker Hub.
 3. The Docker daemon created a new container from that image which runs the
    executable that produces the output you are currently reading.
 4. The Docker daemon streamed that output to the Docker client, which sent it
    to your terminal.

To try something more ambitious, you can run an Ubuntu container with:
 $ docker run -it ubuntu bash

Share images, automate workflows, and more with a free Docker Hub account:
 https://hub.docker.com

For more examples and ideas, visit:
 https://docs.docker.com/engine/userguide/
```

17. There are lots of things going on here. Let's try to understand them one by one:
    - First, let's understand the line that says `Unable to find image 'hello-world:latest' locally`. This line says that you are trying to run a container for an image that does not exist in your Docker host.
    - Docker then downloads the image from Docker Hub (over the Internet) and later uses that image to run a container.
    - You can find this image on Docker Hub here: `https://hub.docker.com/_/hello-world/`. While `hello-world` is the name of the image, `latest` is its tag.
    - Tags are pretty much the same as versions. As you can see, even when we did not provide the `docker` tag in our `docker run` command, Docker automatically used the `latest` tag.
    - After the download, you can see the hello world message. This says that we have successfully run this container and hence successfully installed Docker.

18. If you would like to see the images available on your Docker host, issue the following command:

```
docker images
```

19. You should see something like this:

REPOSITORY	TAG	IMAGE ID	CREATED	SIZE
hello-world	latest	c54a2cc56cbb	7 weeks ago	1.848 kB

20. If you would like to see the containers that are running on your Docker machine, use the following command:

```
docker ps -a
```

21. The -a flag requests Docker to show all containers, including the ones that were stopped. You should see something like this:

CONTAINER ID	IMAGE	COMMAND	CREATED	STATUS	PORTS	NAMES
20181e863c9a	hello-world	"/hello"	8 minutes ago	Exited (0) 8 minutes ago		agitated_tesla

That brings us to the end of this recipe. In the next recipe, we will see how to Dockerize our microservice.

Writing your Dockerfile

So far in this chapter, we have seen how to package our application and how to install Docker. Now that we have our JAR artifact and Docker set up, let's see how to Dockerize our microservice application using Docker.

Getting ready

In order to Dockerize our application, we will have to tell Docker how our image is going to look like. This is exactly the purpose of a Dockerfile. A Dockerfile has its own syntax (or Dockerfile instructions) and will be used by Docker to create images. Throughout this recipe, we will try to understand some of the most commonly used Dockerfile instructions as we write our Dockerfile for the geolocation tracker microservice.

How to do it...

1. First, open your STS IDE and create a new file called `Dockerfile` in the geolocation project. The first line of the Dockerfile is always the `FROM` instruction followed by the base image that you would like to create your image from. There are thousands of images on Docker Hub to choose from. In our case, we would need something that already has Java installed on it. There are some images that are *official*, meaning they are well documented and maintained.

    Docker Official Repositories are very well documented, and they follow best practices and standards. Docker has its own team to maintain these repositories. This is essential in order to keep the repository clear, thus helping the user make the right choice of repository. To read more about Docker Official Repositories, take a look at `https://docs.docker.com/docker-hub/official_repos/`.

2. We will be using the Java official repository. To find the official repository, go to hub.docker.com and search for `java`. You have to choose the one that says official. At the time of writing this, the Java image documentation says it will soon be deprecated in favor of the `openjdk` image. So the first line of our Dockerfile will look like this:

   ```
   FROM openjdk:8
   ```

3. As you can see, we have used version (or tag) `8` for our image. If you are wondering what type of operating system this image uses, take a look at the Dockerfile of this image, which you can get from the Docker Hub page. Docker images are usually tagged with the version of the software they are written for. That way, it is easy for users to pick from. The next step is creating a directory for our project where we will store our JAR artifact. Add this as your next line:

   ```
   RUN mkdir -p /opt/packt/geolocation
   ```

   This is a simple Unix command that creates the `/opt/packt/geolocation` directory. The `-p` flag instructs it to create the intermediate directories if they don't exist. Now let's create an instruction that will add the JAR file that was created in your local machine into the container at `/opt/packt/geolocation`.

   ```
   ADD target/geolocation-0.0.1-SNAPSHOT.jar /opt/packt/geolocation/
   ```

4. As you can see, we are picking up the uber JAR from target directory and dropping it into the `/opt/packt/geolocation/` directory of the container. Take a look at the `/` at the end of the target path. That says that the JAR has to be copied into the directory.

5. Before we can start the application, there is one thing we have to do, that is, expose the ports that we would like to be mapped to the Docker host ports. In our case, the in-memory Tomcat instance is running on port `8080`. In order to be able to map port `8080` of our container to any port on our Docker host, we have to expose it first. For that, we will use the `EXPOSE` instruction. Add the following line to your Dockerfile:

    EXPOSE 8080

6. Now that we are ready to start the app, let's go ahead and tell Docker how to start a container for this image. For that, we will use the `CMD` instruction:

    CMD ["java", "-jar", "/opt/packt/geolocation/geolocation-0.0.1-SNAPSHOT.jar"]

There are two things we have to note here. One is the way we are starting the application and the other is how the command is broken down into comma-separated Strings.

First, let's talk about how we start the application. You might be wondering why we haven't used the `mvn spring-boot:run` command to start the application. Keep in mind that this command will be executed inside the container, and our container does not have Maven installed, only OpenJDK 8. If you would like to use the `mvn` command, take that as an exercise, and try to install Maven on your container and use the `mvn` command to start the application. Now that we know we have Java installed, we are issuing a very simple java – `jar` command to run the JAR. In fact, the Spring Boot Maven plugin internally issues the same command.

The next thing is how the command has been broken down into comma-separated Strings. This is a standard that the CMD instruction follows. To keep it simple, keep in mind that for whatever command you would like to run upon running the container, just break it down into comma-separated Strings (in whitespaces).

Your final Dockerfile should look something like this:

```
FROM openjdk:8
RUN mkdir -p /opt/packt/geolocation
ADD target/geolocation-0.0.1-SNAPSHOT.jar
  /opt/packt/geolocation/
EXPOSE 8080
CMD ["java", "-jar", "/opt/packt/geolocation/geolocation-
  0.0.1-SNAPSHOT.jar"]
```

This Dockerfile is one of the simplest implementations. Dockerfiles can sometimes get bigger due to the fact that you need a lot of customizations to your image. In such cases, it is a good idea to break it down into multiple images that can be reused and maintained separately.

With that said, we've come to the completion of this recipe. There are some best practices to follow whenever you create your own Dockerfile and image. Though we haven't covered that here as it is out of the scope of this book, you still should take a look at them and follow them. To learn more about the various Dockerfile instructions, go to https://docs.docker.com/engine/reference/builder/.

Building your Docker image

In the previous recipe, we created the Dockerfile, which will be used in this recipe to create an image for our microservice. If you are wondering why we would need an image, it is the only way we can ship our software to any system. Once you have your image created and uploaded to a common repository, it will be easier to pull your image from any location.

Getting ready

Before you jump into the actual recipe, it might be a good idea to get yourself familiar with some of the most commonly used Docker commands. In this recipe, we will use the build command. Take a look at this URL to understand the other commands: `https://docs.docker.com/engine/reference/commandline/#/image-commands`. After familiarizing yourself with the commands, open up a new terminal, and change your directory to the root of the geolocation project. Make sure your `docker-machine` instance is running. If it is not running, use the `docker-machine start` command to run your `docker-machine` instance:

```
docker-machine start default
```

If you have to configure your shell for the default Docker machine, go ahead and execute the following command:

```
eval $(docker-machine env default)
```

How to do it...

1. From the terminal, issue the following docker build command:

   ```
   docker build -t packt/geolocation .
   ```

2. We'll try to understand the command later. For now, let's see what happens after you issue the preceding command. You should see Docker downloading the `openjdk` image from Docker Hub.

```
Sending build context to Docker daemon 13.57 MB
Step 1 : FROM openjdk:8
8: Pulling from library/openjdk
357ea8c3d80b: Downloading [===>                                        ] 3.145 MB/51.37 MB
52befadefd24: Downloading [=========>                                  ] 3.538 MB/18.53 MB
3c0732d5313c: Downloading [===>                                        ] 2.569 MB/42.5 MB
557cb7f84eb9: Waiting
831d48be5871: Waiting
fecf7eeb197d: Waiting
e5e3695c1a93: Waiting
a37afaae8f5b: Waiting
```

3. Once the image has been downloaded, you will see that Docker tries to validate each and every instruction provided in the Dockerfile. When the last instruction has been processed, you will see a message saying `Successfully built`. This says that your image has been successfully built.

```
Sending build context to Docker daemon 13.57 MB
Step 1 : FROM openjdk:8
8: Pulling from library/openjdk
357ea8c3d80b: Pull complete
52befadefd24: Pull complete
3c0732d5313c: Pull complete
557cb7f84eb9: Pull complete
831d48be5871: Pull complete
fecf7eeb197d: Pull complete
e5e3695c1a93: Pull complete
a37afaae8f5b: Pull complete
Digest: sha256:1064e0e67166f8859dd7e1aa1104ffc00133bcf19dbd426447cce6f90319031e
Status: Downloaded newer image for openjdk:8
 ---> 69a777edb6dc
Step 2 : RUN mkdir -p /opt/packt/geolocation
 ---> Running in 93f23ec0eebc
 ---> 0af2cef7f04e
Removing intermediate container 93f23ec0eebc
Step 3 : ADD target/geolocation-0.0.1-SNAPSHOT.jar /opt/packt/geolocation/
 ---> 5c6b74af5ea1
Removing intermediate container d6ab5c1730a6
Step 4 : EXPOSE 8080
 ---> Running in 436b4ce51068
 ---> 93ac30784775
Removing intermediate container 436b4ce51068
Step 5 : CMD java -jar /opt/packt/geolocation/geolocation-0.0.1-SNAPSHOT.jar
 ---> Running in 7534d92ccc31
 ---> 2834aa27e5ad
Removing intermediate container 7534d92ccc31
Successfully built 2834aa27e5ad
```

4. Now let's try to understand the command. There are three things to note here:
   - The first thing is the `docker build` command itself. The `docker build` command is used to build a Docker image from a Dockerfile. It needs at least one input, which is usually the location of the Dockerfile.

Dockerfiles can be renamed to something other than `Dockerfile` and can be referred to using the -f option of the docker build command. An instance of this being used is when teams have different Dockerfiles for different build environments, for example, using DockerfileDev for the development environment, DockerfileStaging for the staging environment, and DockerfileProd for the production environment. It is still encouraged as a best practice to use other Docker options (like passing arguments) in order to keep the same Dockerfile for all environments. For more information on how to pass arguments to Dockerfile, please take a look at this documentation:
`https://docs.docker.com/engine/reference/builder/#arg`

- The second thing is the `-t` option. The `-t` option takes the name of the repo and a tag. In our case, we have not mentioned the tag, so by default, it will pick up `latest` as the tag. If you look at the repo name, it is different from the official `openjdk` image name. It has two parts: `packt` and `geolocation`. It is always a good practice to put the Docker Hub account name followed by the actual image name as the name of your repo. For now, we will use `packt` as our temporary account name, but in the next recipe, we will see how to create our own Docker Hub account and use that account name here.
- The third thing is the dot at the end. The dot operator says that the Dockerfile is located in the current directory, or the present working directory to be more precise.

5. Let's go ahead and verify whether our image was created. In order to do that, issue the following command on your terminal:

    docker images

6. The docker images command is used to list down all images available in your Docker host. After issuing the command, you should see something like this:

REPOSITORY	TAG	IMAGE ID	CREATED	SIZE
packt/geolocation	latest	2834aa27e5ad	31 minutes ago	656.6 MB
openjdk	8	69a777edb6dc	11 days ago	643 MB
hello-world	latest	c54a2cc56cbb	7 weeks ago	1.848 kB

As you can see, the newly built image is listed as `packt/geolocation` in your Docker host. The tag for this image is `latest` as we did not specify any. The image ID uniquely identifies your image. Note the size of the image. It is a few megabytes bigger than the `openjdk:8` image. That is most probably because of the size of our executable uber JAR inside the container.

Now that we know how to build an image using an existing Dockerfile, we are at the end of this recipe. This is just a very quick intro to the `docker build` command. There are more options that you can provide to the command, such as CPUs and memory.

To learn more about the `docker build` command, take a look at this page:
`https://docs.docker.com/engine/reference/commandline/build/`

Running your microservice inside a Docker container

In the previous recipe, we successfully created our Docker image in the Docker host. Keep in mind that if you are using Windows or Mac, your Docker host is the VirtualBox VM and not your local computer. In this recipe, we will look at how to spin off a container for the newly created image.

Getting ready

To spin off a new container for our `packt/geolocation` image, we will use the `docker run` command. This command is used to run any command inside your container, given the image. Open your terminal and go to the root of the geolocation project. If you have to start your Docker machine instance, then do so by using the `docker-machine start` command, and set the environment using the `docker-machine env` command.

How to do it...

1. Go ahead and issue the following command on your terminal:

   ```
   docker run packt/geolocation
   ```

2. Right after you run the command, you should see something like this:

   Yay! We can see that our microservice is running as a Docker container. But wait-there is more to it. Let's see how we can access our microservice's in-memory Tomcat instance. Try to run a `curl` command to see if our app is up and running:

3. Open a new terminal instance and execute the following cURL command in that shell:

   ```
   curl -H "Content-Type: application/json" -X POST -d'{"timestamp":
   1468203975, "userId": "f1196aac-470e-11e6-beb8-9e71128cae77", "latitude":
   41.803488, "longitude":-88.144040}' http://localhost:8080/geolocation
   ```

4. Did you get an error message like this?

   ```
   curl: (7) Failed to connect to localhost port 8080:
         Connection refused
   ```

Let's try to understand what happened here. Why would we get a connection refused error when our microservice logs clearly say that it is running on port 8080? Yes, you guessed it right: the microservice is not running on your local computer; it is actually running inside the container, which in turn is running inside your Docker host. Here, your Docker host is the VirtualBox VM called `default`.

So we have to replace localhost in your cURL command with the IP of the container. But getting the IP of the container is not straight-forward. That is the reason we are going to map port 8080 of the container to the same port on the VM. This mapping will make sure that any request made to port 8080 on the VM will be forwarded to port 8080 of the container.

1. Now go to the shell that is currently running your container, and stop your container. Usually, *Ctrl* + *C* will do the job. After your container is stopped, issue the following command:

    ```
    docker run -p 8080:8080 packt/geolocation
    ```

2. The -p option does the port mapping from Docker host to container. The port number to the left of the colon indicates the port number of the Docker host, and the port number to the right of the colon indicates that of the container. In our case, both of them are same. After you execute the previous command, you should see the same logs that you saw before.

3. We are not done yet. We still have to find the IP that we have to use to hit our RESTful endpoint. The IP that we have to use is the IP of our Docker Machine VM. To find the IP of the `docker-machine` instance, execute the following command in a new terminal instance:

    ```
    docker-machine ip default
    ```

4. This should give you the IP of the VM. Let's say the IP that you received was 192.168.99.100. Now, replace `localhost` in your cURL command with this IP, and execute the cURL command again:

    ```
    curl -H "Content-Type: application/json" -X POST -d'{"timestamp":
    1468203975, "userId": "f1196aac-470e-11e6-beb8-9e71128cae77", "latitude":
    41.803488, "longitude":-88.144040}' http://192.168.99.100:8080/geolocation
    ```

5. This should give you an output similar to the following (pretty-printed for readability):

```
{
  "latitude": 41.803488,
  "longitude": -88.14404,
  "userId": "f1196aac-470e-11e6-beb8-9e71128cae77",
  "timestamp": 1468203975
}
```

6. This confirms that you are able to access your microservice from the outside. Before you move on to the next recipe, take a moment to understand how the port mapping is done. The following figure shows how your machine, VM, and container are orchestrated:

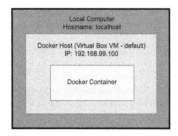

As you can see, the Docker container is running inside the Docker host (VirtualBox VM), which in turn is running on our local computer. This is the hierarchy in which the machines are orchestrated. Our port mapping maps port `8080` on the Docker host to port `8080` of the Docker container.

Pushing your image to Docker Hub

In the previous recipe, we saw how to run your microservice as a Docker container. Your image is not really useful unless you make it easier for shipping. In order for your image to be accessible from other places, you should first host it somewhere.

There are two ways of doing this: either push your image to the Docker Hub central repository, or create your own private Docker registry and push it there. Repositories created on Docker Hub are by default public. You can still purchase various plans to make your repositories private. That is completely up to you and depends on your use case.

Getting ready

1. Before you can push the image to Docker Hub, you will first need a Docker Hub account. If you already have one, skip this step. If you don't have one, go to `https://hub.docker.com/` and start creating an account for yourself. You will need three things:
   - User ID
   - Email associated
   - Password

2. After you have created a new account, log in with your credentials. Take some time to get familiar with the Docker Hub user interface. It is pretty simple and straight-forward.

3. The next thing we have to do is create a repository for our new microservice. This is required before we start trying to push the image to Docker Hub. To create a new repository, click on the `Create Repository` button:

Welcome to Docker Hub
Here are a few things to get you started.

Create Repository   Create Organization   Explore Repositories

4. In the **Create Repository** form, enter the repository name as `geolocation`. Give the short description as `Geo Location Tracking Service` and the full description as `Geo location tracking microservice that will be responsible for collecting and storing geolocations of users`. Mark the visibility of your image as `public`. If you have some sensitive information in your image, it is recommended you use `private`. But since our image is not that sensitive, we will use `public` visibility. Moreover, using the `private` visibility requires additional configuration when you try to pull your image from Marathon and Kubernetes.

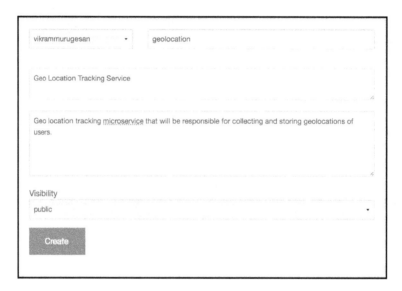

5. After entering all these fields, hit the **Create** button. After the repository is created, you should see a screen similar to this:

As you can see, for consistency, we will use my Docker Hub account throughout the book. Now that we have our repository ready, we just have to push our image to this repository.

How to do it...

1. Before you can push the image to your newly created Docker Hub repo, you have to first tag the image because you will be pushing it to your own repo and not packt. In this case, we will be pushing it to my account, vikrammurugesan. But please change it to your account name wherever you see vikrammurugesan going forward. Open a terminal window and make sure you have docker-machine started. If not, go ahead and start it, and set the environment as well. Execute the following command in your shell:

   docker tag packt/geolocation vikrammurugesan/geolocation

2. To check whether your image was tagged with the new repo name, issue the docker images command and see whether you get something like this:

```
REPOSITORY                    TAG       IMAGE ID        CREATED            SIZE
packt/geolocation             latest    2834aa27e5ad    About an hour ago  656.6 MB
vikrammurugesan/geolocation   latest    2834aa27e5ad    About an hour ago  656.6 MB
openjdk                       8         69a777edb6dc    11 days ago        643 MB
hello-world                   latest    c54a2cc56cbb    7 weeks ago        1.848 kB
```

3. As you can see, there is a new image now with the new repo name we just created. If you look at the image IDs of these two images, they're the same. That is because we just tagged the `packt` image with the new repository's account name without any modifications.

 To learn more about the docker tag command, take a look at its documentation:
`https://docs.docker.com/engine/reference/commandline/tag/`

4. The next step will be pushing the image over to Docker Hub. To do that, execute the following command:

```
docker push vikrammurugesan/geolocation
```

5. You will see that in order to push the image to the repo in my account, authentication is required. This is to make sure another user is not using the same repo.

```
The push refers to a repository [docker.io/vikrammurugesan/geolocation]
62b3303dce44: Preparing
d1fb1f5201c9: Preparing
e4ecd8459633: Preparing
5778f887b92c: Preparing
1a6f9199aa61: Preparing
a0163fd1c828: Waiting
c6952565c883: Waiting
1050aff7cfff: Waiting
66d8e5ee400c: Waiting
2f71b45e4e25: Waiting
unauthorized: authentication required
```

6. To authenticate yourself, you need to use the `docker login` command. Use the following command to authenticate yourself:

```
docker login
```

7. After you execute the previous command, Docker will ask you to enter your credentials. After successful authentication, execute the same `docker push` command again. This time you will see that your image is being uploaded to Docker Hub:

```
The push refers to a repository [docker.io/vikrammurugesan/geolocation]
62b3303dce44: Pushing [===>                                              ] 821.2 kB/13.51 MB
d1fb1f5201c9: Pushing  2.56 kB
e4ecd8459633: Pushing [================================================>]   426 kB
5778f887b92c: Preparing
1a6f9199aa61: Pushing [================================================>] 3.584 kB
a0163fd1c828: Waiting
c6952565c883: Waiting
1050aff7cfff: Waiting
66d8e5ee400c: Waiting
2f71b45e4e25: Waiting
```

8. This process usually takes some time because it is uploading a 656.6 MB file to the Internet. The time taken depends on the speed of your connection. Now that your image has been successfully uploaded to Docker Hub, let's go ahead and verify that your image is available on it. Go to your Docker Hub page from your browser and navigate to the geolocation repo. From there, click on the **Tags** tab and make sure you see a new entry for the latest tag:

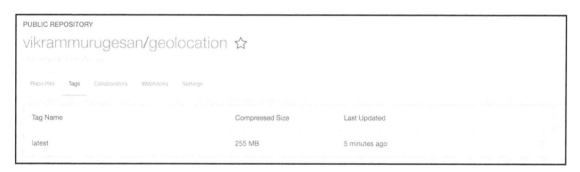

This confirms that your image has been successfully pushed to Docker Hub. Note the size of the image: it is much smaller than the actual size of the image. That is because Docker compresses the image before it uploads it to Docker Hub.

That's it! You have successfully created and uploaded your microservice image to Docker Hub. Your image can now be pulled from any location.

What we have seen so far is just a simple approach to dockerizing your microservice and pushing it to Docker Hub. In a real-life scenario, you will be required to use different docker commands and different techniques. It is strongly recommended that you go through Docker's documentation to understand each and every command and their additional options.

That brings us to the end of this chapter.

3
Deploying Microservices on Mesos

In this chapter, we will learn how to deploy microservices on Mesos, which is an open source cluster management framework from Apache. We will cover the following recipes:

- Setting up a Mesos cluster using Docker
- Understanding the Mesos and Marathon interface
- Deploying your microservice to Mesos using Marathon
- Configuring ports in Marathon
- Configuring volumes in Marathon
- Configuring environment variables in Marathon
- Scaling your microservice in Marathon
- Destroying your microservice in Marathon
- Monitoring your microservice logs in Marathon
- Monitoring your microservice logs in Mesos
- Managing your microservice using Marathon's REST API

Introduction

Before we jump into the recipes and try creating a Mesos cluster, it is very important that you know what Mesos is and why we use it to deploy microservices.

Let's answer the first question: What is Mesos?

Mesos is a cluster management framework that makes resource allocation easier in order to run distributed applications. If you break this sentence down, it will start making more sense. Mesos is called a *cluster management framework* because it groups multiple machines into one single virtual resource pool. Let's say you have 10 machines with 4 GB memory, 4 cores each, and 10 GB disk space. Now you would like to use these machines to do different things, such as the following:

- Run Spark jobs
- Run long running services
- Run Cron jobs
- Run Hadoop
- Run Cassandra

In this case, you would ideally have to go to a whiteboard and draw out an architecture diagram that identifies what is going to run on what machine. You will have machines dedicated for a single purpose. A machine dedicated to run Spark jobs might not be used to run Docker containers unless you go and install Docker on that machine. So as you can see, there is quite a bit of work involved in order to maintain this cluster. At the same time, this setup is not fault tolerant. This is exactly what Mesos solves. If you install Mesos on those 10 machines, you will get a cluster with total resources of 40 GB memory, 40 cores, and 100 GB disk space (keeping in mind that one other machine is used as the master). With that said, Mesos makes it easier to run any type of task on any of these 10 machines.

Now let's move on to *resource allocation*. As Mesos groups all the resources from all the machines (slaves or agents in Mesos terms) into one single virtual resource pool, allocation of resources is automatically taken care of by Mesos. For example, if you would like to spin off a Spark job that needs 2 cores, 2 GB memory and 1 GB disk space, Mesos automatically makes a decision on where this Spark job is going to be submitted based on the availability of resources. This is one of the true wins of Mesos compared to other cluster management frameworks.

Finally, let's talk about *running distributed applications*. Part of this was actually explained in the previous section that talked about Spark job submissions. One example of how Mesos helps run distributed applications is the execution mode of Spark jobs. If you are running Spark jobs on a Mesos cluster, you can choose between two modes: coarse grained and fine grained. Both of these modes define how the cores are shared between multiple Spark tasks. As the name suggests, fine-grained mode is responsible for sharing the cores at a more granular level. At the time of writing this, fine-grained mode has been deprecated by Spark and will soon be removed.

The other example is being able to run multiple instances of the same Docker image from Marathon. By doing so, you are actually scaling your application without having to worry about where your container is running. This will be covered in later recipes in this chapter. These features clearly depict how Mesos helps us run distributed applications.

Now let's answer our second question: Why Mesos to deploy microservices?

We already answered this question in the previous section a little bit. Let's get into the details now. Mesos basically follows a master-slave architecture, where there can be one or more masters and multiple slaves. At any point of time, only one master will be in charge (also called the **leader**). The master's responsibility is to coordinate and delegate offers (resource requests to run tasks) between the framework schedulers and framework executors. Frameworks in Mesos are used to run any particular task on a Mesos cluster. These tasks could be Spark jobs, Cassandra tasks, Docker containers, and so on. The framework that is used to run long-running jobs or Docker containers is called **Marathon**.

In this chapter, we will be learning extensively about Marathon. As we already have our application Dockerized as a Docker image, we will use Marathon and its abilities to expose our microservice.

Setting up a Mesos cluster using Docker

In this recipe, we will be learning how to orchestrate our first Mesos Cluster with Marathon framework configured. We will be orchestrating this cluster in our local machine using Docker and Docker Compose.

Getting ready

Now that we know what Mesos is and why we use it to deploy our microservice, let's orchestrate our first Mesos cluster. In order to do so, we first need to understand the building blocks of Mesos. Mesos is made of the following four components:

- Zookeeper
- Mesos master
- Mesos slaves (also called as agents)
- Mesos frameworks

Zookeeper

Zookeeper is an open source tool from Apache used for centralizing cluster information or other configurations. Mesos uses Zookeeper to store its cluster information. One use of Zookeeper in Mesos is to store information about various masters in the Mesos cluster. Mesos clusters ideally have more than one master to provide fault tolerance; this way, if one master goes down, another master takes charge. Another use of Zookeeper in Mesos is to store slave information to keep track of the slaves that are part of the cluster. In production scenarios, it is always ideal to have a zookeeper cluster instead of standalone zookeeper instances. This makes your cluster more fault tolerant and stable.

Mesos masters and Mesos slaves

The Mesos master is usually responsible for coordinating and delegating offers to deploy tasks to Mesos slaves. Mesos slaves ideally have framework-specific executors, which tell Mesos how to run a specific task on a slave. Schedulers for each framework are responsible for making a decision on whether or not to accept an offer. An offer could be as simple as "run Docker image `jenkins:latest` on Marathon with 1 Core, 2 GB memory, and 10 GB disk space." At the same time, the master is always aware of the resource availability on each slave, which is also sent to the scheduler. As soon as the master sends an offer over to the scheduler, the scheduler takes a decision on whether to accept the offer or decline it based on the resource availability and offer request.

Mesos frameworks

Mesos frameworks are composed of the Scheduler and Executor. While the Scheduler is responsible for making offer decisions, the Executor is responsible for running the actual framework task. Some of the most commonly used frameworks are:

- Spark
- Cassandra
- Aurora
- Marathon
- Chronos

 To get a full list of frameworks, visit
`http://mesos.apache.org/documentation/latest/frameworks/`.

The following diagram depicts the working of a Mesos cluster with multiple frameworks:

In this cluster, there are two or more masters, three or more slaves, and three frameworks. There is also a Zookeeper quorum with three replicated servers. A Zookeeper quorum is a set of replicated Zookeeper servers that have the same configuration. As you can see, the Zookeeper quorum talks to the masters and slaves to elect leaders from masters and keep track of slaves joining the cluster. Also, you can see how one of the masters is marked as **Leader** and is currently active, and the other is grayed out to indicate that it is currently not elected as the leader. Though the framework scheduler is shown as a separate component, it is still part of a framework. As we've discussed already, a framework contains a Scheduler and Executor. For simplicity and understandability, the scheduler and executor are shown as separate components.

> To learn more about the Mesos architecture, take a look at this page:
> `http://mesos.apache.org/documentation/latest/architecture/`

Now we know that we need Zookeeper, a Mesos master, Mesos slaves, and framework to orchestrate a minimal Mesos cluster. In this recipe, we will be using Docker to run our Mesos cluster. This means that Zookeeper, the Mesos master, Mesos slave, and framework will be running as Docker containers in your local machine. In order to do this, we will use Docker Compose. Docker Compose is a utility from Docker that helps you run multiple containers using its powerful `docker-compose` command. To keep our cluster simple and reduce the resource utilization of your local machine, the cluster we are building will consist of one Zookeeper instance, one Mesos master, and one Mesos slave.

How to do it...

1. To create your first `docker-compose` file, open your STS IDE and create a new file called `docker-compose-mesos.yml` in your geolocation project. The first line of your Docker Compose file is usually the version of Docker Compose. In this recipe, we will be using `version2`. So add the following line to your Docker Compose file:

   ```
   version: "2"
   ```

   > At one point, Docker made a change to how the services are described in the Docker Compose YAML file. To indicate the difference, the version property was added as the first line of the YAML files.

    To learn more about the differences, read `https://docs.docker.com/compose/compose-file/#/versioning`.

2. Now let's start defining our services. Go ahead and add the following `services` section to your YAML file:

   ```
   services:
   ```

    Keep in mind that this is a YAML file, so make sure you use blank spaces instead of using tabs. The indentation level used is two blank spaces.

3. The next section in your Docker Compose file is to spin up Zookeeper. At the time of writing this, there are no official Zookeeper images available on Docker Hub. So we will be using my Zookeeper image in this recipe. Go ahead and add the following snippet to define your Zookeeper instance:

   ```
   zookeeper:
     image: vikrammurugesan/zookeeper
     network_mode: host
   ```

- There are three things to note here:

  The first one is the name of the service itself. In this case, we have used Zookeeper as our service name.

  The next important section is the **image**. This says which Docker image should be used to spin off this container (or service).

  The last one is very interesting. The `network_mode` command specifies how to configure the Docker network for this container.

- There are several modes, such as `container`, `host`, `bridged`, and `none`. In this example, for simplicity, we will use `host`. The network mode `host` says that we will be using the host network stack inside the container, which will expose the service via `127.0.0.1`.

  To learn more about Docker network modes, take a look at `https://docs.docker.com/engine/userguide/networking/`.

4. Before we move on to the next step, let's try to validate what we have done so far by starting Zookeeper using `docker-compose`. Your `docker-compose-mesos.yml` file should look something like this:

```
version: "2"
services:
  zookeeper:
    image: vikrammurugesan/zookeeper
    network_mode: host
```

5. Now go to the terminal and change the directory to the root of the geolocation project, where you have created the `docker-compose-mesos.yml` file. Execute the following command:

```
docker-compose -f docker-compose-mesos.yml up
```

  This command is used to bring up any services in your `docker-compose` file. By default, Docker Compose assumes that the name of the Docker Compose file is `docker-compose.yml`. As we have used a different name, we are using the `-f` option to mention the name of our Compose file as `docker-compose-mesos.yml`.

6. If you get errors about the Docker machine being down, start your Docker machine instance, set up the environment, and reissue the same command. You will notice that Docker downloads the Zookeeper image from Docker Hub as it is not available in your Docker host. After the download is complete, Docker Compose will start your Zookeeper server and will show you the logs from the container:

```
Creating geolocation_zookeeper_1
Attaching to geolocation_zookeeper_1
zookeeper_1  | JMX enabled by default
zookeeper_1  | Using config: /etc/zookeeper/conf/zoo.cfg
```

The preceding two log messages confirm that your Zookeeper instance is up and running.

7. Before you move on to the next step, stop and remove the Zookeeper container. You can stop the container either by hitting *Ctrl + C* in the console or using the `docker stop` command.

8. Now let's move on and configure the Compose file to start the Mesos master along with Zookeeper. Again, at the time of writing this, there is no official image for the Mesos master. So we will be picking up an image from Docker Hub. In this recipe, we will use the `mesos-master` image from `mesosphere`. Mesosphere is the company behind the powerful cluster management "operating system" called DC/OS. We will learn more about DC/OS in later chapters.

9. Go ahead and add the following snippet to your Docker Compose file:

```
mesos_master:
  image: mesosphere/mesos-master:1.0.1-2.0.93.ubuntu1404
  network_mode: host
  environment:
    MESOS_ZK: zk://127.0.0.1:2181/mesos
    MESOS_HOSTNAME: 192.168.99.100
  depends_on:
    - zookeeper
```

As you can see, we have used the `mesos-master` image from mesosphere, and the version that we have used is `1.0.1-2.0.93.ubuntu1404`. This version is the latest stable version at the time of writing this book. We already know about `network_mode`.

10. The two new elements are `environment` and `depends_on`. Let's talk about `depends_on` first as it is simpler. The `depends_on` element simply states that the service that is marked with the name `zookeeper` needs to be started before starting this service.

11. Now let's talk about environment. The `environment` element is used to add any environment variables to the container.

12. For example, in the previous case, we see two variables, `MESOS_ZK` and `MESOS_HOSTNAME`. `MESOS_ZK` has the value `zk://127.0.0.1:2181/mesos`, which specifies how to look up Mesos configs on Zookeeper. And the `MESOS_HOSTNAME` environment variable is used to indicate the IP or hostname to which the Mesos master will be bound.

13. In our case, we have used the IP of our Docker host, `192.168.99.100`. If you are using a `docker-machine` instance with a different IP, use that IP here. Your `docker-compose-mesos.yml` file will look like this:

```
version: "2"
services:
  zookeeper:
    image: vikrammurugesan/zookeeper
    network_mode: host
  mesos_master:
    image: mesosphere/mesos-master:1.0.1-2.0.93.ubuntu1404
    network_mode: host
    environment:
      MESOS_ZK: zk://127.0.0.1:2181/mesos
      MESOS_HOSTNAME: 192.168.99.100
    depends_on:
      - zookeeper
```

14. Now that we have our Zookeeper instance and Mesos master, let's validate our work so far. To do so, start your services using the `docker-compose` command:

```
docker-compose -f docker-compose-mesos.yml up
```

After you execute the preceding command, you should see something like this:

These logs are just a portion of the logs that your containers show, but they should look similar. As you can see, logs from different containers are marked with their name and are color-coded.

15. Now let's verify that our Mesos cluster is up and running by accessing its web interface. Mesos' web UI is very easy to use and has all the information you will need to know about your cluster. Though you will not be using this very often, it is still a good idea to take a look at it. You should be able to access the Mesos web UI using this URL: `http://192.168.99.100:5050`. 5050 is the default port used by Mesos unless you change it via `config`. You should see something like this:

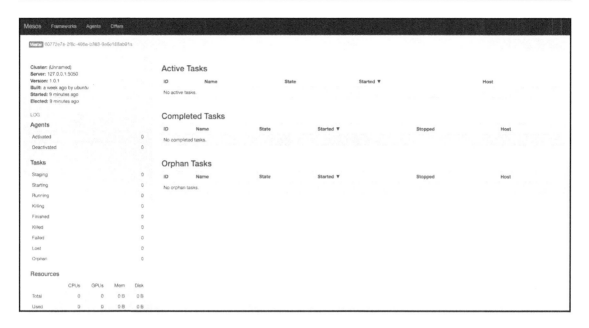

16. On the left hand side, you can see that there are zero agent nodes available (an agent is the same thing as a slave or worker). This is because we haven't added any Mesos slaves to the cluster. At this time, our cluster is not useful, as it does not have any slaves. Before you move on to the next step, stop and remove all containers running in your host. You already know how to stop the containers. You can remove the containers by running the following command:

```
docker rm $(docker ps -a -q)
```

The preceding command can be broken down into two parts. We first list down all the containers using the `ps` command. We pass `-q` (quiet mode) argument to list only the container IDs. The container IDs are then passed to the `rm` command for removal.

17. Now let's add our first Mesos slave to the cluster. In order to do that, add the following snippet to the Docker Compose file:

```
mesos_slave:
  image: mesosphere/mesos-slave:1.0.1-2.0.93.ubuntu1404
  network_mode: host
  environment:
    MESOS_MASTER: zk://127.0.0.1:2181/mesos
    MESOS_WORK_DIR: /tmp
    MESOS_CONTAINERIZERS: docker
    MESOS_HOSTNAME: 192.168.99.100
```

```
    MESOS_PORT: 5051
volumes:
  - /sys/fs/cgroup:/sys/fs/cgroup
  - /var/run/docker.sock:/var/run/docker.sock
  - /usr/local/bin/docker:/usr/bin/docker
depends_on:
  - zookeeper
```

There are a few things to note here: first, the name of the service. As the name indicates, this service will be our mesos_slave. The image is different from that of the master by its name. The version is exactly the same. Again, we are taking this image from mesosphere. There are four environment variables. The MESOS_MASTER environment variable tells the slave how to look up the Mesos master config from Zookeeper.

In the previous snippet, we have used zk://127.0.0.1:2181/mesos. See how 127.0.0.1 is being used as the hostname for Zookeeper. MESOS_WORK_DIR is the directory on the slave that will be used for storing any temp files or any other files created by the executor. We have used /tmp for this. As for MESOS_CONTAINERIZERS, though the name might be pretty straightforward, there are a few things that you need to know about it.

To know more about this property, take a look at this page:
http://mesos.apache.org/documentation/latest/containerizer/

In our example, we have used just docker. The MESOS_HOSTNAME environment is used to indicate the IP or hostname to which the slave should be bound. In the snippet, we have used the IP of our docker-machine instance, 192.168.99.100. If the IP of your docker-machine instance is different, use that IP here. The MESOS_PORT environment variable defines the port where your agent or slave is listening.

18. The volumes section is pretty interesting. Volumes are used to map mount paths and any named volumes to any path on the Docker host. In the preceding example, we have three different mappings. These mappings are required to run a Docker container inside the slave, which is again a Docker container. The mappings to the docker.sock file (/var/run/docker.sock) and the Docker binary (/usr/bin/docker) are used to make this happen. The cgroup mapping (/sys/fs/cgroup) is required by Mesos itself. Finally, the depends_on section is something we saw earlier.

Your `docker-compose-mesos.yml` file will look like this:

```
version: "2"
services:
  zookeeper:
    image: vikrammurugesan/zookeeper
    network_mode: host
  mesos_master:
    image: mesosphere/mesos-master:1.0.1-2.0.93.ubuntu1404
    network_mode: host
    environment:
      MESOS_ZK: zk://127.0.0.1:2181/mesos
      MESOS_HOSTNAME: 192.168.99.100
    depends_on:
      - zookeeper
  mesos_slave_one:
    image: mesosphere/mesos-slave:1.0.1-2.0.93.ubuntu1404
    network_mode: host
    environment:
      MESOS_MASTER: zk://127.0.0.1:2181/mesos
      MESOS_WORK_DIR: /tmp
      MESOS_CONTAINERIZERS: docker
      MESOS_HOSTNAME: 192.168.99.100
      MESOS_PORT: 5051
    volumes:
      - /sys/fs/cgroup:/sys/fs/cgroup
      - /var/run/docker.sock:/var/run/docker.sock
      - /usr/local/bin/docker:/usr/bin/docker
    depends_on:
      - zookeeper
```

19. Now let's check whether we can see our new slave detected by Mesos. To do so, issue the `docker compose up` command on your console:

```
docker-compose -f docker-compose-mesos.yml up
```

This time, you should see some additional log messages from the Mesos slave container:

```
zookeeper_1    | JMX enabled by default
zookeeper_1    | Using config: /etc/zookeeper/conf/zoo.cfg
mesos_slave_1  | WARNING: Logging before InitGoogleLogging() is written to STDERR
mesos_slave_1  | I0905 18:10:23.883550    1 main.cpp:243] Build: 2016-08-26 23:00:07 by ubuntu
mesos_slave_1  | I0905 18:10:23.883646    1 main.cpp:244] Version: 1.0.1
mesos_slave_1  | I0905 18:10:23.883649    1 main.cpp:247] Git tag: 1.0.1
mesos_slave_1  | I0905 18:10:23.883651    1 main.cpp:251] Git SHA: 3611eb0b7eea8d144e9b2e840e0ba16f2f659ee3
mesos_master_1 | WARNING: Logging before InitGoogleLogging() is written to STDERR
mesos_master_1 | I0905 18:10:23.883477    1 main.cpp:263] Build: 2016-08-26 23:00:07 by ubuntu
mesos_master_1 | I0905 18:10:23.883592    1 main.cpp:264] Version: 1.0.1
mesos_master_1 | I0905 18:10:23.883596    1 main.cpp:267] Git tag: 1.0.1
mesos_master_1 | I0905 18:10:23.883597    1 main.cpp:271] Git SHA: 3611eb0b7eea8d144e9b2e840e0ba16f2f659ee3
mesos_master_1 | I0905 18:10:23.887123    1 main.cpp:370] Using 'HierarchicalDRF' allocator
mesos_master_1 | 2016-09-05 18:10:23,887:1(0x7f90c4e09700):ZOO_INFO@log_env@726: Client environment:zookeeper.version=zookeeper C client 3.4.8
mesos_master_1 | 2016-09-05 18:10:23,887:1(0x7f90c4e09700):ZOO_INFO@log_env@730: Client environment:host.name=default
mesos_master_1 | 2016-09-05 18:10:23,887:1(0x7f90c4e09700):ZOO_INFO@log_env@737: Client environment:os.name=Linux
mesos_master_1 | 2016-09-05 18:10:23,887:1(0x7f90c4e09700):ZOO_INFO@log_env@738: Client environment:os.arch=4.4.16-boot2docker
mesos_master_1 | 2016-09-05 18:10:23,887:1(0x7f90c4e09700):ZOO_INFO@log_env@739: Client environment:os.version=#1 SMP Fri Jul 29 00:13:24 UTC 2016
mesos_master_1 | 2016-09-05 18:10:23,887:1(0x7f90c4e09700):ZOO_INFO@log_env@747: Client environment:user.name=(null)
mesos_master_1 | 2016-09-05 18:10:23,888:1(0x7f90c4e09700):ZOO_INFO@log_env@755: Client environment:user.home=/root
mesos_master_1 | 2016-09-05 18:10:23,888:1(0x7f90c4e09700):ZOO_INFO@log_env@767: Client environment:user.dir=/
```

Now that our Mesos cluster is running, access the web UI from a browser using the URL `http://192.168.99.100:5050`:

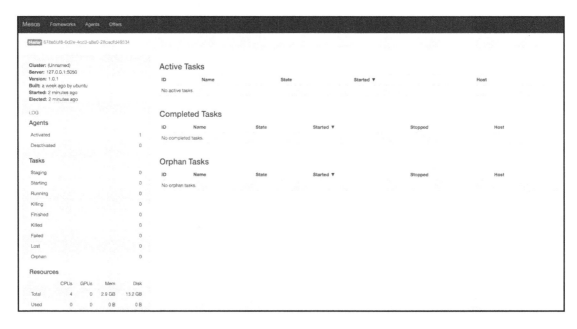

20. As you can see, now there is one new slave (or agent) that is activated. You can also see that the **Resources** section reflects the amount of resources available for this cluster. The amount of resources depends on the size of our Docker host. If you would like to increase the resources allocated to your Docker host, you have to recreate your VM with more resources using the `docker-machine create` command.

 If you want another slave, feel free to copy the `mesos_slave` section and paste it in the Docker Compose file again with a different `MESOS_PORT` number. At the same time, you will have to change the service name.

With that said, can we say that we now have a fully functional cluster? Maybe. That is because we still do not have a framework installed. As we will be using this Mesos cluster to deploy our Dockerized microservice, we will be installing the Marathon framework on this cluster.

21. To register the Marathon framework, add the following snippet to your Docker Compose file:

```
marathon:
  image: mesosphere/marathon:v1.1.2
  network_mode: host
  environment:
    MARATHON_MASTER: zk://127.0.0.1:2181/mesos
  depends_on:
    - zookeeper
```

The image that we have used is again from mesosphere, and the name of the image is marathon. See that we have used a version different than that of the Mesos master and slave. This is because the frameworks are not tied to any one version of master or slave images. The only environment variable that is used is `MARATHON_MASTER`, which is set to `zk://127.0.0.1:2181/mesos`, specifying how to look up the Mesos configs on Zookeeper. Finally, this service depends on the Zookeeper service.

22. Your final `docker-compose-mesos.yml` file will look something like this:

```
version: "2"
services:
  zookeeper:
    image: vikrammurugesan/zookeeper
    network_mode: host
  mesos_master:
    image: mesosphere/mesos-master:1.0.1-2.0.93.ubuntu1404
    network_mode: host
    environment:
      MESOS_ZK: zk://127.0.0.1:2181/mesos
      MESOS_HOSTNAME: 192.168.99.100
    depends_on:
      - zookeeper
  mesos_slave_one:
    image: mesosphere/mesos-slave:1.0.1-2.0.93.ubuntu1404
    network_mode: host
    environment:
      MESOS_MASTER: zk://127.0.0.1:2181/mesos
      MESOS_WORK_DIR: /tmp
      MESOS_CONTAINERIZERS: docker
      MESOS_HOSTNAME: 192.168.99.100
      MESOS_PORT: 5051
    volumes:
      - /sys/fs/cgroup:/sys/fs/cgroup
      - /var/run/docker.sock:/var/run/docker.sock
      - /usr/local/bin/docker:/usr/bin/docker
    depends_on:
      - zookeeper
  marathon:
    image: mesosphere/marathon:v1.1.2
    network_mode: host
    environment:
      MARATHON_MASTER: zk://127.0.0.1:2181/mesos
    depends_on:
      - zookeeper
```

23. With that said, we are now ready to validate whether we have Marathon installed on our cluster. Stop and remove any containers that are already running. Now execute the following command on your console to start the Mesos cluster:

```
docker-compose -f docker-compose-mesos.yml up
```

This time, you will see some additional logs from Marathon:

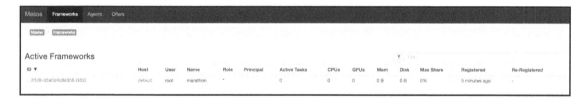

24. Now let's verify whether Marathon is registered as a Mesos framework on our cluster. To do that, open the Mesos web UI from your browser and click on the **Frameworks** tab. You should now see a new entry in the **Active Frameworks** grid for Marathon. You can see the name of the framework in the **Name** column:

Mesos	Frameworks	Agents	Offers										

Active Frameworks

ID ▼	Host	User	Name	Role	Principal	Active Tasks	CPUs	GPUs	Mem	Disk	Max Share	Registered	Re-Registered
...8109-d3a0a4c8a356-0000	default	root	marathon	*		0	0	0	0 B	0 B	0%	5 minutes ago	-

That's it! You have successfully created your first Mesos cluster using Docker. Now, it is time to play with this cluster by spinning off some Marathon tasks.

Understanding the Mesos and Marathon interface

Now that we have a fully functional Mesos cluster with the Marathon framework, we are ready to spin off new tasks (or Docker containers) to Marathon. Before we do that, it is highly important that we understand the Mesos and Marathon web interface.

Getting ready

We already know that the Mesos web UI is located at port 5050. To access the web UI, open `http://192.168.99.100:5050` in a web browser. Similarly, Marathon has a sophisticated web interface located at port 8080. To access the Marathon web UI, open `http://192.168.99.100:8080` in another tab of your web browser.

How to do it...

First, let's try to get familiar with the Mesos interface.

The Mesos interface

There are four tabs in the Mesos web UI. Let's go one by one. The first one is the Mesos home page.

The Mesos home page

This is where you actually get to see most of the information about your tasks. Let's start with the left-hand side menu pane. The first section of the pane is the cluster information. It has information such as cluster name, master URL, version, when this version was built, when this master was started, and when this master was elected as leader. These are the options that are available in this particular version of Mesos. This list is prone to change if you use any other version of Mesos. It will look something like this:

Cluster: (Unnamed)
Server: 127.0.0.1:5050
Version: 1.0.1
Built: a week ago by *ubuntu*
Started: 19 minutes ago
Elected: 19 minutes ago

The cluster name is (Unnamed) because we did not pass the MESOS_CLUSTER environment variable to the master. If we had set that environment variable in the Docker Compose file for the master, then that cluster name would have been displayed here. In production systems, this is very important when you have multiple masters. We have not done that in order to make the cluster configuration simple.

Right following the **Cluster** section, you will see a hyperlink called LOG. This is used to look at the logs of the master. If you click on this, you will see the following error:

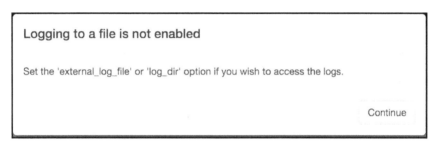

This is because we have not set the config property that specifies where we would like the log files to be created.

To configure that, we have to set the MESOS_LOG_DIR environment variable in the Docker Compose file for the Mesos master.

Agents

The next section is **Agents**. Mesos started adopting the term "agents" for slaves recently. Wherever you see the term *agents* henceforth, keep in mind that they are synonymous with slaves. This section is where you will see the number of slaves that are activated and the number of slaves that are deactivated. It will look something like this:

Agents	
Activated	1
Deactivated	0

Tasks

This next section, **Tasks**, shows the number of tasks grouped by their statuses on all slaves. Mesos has been adding new statuses recently to provide a more granular understanding of where each task is. At the time of writing this, there are nine statuses: **Staging, Starting, Running, Killing, Finished, Killed, Failed, Lost, Orphan**. In your Mesos web UI, this looks something like the following:

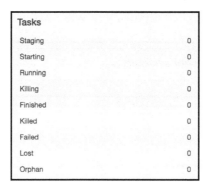

As you can see in the preceding picture, none of the resources are being used or offered because we have not run any tasks on the cluster yet. Moving on to the main section of the home page is the **Tasks** breakout. By default, you have three grids: **Active Tasks**, **Completed Tasks**, and **Orphan Tasks**.

Resources

The next section is the **Resources** section, which shows the resource utilization by task and resource availability in the slaves. Resources include CPUs, GPUs, memory, and disk space. Let's talk about **graphics processing unit** (**GPU**) as it is new to this list. Now that Mesos is being used for more advanced use cases such as graphics and video processing, Mesos and Nvidia have come together to include GPUs in Mesos. This section will look something like this:

Task types

Active tasks are tasks that are currently executing. Completed tasks are tasks that have finished execution (either completed successfully or failed or killed). Orphan tasks are tasks that are orphaned after a master failure when the framework fails to reregister. As we do not have any tasks now, this section is empty. But ideally, you will see that for each task, there is a new entry in one of these grids:

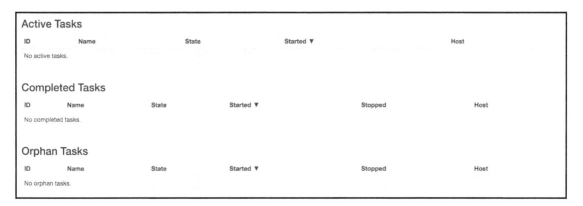

Frameworks

The second tab is the **Frameworks** tab. The **Frameworks** tab mainly shows the list of active, completed, and inactive frameworks in the cluster. The frameworks can be anything, such as Spark, Cassandra, Aurora, Marathon, and Chronos:

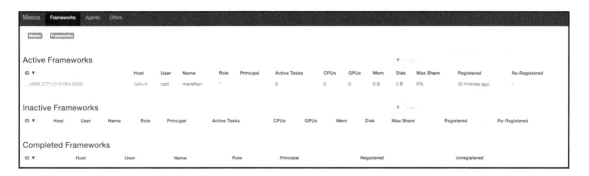

Agents

The **Agents** tab usually displays the list of all slaves registered in the cluster. In our cluster, we have only one slave registered. You should see something like this:

Offers

The last tab is the **Offers** tab, which lists down all the offers that are currently open for a slave to be picked up:

That's pretty much everything on the Mesos web interface. Though you will not be using this interface a lot, it is still a good idea to become familiar with this interface so that you can use it for debugging. Debugging situations can happen when one of your tasks keeps restarting or when you would like to know whether you have enough resources to spin off more tasks.

The Marathon web UI

Now let's open up the Marathon web UI and understand the main screen. As we still haven't learned how to deploy Docker containers in Marathon, we will just understand the basic sections of the Marathon web UI. We will learn about the other screens as we deploy our application.

Open the tab that you already had for Marathon. If you closed it by mistake, use this URL to open it: `http://192.168.99.100:8080`:

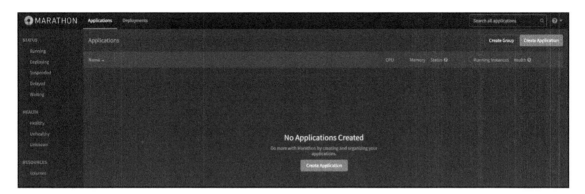

As you can see, it is a very simple interface with some useful filters on the left-hand side menu. The filters are based mainly on the status, health, and volumes. The **Create Application** button is used to deploy your Docker container on the Mesos cluster using Marathon. Right now, we do not have any new applications already deployed. If we had one, it would be displayed in the **Applications** section of the page. You can also create groups to group your applications.

With that said, we come to the end of this recipe. We will get to play with the Marathon interface in the rest of this chapter.

Deploying your microservice to Mesos using Marathon

Now that we have a fully functional Mesos cluster with the Marathon framework, we are ready to spin off new tasks (or Docker containers) on Marathon. In this recipe, we will deploy our Dockerized geolocation microservice on Marathon.

Getting ready

Before you start, make sure your Mesos cluster is up and running. You can do this by executing the `docker ps -a` command. You should see four containers running: Mesos master, Mesos slave, Marathon, and Zookeeper:

Sometimes, it is possible that either the Mesos master or slave, or even the Marathon container, might go down. This usually happens when it runs out of resources or probably when you restart your computer and they try to come back up, but they might not be able to orchestrate properly. In those cases, make sure you stop the whole cluster and perform a clean start. You can do that by running the following command:

```
docker stop $(docker ps -a -q) && docker rm $(docker ps -a -q) && docker-compose -f docker-compose-mesos.yml up
```

The command uses `&&` to combine three different commands. The first one is used to stop all running and stopped containers. The second one removes all the containers that were stopped by the previous command (including the ones that were previously stopped, if any), and the third command starts the cluster back up.

Now that your cluster is up and running, open a browser and navigate to the Marathon web interface at `http://192.168.99.100:8080`.

How to do it...

1. Let's start by understanding the Marathon interface. Marathon's user interface has improved a lot lately and is very easy to use. Click on the **Create Application** button. You should see a modal similar to this:

As you can see, there are several sections on the left-hand side, such as **General**, **Docker Container**, **Ports**, **EnvironmentVariables**, **Labels**, **Health Checks**, and **Volumes**.

2. Let's start with the **General** section. The first field that is required in this section is the **ID** field. The value of **ID** uniquely identifies the application in Marathon. In our case, as we are deploying the geolocation application, we can probably use `geolocation` as the ID of our application. The other fields in this modal that we should care about now are **CPUs**, **Memory**, and **Disk Space**.

   - The default CPU value of **1** should be more than enough for our application. Mesos' **CPUs** parameter is a little tricky to understand. You can even assign values such as `0.1` or `0.25` to the **CPUs** field. It mainly helps you identify how many resources are left in your cluster rather than limiting access to the CPU itself. Even though you set the value of **CPUs** to `1`, your application will have access to all the other CPUs in your slave.

- The **Memory** field is set at 128 MB by default. For our application, we could go a little higher and assign it 512 MB. In production scenarios, 512 MB might not be sufficient, and you might have to go with a minimum of 4 GB of memory based on your application's usage. If, for some reason, you are forced to allocate more than 4 GB of memory for a similar application, it is a signal that there could either be an architectural refactor that could reduce your memory allocation, or your application is becoming more monolithic, thereby defeating the purpose of building a microservice. Here, the 4 GB limit was picked as an example that is used for the geolocation application, but the point is to make sure you don't build an application that is monolithic or follows bad architectural design.

- The **Disk Space** field is also really important when you create a new application in Marathon. Though it might not matter a lot in our case, it becomes super important when you are deploying a container that stores information in the filesystem. For example, if you are running Kafka or a database as a container, you definitely don't want to allocate it 1 GB of disk space. It is definitely going to run out of disk space sooner or later. For the geolocation application, as it is not going to write anything to the filesystem, let's allocate it 1 GB of disk space.

3. To summarize, these are the fields and their respective values:
    - **ID**: `geolocation`
    - **CPUs**: `1`
    - **Memory**: `512`
    - **Disk Space**: `1024`
    - **Instances**: `1`
    - **Command**: Leave this field empty

4. Now, let's move on to the important section: the Docker container section. The Docker container section is where we get to provide the container information to Marathon. There are five important fields in this section:

    - The **Image** field tells Marathon, the name and tag of the Docker image that it has to pull from Docker Hub. By default, Marathon tries to pull the image from the public Docker Hub. But if you have your own private Docker Hub, you have to make a few changes to your deployment to instruct Marathon to authenticate and get the image from your private repository. In our case, we will use the public repository, and the name of our image is `vikrammurugesan/geolocation`. Please keep in mind that this is my Docker Hub account, and you should be using the image in your account. We don't have to provide the `latest` tag as Marathon uses it as the default tag if you don't provide one.
    - The **Network** mode can either be **Bridged** or **Host**. For now, we will use **Bridged** mode. We will learn more about the bridged networking mode in later recipes in this chapter. The **Force pull image on every launch** option is pretty self-explanatory. You don't have to check this option. The **Extend run-time privileges** option lets you run the container in privileged mode. You can use this option if you are going to run Docker inside this Docker container. For now, we will not need it.

For more information on privileged containers, take a look at this page: `https://docs.docker.com/engine/reference/run/#/runtime-privilege-and-linux-capabilities`

- The **Parameters** are nothing but Docker environment variables. If your application needs environment variables, you can list them here. For now, the configurations we have done so far will let us start the application on Marathon. We will look at other sections in later recipes in this chapter. With that said, the **Docker Container** section should look something like this:

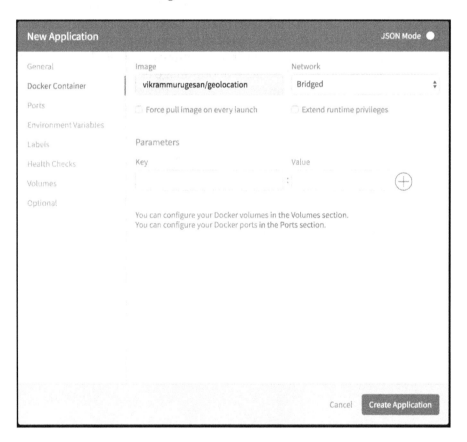

5. Now that you have everything set up right, click on the **Create Application** button. You should see that Marathon is trying to deploy our microservice. You can confirm this by looking at the status of your application. It should show up as **Deploying**. During this step, the slave will try to pull the image from Docker Hub and start the container with the configurations we provided in the **Create Application** modal:

6. A few seconds later, you should see that the application's status changes from **Deploying** to **Running**, indicating that it is ready to be consumed:

7. Without wasting any more time, let's test our service. Before that, how do you know which host your application is running on? To find out, you will need the IP of your Mesos slave. Marathon makes it easy for you to find the host and port your application is running on. From Marathon's home page, click on your application name. It should take you to the application details page for the geolocation application:

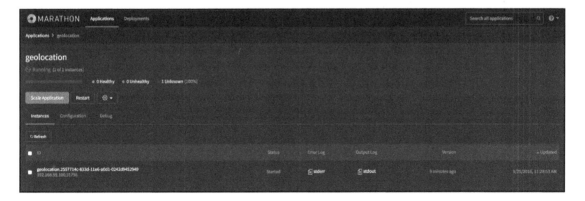

8. There are lots of things on this page. But let's just focus on the **Instances** grid. Right following the ID of the application instance, we can see a `<hostname>:<port>` combination. The hostname is something you are already familiar with. That is the IP of our Docker host (VirtualBox VM). The port is a random port that Marathon has elected to expose our application on.

9. Execute a `curl` command to `GET` all geolocations saved in the application. Since this is a brand new deployment, you should get an empty array back, indicating there are no geolocations saved in the system:

    `curl http://192.168.99.100:31756/geolocation`

10. The output should be something like this:

    `curl: (7) Failed to connect to 192.168.99.100 port  31756: Connection refused`

11. What just happened here? We are not able to connect to our service on host `192.168.99.100` and port `31756`. With that said, we now clearly know that the port number we have is not right. There is definitely a way to configure our application in such a way that it exposes the API on the right port. We will look at that in our next recipe.

Configuring ports in Marathon

In the previous recipe, we saw how to deploy our microservice in Marathon. We were able to deploy the geolocation microservice on Marathon, but it was not really useful because we haven't figured out how to talk to our microservice via its RESTful API. In this recipe, we will learn how to configure our application's service and host ports in Marathon to expose the RESTful APIs.

Getting ready

If you don't have your cluster up and running, bring it back up. Also make sure you have the geolocation application up and running in your cluster. You can verify that from the Marathon web interface.

How to do it…

1. From the **Instances** grid, click on the application instance and go to the **Configuration** tab. The **Configuration** tab is used to show the Marathon configurations for your application. You will see several configurations, such as the memory, CPU, disk space, Docker container, and health checks:

2. In the **Container** section, you will see JSON code similar to this:

```
{
  "type": "DOCKER",
  "volumes": [],
  "docker": {
    "image": "vikrammurugesan/geolocation",
    "network": "BRIDGE",
    "portMappings": [
      {
        "containerPort": 0,
        "hostPort": 0,
        "servicePort": 10000,
        "protocol": "tcp",
        "labels": {}
      }
    ],
    "privileged": false,
    "parameters": [],
    "forcePullImage": false
  }
}
```

The one that we are really concerned about is `portMappings` in the Container section. In some versions of Marathon, the `portMappings` will be listed under **Port Definitions** property. So don't panic if your interface looks different. The instructions in this recipe are still going to be the same. You can see that the `containerPort` is marked as `0`. Ideally, we should expect `8080` there, as that's where our API is listening.

The `hostPort` is the port on the Docker host to which Marathon will bind this `containerPort`. The `hostPort` can also take the value `0`, instructing Marathon to choose a random port number. In most cases, the `hostPort` is the port number on the Mesos slave that is running this container. Again, identifying the slave IP on a cluster with hundreds of slaves is not ideal.

That's where the `servicePort` comes to the rescue. The `servicePort` is currently set to `10000` by default. In production environments, the `servicePort` is manually set to a well-known value, such as `8899` or `8181`. Once you set the `servicePort` to a well-known value that you can remember, you can then use service discovery tools such as Consul or tools such as HAProxy to perform a forwarding from the `hostPort` to the `servicePort`. Marathon previously provided a script called `haproxy-marathon-bridge` to do exactly this. It creates a HAProxy config file that can be used with HAProxy to make this balancing happen. At the time of writing this, this script has been deprecated in favor of the **Marathon Load Balancer (LB)**. We will learn more about Marathon LB in Chapter 5, *Service Discovery and Load Balancing Microservices*. After you enable service discovery and configure Marathon, you will be able to access your service from `mesosMasterHostName:servicePort`. If you have multiple masters, it is recommended that you have a common hostname that always points to the active master.

The protocol can be UDP or TCP. You won't have to use UDP in most cases. We will stick to TCP throughout this book.

3. Now let's modify the application's Marathon configuration to include the `hostPort` and `servicePort`. In order to do that, click on the **Edit** button on the **Configuration** screen, and go to the **Ports** section. Enter the **Container Port** value as `8080`. Leave the protocol value as `tcp`:

4. Now, if you are wondering where `hostPort` and `servicePort` are, Marathon leaves those as advanced configurations, and the only way to configure the advanced configurations is using JSON mode. In order to use JSON mode, click on the toggle button in the top right of the modal that says **JSON Mode**. You should see the JSON that Marathon uses to post to its REST service, which in turn converts it into a Mesos task request. In the `portMappings` section, you should now see that `containerPort` is populated with the value `8080`. Go ahead and add these two fields to this port mapping object:

```
"hostPort": 0,
"servicePort": 8899
```

This will tell Marathon to use any random port as the host port and use 8899 as the service. Like we saw earlier, it is our responsibility to perform a port forwarding from the host port to the service port using tools such as HAProxy or Marathon LB, which we will be looking at in later chapters. For now, what this will do is expose the RESTful services in the geolocation application on any random port on the host machine. In our case, the host machine is the Virtual Box VM at 192.168.99.100.

With that said, click on **Change and deploy configuration**. Usually, it takes a few seconds to finish the deployment. You can look at the pending deployments from the **Deployments** tab of Marathon. You can make sure that your configurations are updated by looking at the Docker container setting in the Configuration tab. It should include the servicePort and hostPort:

```
{
  "type": "DOCKER",
  "volumes": [],
  "docker": {
    "image": "vikrammurugesan/geolocation",
    "network": "BRIDGE",
    "portMappings": [
      {
        "containerPort": 8080,
        "hostPort": 0,
        "servicePort": 8899,
        "protocol": "tcp",
        "labels": {}
      }
    ],
    "privileged": false,
    "parameters": [],
    "forcePullImage": false
  }
}
```

5. Now, let's test our service using the `curl` command. Before that, you have to know what host port your service is running on. You can get that from the **Instances** section:

As you can see, it is running on port `31434`. Yours might be different as it gets randomly generated. So please make sure you use your port number in the next cURL command.

6. Now, open a new terminal session and issue the following `curl` command:

```
curl -H "Content-Type: application/json" -X POST -d '{"timestamp":
1468203975, "userId": "f1196aac-470e-11e6-beb8-9e71128cae77", "latitude":
41.803488, "longitude": -88.144040}'
http://192.168.99.100:31434/geolocation
```

7. This should give you an output similar to the following (pretty-printed for readability):

```
{
  "latitude": 41.803488,
   "longitude": -88.14404,
  "userId": "f1196aac-470e-11e6-beb8-9e71128cae77",
   "timestamp": 1468203975
}
```

Configuring ports in Marathon is trickier than you think. You have to understand the usage of `servicePorts`, `hostPorts`, and `requirePorts` as well as the various networking modes, such as **HOST** and **BRIDGE**. It is strongly recommended you take a look at `https://mesosphere.github.io/marathon/docs/ports.html` before you start playing with them on your production cluster.

That brings us to the end of this recipe. You now know how to deploy your own microservice on a Mesos cluster using Marathon.

Configuring volumes in Marathon

So far, we have learned how to deploy our microservice on a Mesos cluster using Marathon and configure ports using Marathon's web UI. One of the most common things you would want to do is be able to map volumes in your container to the host machine. Though this is not something that is super important to our geolocation application, when you deal with applications that save files on the filesystem, this is critical. You wouldn't want to lose your data, would you? In this recipe, we will look at how to map volumes using Marathon.

Getting ready

In order to learn how to configure volume mapping in Marathon, let's make our application save something to the filesystem. Let's say the geolocation application would like to store the geolocation JSON to the filesystem as it receives them. It might not be a great design, but for our understanding, let's make our geolocation application store the geolocation JSON files in a dedicated data directory as and when they arrive. In order to do so, let's open up our STS IDE.

How to do it...

In order to create this data directory, we have to do two things:

- Create the directory on the host machine and make it accessible
- Make the `GeoLocationRepository.java` file write any new geolocation JSON to the data directory

Before we can implement this in the container, let's try to do it locally:

1. Issue the following two commands on your terminal:

```
mkdir -p /opt/packt/geolocation/data
chmod -R 777 /opt
```

> Use sudo if needed. The mkdir command creates the given directory structure in your local filesystem, and the chmod command gives everyone read, write, and execute permissions on the /opt directory and its subdirectories. You can verify this by running the ls -l command. Setting 777 privileges is not a safe approach as it opens up security risks. When you are doing something similar in your application, make sure that you give just the required privileges.

2. Now that our directory is ready, let's make changes in our repository class to start writing geolocations to this directory. As we would need one file per geolocation, we have to come up with a naming convention so that the files don't get overwritten. The timestamp will more or less be unique for all geolocations. But what happens when you are writing geolocations for multiple users at the same time? So, maybe a combination of timestamp and user ID? Yes, that should work for now. To differentiate the user ID from the timestamp, we could use the following convention:

```
user<userId>_t<timestamp>
```

3. Let's make changes to the GeoLocationRepository.java file to follow this naming convention. The first thing that we will need is an object-to-JSON string serializer. We will use com.fasterxml.jackson.databind.ObjectMapper as it is already used by Spring MVC. The ObjectMapper.writeValue(File, String) method is used to write a file with the given string content, which suits our needs perfectly.

4. Go ahead and use this method in the GeoLocationRepository class' addGeoLocation method. After you are done, your GeoLocationRepository.java class will look something like this:

```
package com.packt.microservices.geolocation;
import java.io.File;
import java.util.ArrayList;
import java.util.Collections;
import java.util.List;

import org.springframework.stereotype.Repository;
```

```
import com.fasterxml.jackson.databind.ObjectMapper;

@Repository
public class GeoLocationRepository {

    private List<GeoLocation> geolocations = new ArrayList<GeoLocation>();

    private static final ObjectMapper MAPPER = new ObjectMapper();

    public void addGeoLocation(GeoLocation geolocation) {
        geolocations.add(geolocation);

        try {
            MAPPER.writeValue(new File("/opt/packt/geolocation/data/user" +
geolocation.getUserId() + "_t" + geolocation.getTimestamp()), geolocation);
        } catch (Exception e) {
            e.printStackTrace();
        }
    }

    public List<GeoLocation> getGeoLocations() {
    return Collections.unmodifiableList(geolocations);
    }
}
```

5. Now that both our directory and code are ready, let's test the application. Start your `GeoLocationApplication.java` application as a Spring Boot application from your STS IDE. Now issue the following `curl` command to create a geolocation:

```
curl -H "Content-Type: application/json" -X POST -d'{"timestamp":
1468203975, "userId": "f1196aac-470e-11e6-beb8-9e71128cae77", "latitude":
41.803488, "longitude": -88.144040}' http://localhost:8080/geolocation
```

This should have given you an output similar to the following (pretty-printed for readability):

```
{
  "latitude": 41.803488,
  "longitude": -88.14404,
  "userId": "f1196aac-470e-11e6-beb8-9e71128cae77",
  "timestamp": 1468203975
}
```

Also, this should have created the data file at the
`/opt/packt/geolocation/data` directory. Let's verify that. Issue the
following command to look at the contents of the data file:

```
cat /opt/packt/geolocation/data/userf1196aac-470e-11e6-
beb8-9e71128cae77_t1468203975
```

6. This should have given you an output similar to the following (pretty-printed for
readability):

```
{
    "latitude": 41.803488,
    "longitude": -88.14404,
    "userId": "f1196aac-470e-11e6-beb8-9e71128cae77",
    "timestamp": 1468203975
}
```

7. Now that our code works great, the next steps are as follows:

    1. Build the project to generate a new JAR artifact

    2. Create a new Docker image because our code has changed

    3. Upload the new image to Docker Hub

    4. Redeploy the new image with volume configurations

    5. Verify whether the volume is mapped

8. Go ahead and build your project using the `mvn clean package` command. This
should create a new `geolocation-0.0.1-SNAPSHOT.jar` artifact in the target
directory.

9. In order to create the new image, we have to add two new lines to the Dockerfile
to create the data directory and give it write privileges. Add the following two
lines to your Docker file:

```
RUN mkdir -p /opt/packt/geolocation/data
RUN chmod -R 777 /opt
```

10. After you add this, your Docker file will look something like this:

```
FROM openjdk:8
RUN mkdir -p /opt/packt/geolocation/data
RUN chmod 777 /opt
ADD target/geolocation-0.0.1-SNAPSHOT.jar
 /opt/packt/geolocation/
```

```
EXPOSE 8080
CMD ["java", "-jar", "/opt/packt/geolocation/geolocation-
   0.0.1-SNAPSHOT.jar"]
```

11. Now let's build the image with new code. Keep in mind that in addition to creating the data directory, the other change in the image is `geolocation-0.0.1-SNAPSHOT.jar`. This file would have been automatically created by your IDE when you made the change to your `GeoLocationRepository.java` file. Though I didn't explicitly mention earlier, be aware that it is also getting changed in your image.

12. Before we build the new image, let's remove the image we already have. To do that, run the following two commands one by one:

```
docker rmi packt/geolocation
docker rmi vikrammurugesan/geolocation
```

> We are removing the `packt/geolocation` image as it references the `vikrammurugesan/geolocation` image. If you try to remove the `vikrammurugesan/geolocation` image without removing the `packt/geolocation` image, Docker will complain about references and will not remove the image. To build our image, issue the following command on your terminal:

```
docker build -t vikrammurugesan/geolocation .
```

> Remember to use your account name instead of mine in this command. After your image has been built, push your Docker image to Docker Hub using the following command. You may be asked to log in to your Docker Hub account if you haven't already done so.

```
docker push vikrammurugesan/geolocation
```

> Again, make sure you use your account name instead of mine. After the image has been uploaded successfully, go to Docker Hub and verify that the last updated time of your image shows something more recent.

13. Now that our image is ready to be used, let's spin off our microservice on Mesos using Marathon. Make sure your Mesos cluster is up and running. If it is down, kill your cluster and start it again. Once your cluster is back up, open the Marathon web UI on your browser. Click on the **Create Application** button and go into JSON mode. We will be using JSON mode to quickly populate the modal.

In JSON mode, delete the existing JSON and paste the following:

```
{
  "id": "/geolocation",
  "cmd": null,
  "cpus": 1,
  "mem": 512,
  "disk": 1024,
  "instances": 1,
  "container": {
    "type": "DOCKER",
    "docker": {
      "image": "vikrammurugesan/geolocation",
      "network": "BRIDGE",
      "portMappings": [
        {
          "containerPort": 8080,
          "hostPort": 0,
          "servicePort": 8899,
          "protocol": "tcp",
          "labels": {}
        }
      ],
      "privileged": false,
      "parameters": [],
      "forcePullImage": false
    }
  }
}
```

14. Now go back to UI mode by toggling the **JSON Mode** button. Navigate to the **Volumes** section. In the **Volumes** section, you will see two things. One is **Persistent Volumes**, which is mostly used in applications that need stateful behavior. The next one is the **Docker Container Volumes**, which is used to map volumes between the container and host. In our case, we have to add a Docker container volume. Add the following entries to the **Docker Container Volumes** section and hit **Create Application**:

- **Container Path**: /opt/packt/geolocation/data
- Host Path: /opt/packt/geolocation/data
- Mode: **Read and Write**

    As you can see, we are using the same path in the container and the host. Marathon will deploy the application with the newer version of your image.

15. Now that our application is ready to test, let's create two geolocations using `curl`. Make sure the port number that you use is the same port number that is advertised in Marathon. In my case, the port number was changed from `31434` to `31758`. That's because we redeployed the application.

```
        curl -H "Content-Type: application/json" -X POST -d'{"timestamp":
1474843159, "userId": "f1196aac-470e-11e6-beb8-9e71128cae77", "latitude":
41.803488, "longitude": -88.144040}'
http://192.168.99.100:31758/geolocation
        curl -H "Content-Type: application/json" -X POST -d
'{"timestamp": 1474843900, "userId": "f1196aac-470e-11e6-
beb8-9e71128cae77", "latitude": 42.803488, "longitude":-87.144040}'
http://192.168.99.100:31758/geolocation
```

These two commands should have created two files in the `/opt/packt/geolocation/data` directory of the container as well as the host.

16. First, let's verify that the file is created in the container. To list the files in the `/opt/packt/geolocation/data` directory, we have to find out the ID of the container. Ideally, when you have a real non-dockerized Mesos cluster, your container will be running on a remote Mesos slave. But as our installation is a Dockerized version, the geolocation application will be running as a container on our Docker host. You can verify that using the `docker ps -a` command:

```
CONTAINER ID    IMAGE                                              COMMAND
924b3f748273    vikrammurugesan/geolocation                        "java -jar /opt/packt"
3017b
f6827c9e632e    mesosphere/mesos-master:1.0.1-2.0.93.ubuntu1404    "mesos-master --regis"
1ea0b0d1fe10    mesosphere/marathon:v1.1.2                         "./bin/start"
0d44f67fd69d    mesosphere/mesos-slave:1.0.1-2.0.93.ubuntu1404     "mesos-slave"
187269de7d8f    vikrammurugesan/zookeeper                          "/usr/share/zookeeper"
```

In this screenshot, some portion of the console has been cropped out to highlight only the relevant information. But as you can see, the geolocation application is running as a Docker container, and its ID is `924b3f748273`. Now that we know the container ID, issue the following Docker command to list the contents of the data directory and the data files themselves:

```
docker exec 924b3f748273 ls /opt/packt/geolocation/data
```

This should show something like the following:

```
userf1196aac-470e-11e6-beb8-9e71128cae77_t1474843159
userf1196aac-470e-11e6-beb8-9e71128cae77_t1474843900
```

17. To verify the contents of the files, issue the following commands one by one:

```
docker exec 924b3f748273
cat/opt/packt/geolocation/data/userf1196aac-470e-11e6-
beb8-9e71128cae77_t1474843159
```

18. You should see this output (pretty-printed for readability):

```
{
    "latitude":41.803488,
    "longitude":-88.14404,
    "userId":"f1196aac-470e-11e6-beb8-9e71128cae77",
    "timestamp":1474843159
}
```

```
docker exec 924b3f748273 cat
/opt/packt/geolocation/data/userf1196aac-470e-11e6-beb8-
9e71128cae77_t1474843900
```

19. You should see this output (pretty-printed for readability):

```
{
    "latitude":42.803488,
    "longitude":-87.14404,
    "userId":"f1196aac-470e-11e6-beb8-9e71128cae77",
    "timestamp":1474843900
}
```

> With that, we have verified that our application creates the data files in the data directory of the container.

20. In order to verify that our volume mappings work, we have to check whether those files are available in the Docker host. Keep in mind that as we are using Docker Machine, the Docker host in this case is the Oracle VirtualBox VM and not our local computer. In order to look at the contents of the VM, we have to first SSH into the VM. Docker Machine has an `ssh` command that lets you SSH into the VM. Go ahead and issue the following command to SSH into the VM:

```
docker-machine ssh default
```

You should see something like this:

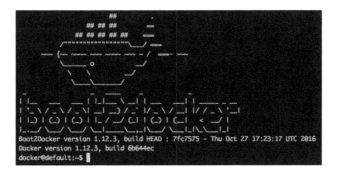

21. List the files in the `/opt/packt/geolocation/data` directory using the `ls` command:

    ls -l /opt/packt/geolocation/data

    You should see that two files have been created with the same names as in the container:

```
docker@default:~$ ls -l /opt/packt/geolocation/data
total 8
-rw-r--r--    1 root     staff          115 Sep 25 23:27 userf1196aac-470e-11e6-beb8-9e71128cae77_t1474843159
-rw-r--r--    1 root     staff          115 Sep 25 23:27 userf1196aac-470e-11e6-beb8-9e71128cae77_t1474843900
docker@default:~$
```

    If you would like to look at the contents, execute the cat command to look at the contents of the data files. That's it! We have learned how to map volumes using Marathon. In a real-time scenario, it is worth using volume mapping to take backups of any critical data such as DB data files, sensitive log files, and raw machine data. Some organizations utilize Mesos frameworks such as Chronos to perform data backups of these data.

    To learn more about Chronos, take a look at this page:
    https://mesos.github.io/chronos/

Configuring environment variables in Marathon

Environment variables play a vital role in any container. Be it your database or messaging server or your own RESTful API, environment variables can be used to store configurations of your container. So far in our geolocation microservice, we haven't come across a scenario to use environment variables as it is a standalone application and does not have to talk to any other server or middleware. But in production scenario where you microservice has to talk to a database or Kafka broker, you have to store the configurations of your database or broker somewhere. That's where developers prefer using environment variables. In this recipe we will take a look at how to configure our geolocation application to use an environment variable and also see how to pass that variable using Marathon.

Getting ready

Before we move on, we first need to know the environment variable that we are going to parameterize and how the geolocation application is going to use it. One use case could be getting the location of the data files as an environment variable. Let's go ahead and do that! As we will have to make some code changes, go ahead and open up STS IDE.

How to do it...

Open the `GeolocationRepository.java` file that is responsible for creating the geolocations and persisting the geolocation JSONs to the local file system. In this recipe we will be parameterizing the path to the data directory `/opt/packt/geolocation/data`. Create a new constant called `DATA_FILES_DIR` and assign it with the value of the environment variable `GEOLOCATION_DATA_FILES_DIR`.

```
private static final String DATA_FILES_DIR =
    System.getenv("GEOLOCATION_DATA_FILES_DIR");
```

But wait, what if the person that deploys the application forgets to pass this environment variable? So it is always safer to give a default value to environment values if they are null (while they are non-nullable). With that said, lets go ahead and rewrite the preceding line with this:

```
private static final String DATA_FILES_DIR =
    System.getenv("GEOLOCATION_DATA_FILES_DIR") != null        ?
    System.getenv("GEOLOCATION_DATA_FILES_DIR") :
    "/opt/packt/geolocation/data";
```

As you can see we have defaulted the value to `/opt/packt/geolocation/data`. Now modify the `addGeoLocation` method to use this variable. After modification, this class will look something like this:

```
package com.packt.microservices.geolocation;

import java.io.File;
import java.util.ArrayList;
import java.util.Collections;
import java.util.List;

import org.springframework.stereotype.Repository;

import com.fasterxml.jackson.databind.ObjectMapper;

@Repository
public class GeoLocationRepository {

  private List<GeoLocation> geolocations = new
    ArrayList<GeoLocation>();
  private static final ObjectMapper MAPPER = new
    ObjectMapper();
  private static final String DATA_FILES_DIR =
    System.getenv("GEOLOCATION_DATA_FILES_DIR") != null
      ? System.getenv("GEOLOCATION_DATA_FILES_DIR") :
        "/opt/packt/geolocation/data";
  public void addGeoLocation(GeoLocation geolocation) {
    geolocations.add(geolocation);
    try {
      MAPPER.writeValue(new File(DATA_FILES_DIR + "/user" +
        geolocation.getUserId() + "_t" +
        geolocation.getTimestamp()), geolocation);
    } catch (Exception e) {
      e.printStackTrace();
    }
    }
    public List<GeoLocation> getGeoLocations() {
    return Collections.unmodifiableList(geolocations);
  }
}
```

Now that our code is ready, let's go ahead and test the application. Start your application `GeoLocationApplication.java` as a Spring Boot application from your STS IDE. Now issue the following cURL command to create a geolocation:

```
curl -H "Content-Type: application/json" -X POST -d '{"timestamp":
1468203975, "userId": "f1196aac-470e-11e6-beb8-9e71128cae77",
```

```
"latitude": 41.803488,"longitude":-88.144040}'
http://localhost:8080/geolocation
```

This should have given you an output similar to (output has been pretty printed for readability purposes):

```
{
    "latitude": 41.803488,
    "longitude": -88.14404,
    "userId": "f1196aac-470e-11e6-beb8-9e71128cae77",
    "timestamp": 1468203975
}
```

Also, this should have created the data file at /opt/packt/geolocation/data directory. Let's go ahead and verify that. Issue the following command to look at the contents of the data file:

```
cat /opt/packt/geolocation/data/userf1196aac-470e-11e6-beb8
-9e71128cae77_t1468203975
```

This should have given you an output similar to (output has been pretty printed for readability purposes):

```
{
    "latitude": 41.803488,
    "longitude": -88.14404,
    "userId": "f1196aac-470e-11e6-beb8-9e71128cae77",
    "timestamp": 1468203975
}
```

Now that our code works great, the next steps are:

1. Build the project to generate a new JAR artifact.
2. Creating a new Docker Image as our code has changed.
3. Upload the new image to Docker Hub.
4. Redeploy the new image with environment variable.
5. Verify if the environment variable is being used.

Go ahead and build your project using the mvn clean package command. This should create a new geolocation-0.0.1-SNAPSHOT.jar artifact in the target directory.

Before we build the new image, let's go ahead and remove the existing image that we already have. To do that go ahead and run the following command:

```
docker rmi vikrammurugesan/geolocation
```

To build our image, issue the following command on your terminal:

```
docker build -t vikrammurugesan/geolocation .
```

Please use your account name instead of the author's in the preceding commands. After your image has been built, go ahead and push your Docker image to the Docker Hub using the following command. You might be asked to log in to your Docker Hub account if you haven't already done so.

```
docker push vikrammurugesan/geolocation
```

Again make sure you use your account name instead of mine. After the image has been uploaded successfully, go to Docker Hub and verify that the "Last Updated" time of your image shows something more recent. Now that our image is ready to be used, let's go ahead and spin off our microservice on Mesos using Marathon. Make sure your Mesos cluster is up and running. If it is down, please kill your cluster and start it again. Once your cluster is back up, go ahead and open up Marathon web UI on your browser. Click on the **Create Application** button and go to the JSON mode. We will be using the JSON mode to quickly populate the modal. In the JSON mode, delete the existing JSON and paste the following JSON.

```
{
    "id": "/geolocation",
    "cmd": null,
    "cpus": 1,
    "mem": 512,
    "disk": 1024,
    "instances": 1,
    "container": {
      "type": "DOCKER",
      "docker": {
        "image": "vikrammurugesan/geolocation",
        "network": "BRIDGE",
        "portMappings": [
          {
            "containerPort": 8080,
            "hostPort": 0,
            "servicePort": 8899,
            "protocol": "tcp",
            "labels": {}
          }
        ],
        "privileged": false,
        "parameters": [],
        "forcePullImage": false
      }
```

```
        }
    }
```

Now flip back to the friendly form view and go to the **Environment Variables** section. In the environment variables section, add the following entry and hit **Create Application**.

- **Key**: GEOLOCATION_DATA_FILES_DIR
- **Value**: /opt/packt/geolocation/data

To verify if the environment variable has created correctly, go ahead and take a look at the **Configuration** section of the application on Marathon. You should see something like this:

```
Container    {
                "type": "DOCKER",
                "volumes": [],
                "docker": {
                    "image": "vikrammurugesan/geolocation",
                    "network": "BRIDGE",
                    "portMappings": [
                        {
                            "containerPort": 8080,
                            "hostPort": 0,
                            "servicePort": 8899,
                            "protocol": "tcp",
                            "labels": {}
                        }
                    ],
                    "privileged": false,
                    "parameters": [],
                    "forcePullImage": false
                }
            }

CPUs    1
Environment  GEOLOCATION_DATA_FILES_DIR=/opt/packt/geolocation/data
```

As a next step, let's go ahead and create two geolocations using the POST API and verify if the files were created on the right directory of the container. Go ahead and issue the following two cURL commands one by one on your terminal window:

```
curl -H "Content-Type: application/json" -X POST -d '{"timestamp":
1474843159, "userId": "f1196aac-470e-11e6-beb8-9e71128cae77", "latitude":
41.803488, "longitude": -88.144040}'
http://192.168.99.100:31758/geolocation
    curl -H "Content-Type: application/json" -X POST -d '{"timestamp":
1474843900, "userId": "f1196aac-470e-11e6-beb8-9e71128cae77", "latitude":
42.803488, "longitude": -87.144040}'
http://192.168.99.100:31758/geolocation
```

Please note that the port number of the container might be different on your installation. In the preceding command we have used `31758` as that's what Marathon uses for this instance. Now issue the following `docker exec` command to verify the contents of the data directory inside the container:

```
docker exec 1d52a2617a8e ls /opt/packt/geolocation/data
```

This should show something like this:

```
userf1196aac-470e-11e6-beb8-9e71128cae77_t1474843159
userf1196aac-470e-11e6-beb8-9e71128cae77_t1474843900
```

Again note the container ID in the preceding command. Please find your container's ID using the `docker ps` command and use that container ID in the preceding command.

With that said we now know how to configure environment variables in Marathon. Though we don't have a solid use case of the environment variable in this example, we will be using environment variables heavily in our future chapters.

Scaling your microservice in Marathon

One of the most important design decisions in building a microservice is scalability. If your microservice is not scalable, there is no point in deploying it as a microservice; it could in fact be a huge monolithic application. There are several ways to scale a microservice. It also depends on the transport type your microservice uses. If your microservice uses HTTP, you should consider load-balancing your HTTP endpoints in various instances of your microservice. Another approach is using an asynchronous messaging system, such as ActiveMQ, Kafka, RabbitMQ, and ZeroMQ.

Getting ready

The geolocation microservice uses RESTful APIs to expose its endpoints. We should be considering load-balancing tools to load-balance the endpoints across instances of the geolocation application. In order to scale our application, let's first bring up the Marathon web interface.

How to do it...

1. Once the Marathon web UI is up and running, deploy the application if it is not already running. Instead of running the application from the **Create Application** modal, using JSON mode is always quicker and simpler. Use the following JSON to create your application:

```json
{
    "id": "/geolocation",
    "cmd": null,
    "cpus": 1,
    "mem": 512,
    "disk": 1024,
    "instances": 1,
    "container": {
        "type": "DOCKER",
        "volumes": [
            {
                "containerPath": "/opt/packt/geolocation/data",
                "hostPath": "/opt/packt/geolocation/data",
                "mode": "RW"
            }
        ],
        "docker": {
            "image": "vikrammurugesan/geolocation",
            "network": "BRIDGE",
            "portMappings": [
                {
                    "containerPort": 8080,
                    "hostPort": 0,
                    "servicePort": 8899,
                    "protocol": "tcp",
                    "labels": {}
                }
            ],
            "privileged": false,
            "parameters": [],
            "forcePullImage": false
        }
    }
}
```

2. After the geolocation application starts, click on the application from the applications grid, and go to the geolocation-specific page. There, you should see the **Scale Application** button. Click on it. It should open a modal like this:

3. Choose **4** from the dropdown and hit **Scale Application**. You should now see that Marathon has deployed the application as four different instances, each exposing different ports:

If you would like to verify that the app is running on these ports, test them one by one using the `curl` command. If you do not have enough resources in your cluster, scaling might not work. Please try increasing the resources by recreating your Docker Machine VM.

4. All this time, we have been interfacing with the Marathon web UI. For a change, let's look at the Mesos web UI at `http://192.168.99.100:5050`. You should see that there are four different tasks running, each of them indicating the various geolocation instances:

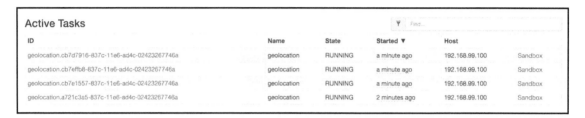

5. We just learned how to scale up applications using Marathon. Let's say you would like to scale the geolocation application back to just one instance; in other words, scale it down. You can use the same **Scale Application** modal to scale it down to **1** instance. After you scale it down, you should now see that there is only one instance of the application running. You have no control over which three out of the previous four will get destroyed. This decision is made by Mesos based on the resource availability on the Mesos slaves:

6. Now go back to the Mesos web interface, and you will notice that three tasks are in **KILLED** status:

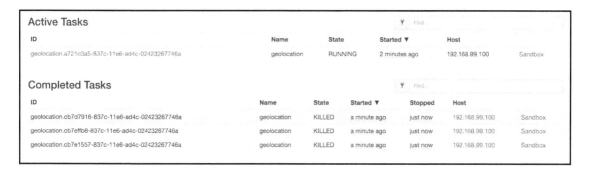

Destroying your microservice in Marathon

There might be times you want to destroy a microservice or application that is already running on Marathon either because you want to free up some resources or because you would like to redeploy the application with a different set of Marathon configurations. This can be easily achieved from the application-specific page in Marathon.

Getting ready

Open the Marathon web interface in your browser, and navigate to the geolocation application page. If you don't have the application up and running, use JSON mode and deploy the application using the JSON that was used in previous recipe *Scaling your Microservice in Marathon*.

How to do it...

1. Marathon applications can either be suspended or destroyed. Suspended applications can be redeployed, while destroyed applications cannot. Click on the button that looks like a gear. This button has two options: **Suspend** and **Destroy**. Let's try to suspend the application:

As you can see, the status of the application is marked as **Suspended**, and there are no active instances of the application running. In order to redeploy the application, we will have to scale it.

2. Scale the application using the **Scale Application** modal with a scaling factor of **1**. Within a few seconds, you should see a brand new instance of the geolocation application up and running. The **Suspend** option is often used to temporarily bring down a service. When you suspend your application, Marathon saves the configurations of your application so that you can bring it back up with the same set of configurations without having to re-enter them.

3. The next option we are interested in is **Destroy**. Unlike **Suspend**, the **Destroy** option removes the application and its configurations completely from Marathon. Like we saw earlier, you may want to destroy your application either to free up some resources or redeploy the application with a new set of configurations.

4. Go ahead and click on the gear button, and then hit the **Destroy** button. Marathon will ask you for confirmation as you cannot recover from this step:

If you confirm that you would like to destroy the application, you will be taken to the Marathon main screen, and you will not see any applications running:

Monitoring your microservice logs in Marathon

So far, we have learned how to deploy, scale, suspend, and destroy our microservice in a Mesos cluster using Marathon. All these steps are part of your deployment process, but there is one thing you would want to do post deployment: monitor the logs. In this recipe, we will look at how to monitor our application logs using Marathon.

Getting ready

Fortunately, there is an easy way to look at your application's log files using Marathon's web interface. Though it is not very user friendly, it is still possible. To illustrate this, let's deploy the geolocation microservice using Marathon. If you have to restart your Mesos cluster, do so. In Marathon, use JSON mode and the JSON that was used in recipe *Scaling your Microservice in Marathon* to deploy the application.

How to do it…

1. Once your application has started, go to the geolocation application's page in Marathon. You will see that one instance of your application is running. Click on the running instance of the geolocation application. You will see something like this:

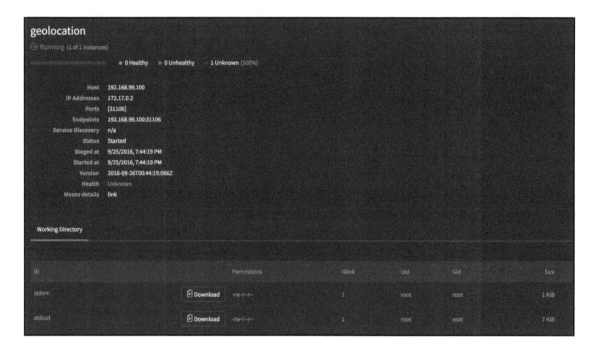

The first section, at the top, provides information such as the host on which your application is deployed, the IP address of your Docker container, ports exposed, and endpoints exposed. The section that really matters to us now is Working Directory. It shows two files here: stdout and stderr. Both of them have the same permissions, rw/r/r.

2. Marathon uses Docker's logging behavior to consume and display the logs. Any standard output logged by the Docker container goes into stdout, and any standard error logged by Docker container goes into stderr. The version of Marathon we are using does not let you view the logs on the screen. The only way to look at them is to download them first and open them with your preferred editor.

3. Hit the **Download** button on stdout. This should download the 7 KB file. Open the downloaded file with your preferred editor. In the following screenshot, I have used OS X's TextEdit application:

As you can see, there are some Spring Boot logs in stdout. Towards the end of the logs, you can see the in-memory Tomcat service started on port 8080 exposing our REST APIs.

4. Similarly, download `stderr` and take a look at its contents:

```
● ● ●                                                   stderr
I0926 00:44:19.251945   458 exec.cpp:161] Version: 1.0.1
I0926 00:44:19.255882   463 exec.cpp:236] Executor registered on agent 365f9aa3-1e12-41a1-ab98-3d6b5c8cb278-S0
I0926 00:44:19.257060   462 docker.cpp:809] Running docker -H unix:///var/run/docker.sock run --cpu-shares 1024 --memory 536870912 -e
MARATHON_APP_VERSION=2016-09-26T00:44:19.066Z -e HOST=192.168.99.100 -e MARATHON_APP_RESOURCE_CPUS=1.0 -e MARATHON_APP_DOCKER_IMAGE=vikrammurugesan/
geolocation -e MESOS_TASK_ID=geolocation.5bd45ced-8382-11e6-ad4c-024232677746a -e PORT=31106 -e MARATHON_APP_RESOURCE_MEM=512.0 -e PORTS=31106 -e
MARATHON_APP_RESOURCE_DISK=1024.0 -e MARATHON_APP_LABELS= -e PORT_8080=31106 -e MARATHON_APP_ID=/geolocation -e PORT0=31106 -e MESOS_SANDBOX=/mnt/mesos/
sandbox -e MESOS_CONTAINER_NAME=mesos-365f9aa3-1e12-41a1-ab98-3d6b5c8cb278-S0.d013b85e-a68f-4149-b59b-86430c653797 -v /opt/packt/geolocation/data:/opt/
packt/geolocation/data:rw -v /tmp/slaves/365f9aa3-1e12-41a1-ab98-3d6b5c8cb278-S0/frameworks/365f9aa3-1e12-41a1-ab98-3d6b5c8cb278-0000/executors/
geolocation.5bd45ced-8382-11e6-ad4c-024232677746a/runs/d013b85e-a68f-4149-b59b-86430c653797:/mnt/mesos/sandbox --net bridge -p 31106:8080/tcp --name
mesos-365f9aa3-1e12-41a1-ab98-3d6b5c8cb278-S0.d013b85e-a68f-4149-b59b-86430c653797 vikrammurugesan/geolocation
```

There are some log messages from some C++ files, showing that the Docker container was started.

Though using the Marathon web interface to view logs is not very convenient, it is one step toward viewing your logs. In the future, we can expect a more sophisticated interface from Marathon. The intended use of **Working Directory** is when you would like to expose some resource files used by your application. In our geolocation application, we do not have any files in the working directory.

Monitoring your microservice logs in Mesos

We've already seen that viewing logs in Marathon is not very easy. Oftentimes, you will want to perform more advanced operations, such as tailing logs, viewing logs on screen, or viewing multiple logs at the same time. Fortunately, you can do this using Mesos. In this recipe, we will learn how to monitor application logs-in other words, task logs-using the Mesos web UI.

Getting ready

To check this out, deploy the geolocation microservice using Marathon. If you have to restart your Mesos cluster, do so. In Marathon, use JSON mode and the JSON that was used in recipe *Scaling your Microservice in Marathon* to deploy the application.

How to do it…

1. Once your application has started, go to the Mesos web interface using the URL `http://192.168.99.100:5050`, and verify that your application's task is running:

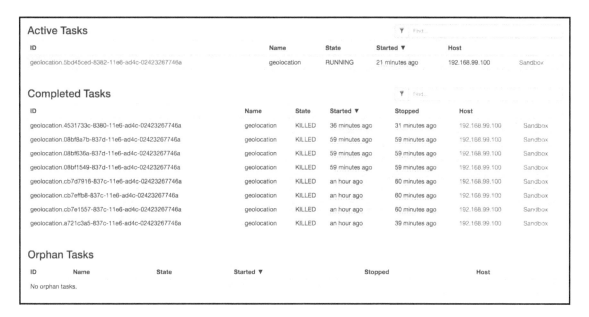

2. From the preceding screenshot, you can see that there is one active task and several completed tasks for the geolocation microservice. The completed tasks were from previous executions, and the running task is the one that we are concerned about. In fact, you can still look at the logs of the completed tasks, but in this recipe, we will be looking at the active task's logs, as the steps are exactly the same. In **Active Tasks**, there is a hyperlink called **Sandbox**. Click on it. You should see a screen that displays two items: `stdout` and `stderr`.

This is pretty much the same thing we saw in Marathon. You can do two things: either download the logs using the **Download** button and take a look at them using your favorite text editor, or tail the logs by clicking on the file names.

3. Go ahead and click on **stdout**. You will see that a popup window opens up with the contents of `stdout`:

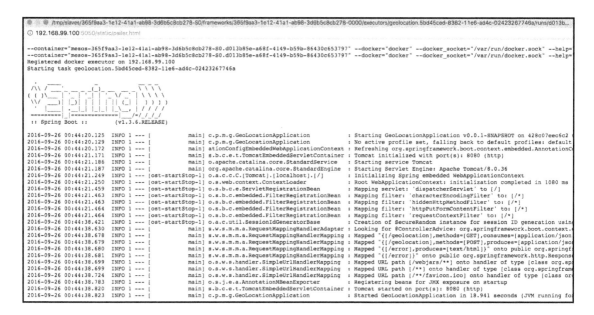

A great advantage of this view is that it constantly tails any new `stdout` calls. You can keep this window open to look at the live logs as they come.

4. Similarly, click on **stderr** to look at the contents of `stderr`:

```
/tmp/slaves/365f9aa3-1e12-41a1-ab98-3d6b5c8cb278-S0/frameworks/365f9aa3-1e12-41a1-ab98-3d6b5c8cb278-0000/executors/geolocation.5bd45ced-8382-11e6-ad4c-0...
192.168.99.100:5050/static/pailer.html

I0926 00:44:19.251945   458 exec.cpp:161] Version: 1.0.1
I0926 00:44:19.255882   463 exec.cpp:236] Executor registered on agent 365f9aa3-1e12-41a1-ab98-3d6b5c8cb278-S0
I0926 00:44:19.257060   462 docker.cpp:809] Running docker -H unix:///var/run/docker.sock run --cpu-shares 1024 --memory 536870912 -e MARATHON
```

The tailing feature is especially helpful when you are monitoring logs of multiple applications. Keep in mind that this is a feature of Mesos, and Mesos lets you look at logs on tasks deployed using any framework: Spark, Chronos, Marathon, Aurora, Cassandra, and so on.

In this recipe, we learned two ways of monitoring the logs of applications that are deployed in Marathon. With this recipe, you have finished learning the basics of Mesos and Marathon. You can now start playing around with Mesos and Marathon to fit your needs.

Managing your microservice using Marathon's REST API

Marathon's web interface is definitely one of the best user interfaces. It is very intuitive and sophisticated. So far, we have been using the web interface because it was the easiest way to get you up to speed. Using the web interface might not be scalable when you are dealing with hundreds of microservices, though. Mesos and Marathon are now production ready. In fact, a lot of organizations have been using Mesos and Marathon to deploy hundreds of microservices. In this recipe, we will look at how to deploy microservices in Marathon using its REST API. This enables you to implement continuous deployments.

Continuous deployments have been picking up traction lately. Continuous deployment is a process in which you deploy your application to production as soon as it has been checked in, packaged, tested, and validated. Organizations use **continuous integration** (**CI**) tools such as Jenkins, Hudson, Bamboo, and Travis CI to automate their deployments. If you have the right set of test cases and the right tools to validate and automate your tests, you can confidently deploy your application after it has been tested and validated. With the recent improvements in the aforementioned tools, it is now possible to automate deployments easily. Before Mesos or Kubernetes, deployments were done using build frameworks such as Maven, Gradle, and Ant. One such example is the Cargo plugin. The Cargo plugin for Maven, Ant, and Gradle can deploy your artifacts to several web and application servers, including but not limited to Tomcat, WildFly, Glassfish, Weblogic, and Websphere. If you have used the Cargo plugin, you will know that it is not very easy to configure.

Getting ready

In this recipe, we will learn how to use the various RESTful APIs of Marathon. This will be particularly useful when you are automating your deployments to Mesos and Marathon. Before we start this recipe, let's rebuild the Mesos cluster. As our Mesos cluster is Dockerized, I suggest you restart the cluster every once in a while. This is because, sometimes the containers tend to run out of resources. However you don't have to worry about this in production if you have sufficient resources. Once your cluster is up and running, open the Marathon web interface in a browser. We will be using the terminal to hit Marathon's API using `curl` commands. So keep a terminal window open all the time.

How to do it...

In this recipe, we will be looking at several Marathon REST APIs that let you:

- Deploy an application
- Scale an application
- List all instances of a given application
- Destroy an application

1. First, let's take a look at how we can deploy the geolocation application using Marathon's REST endpoint. All the application-related APIs are listed under the `/apps` domain. The most recent version of the Marathon REST endpoints is `v2`. Hence, the `/apps` domain APIs are listed under the path `/v2/apps`. To create a new application on Marathon, all you have to do is `POST` the JSON representation of your application to the URL `http://192.168.99.100:8080/v2/apps`.

   The schema for this JSON is exactly the same one we used in JSON mode from previous recipes:

```
{
  "id": "/geolocation",
 "cmd": null,
 "cpus": 1,
  "mem": 512,
  "disk": 1024,
  "instances": 1,
  "container": {
    "type": "DOCKER",
    "volumes": [
      {
        "containerPath": "/opt/packt/geolocation/data",
```

```
        "hostPath": "/opt/packt/geolocation/data",
        "mode": "RW"
      }
    ],
    "docker": {
      "image": "vikrammurugesan/geolocation",
      "network": "BRIDGE",
      "portMappings": [
        {
          "containerPort": 8080,
          "hostPort": 0,
          "servicePort": 8899,
          "protocol": "tcp",
          "labels": {}
        }
      ],
      "privileged": false,
      "parameters": [],
      "forcePullImage": false
    }
  }
}
```

2. As we will be using `curl` as our client, let's make the whole JSON wrap into one single line. You can use your favorite text editor to do this. The final `curl` command will look something like this:

```
curl -H "Content-Type: application/json" -X POST -d '{"id":
"/geolocation", "cmd": null, "cpus": 1, "mem": 512, "disk": 1024,
"instances": 1, "container": {"type": "DOCKER", "volumes":
[{"containerPath": "/opt/packt/geolocation/data", "hostPath":
"/opt/packt/geolocation/data", "mode": "RW"} ], "docker": {"image":
"vikrammurugesan/geolocation", "network": "BRIDGE", "portMappings":
[{"containerPort": 8080, "hostPort": 0, "servicePort": 8899, "protocol":
"tcp", "labels": {} } ], "privileged": false, "parameters": [],
"forcePullImage": false } } }' http://192.168.99.100:8080/v2/apps
```

3. You should get a response saying your application has been queued for deployment (pretty-printed for readability):

```
{
  "id": "/geolocation",
  "cmd": null,
  "args": null,
  "user": null,
  "env": {},
  "instances": 1,
```

```json
    "cpus": 1,
    "mem": 512,
    "disk": 1024,
    "executor": "",
    "constraints": [],
    "uris": [],
"fetch": [],
    "storeUrls": [],
    "ports": [
      8899
    ],
    "portDefinitions": [
      {
        "port": 8899,
        "protocol": "tcp",
        "labels": {}
      }
    ],
"requirePorts": false,
"backoffSeconds": 1,
"backoffFactor": 1.15,
 "maxLaunchDelaySeconds": 3600,
 "container": {
    "type": "DOCKER",
    "volumes": [
      {
        "containerPath": "/opt/packt/geolocation/data",
        "hostPath": "/opt/packt/geolocation/data",
        "mode": "RW"
      }
    ],
    "docker": {
      "image": "vikrammurugesan/geolocation",
      "network": "BRIDGE",
      "portMappings": [
        {
          "containerPort": 8080,
          "hostPort": 0,
          "servicePort": 8899,
          "protocol": "tcp",
          "labels": {}
        }
      ],
      "privileged": false,
      "parameters": [],
      "forcePullImage": false
    }
  },
```

```
"healthChecks": [],
"readinessChecks": [],
"dependencies": [],
"upgradeStrategy": {
    "minimumHealthCapacity": 1,
    "maximumOverCapacity": 1
},
"labels": {},
"acceptedResourceRoles": null,
"ipAddress": null,
"version": "2016-09-26T02:03:43.284Z",
"residency": null,
"tasksStaged": 0,
"tasksRunning": 0,
"tasksHealthy": 0,
"tasksUnhealthy": 0,
"deployments": [
    {
        "id": "6f569b52-181f-4909-974a-23666d7a2c6f"
    }
],
"tasks": []
}
```

4. Go to Marathon and make sure that your application is up and running.
5. Now let's scale our application to a factor of 2. To do this, we will use the PUT method and the path /v2/apps/geolocation, where /geolocation is the unique ID of our application in Marathon. If you look at the following request body, it is exactly the same as the previous request, except for the number of instances. Here, we've set the value of instances to 2:

```
{
  "id": "/geolocation",
  "cmd": null,
  "cpus": 1,
  "mem": 512,
  "disk": 1024,
  "instances": 2,
  "container": {
    "type": "DOCKER",
    "volumes": [
      {
        "containerPath": "/opt/packt/geolocation/data",
        "hostPath": "/opt/packt/geolocation/data",
        "mode": "RW"
      }
    ],
```

```
        "docker": {
          "image": "vikrammurugesan/geolocation",
          "network": "BRIDGE",
          "portMappings": [
            {
              "containerPort": 8080,
              "hostPort": 0,
              "servicePort": 8899,
              "protocol": "tcp",
              "labels": {}
            }
          ],
          "privileged": false,
          "parameters": [],
          "forcePullImage": false
        }
      }
    }
```

6. Go ahead and execute the following `curl` command:

```
        curl -H "Content-Type: application/json" -X PUT -d '{"id":
"/geolocation", "cmd": null, "cpus": 1, "mem": 512, "disk": 1024,
"instances": 2, "container": {"type": "DOCKER", "volumes":
[{"containerPath": "/opt/packt/geolocation/data", "hostPath":
"/opt/packt/geolocation/data", "mode": "RW"} ], "docker": {"image":
"vikrammurugesan/geolocation", "network": "BRIDGE", "portMappings":
[{"containerPort": 8080, "hostPort": 0, "servicePort": 8899, "protocol":
"tcp", "labels": {} } ], "privileged": false, "parameters": [],
"forcePullImage": false } } }'
http://192.168.99.100:8080/v2/apps/geolocation
```

You should have received a response similar to this, indicating the deployment ID for the request (pretty-printed for readability):

```
{
  "version": "2016-09-26T02:09:51.476Z",
  "deploymentId": "1eb0ae12-8ce9-497a-b0df-0e07261e993a"
}
```

7. Now if you go to Marathon, you will see that there are two instances of geolocation showing up as running:

8. You can scale down the application by posting the same PUT request with a scaling factor of 1. You might want to list down the instances that are running for the given application. You can do that by using the GET method and URL path /v2/apps/geolocation. Execute the following curl command on your console:

```
curl http://192.168.99.100:8080/v2/apps/geolocation
```

9. You should get the following response, indicating that two instances of the same application are running in Marathon (parts of the response have been truncated for readability):

```
{
  "app": {
    "id": "/geolocation",
    .
    .
    .
    "container": {
      "type": "DOCKER",
      "volumes": [
        {
```

```
              "containerPath": "/opt/packt/geolocation/data",
              "hostPath": "/opt/packt/geolocation/data",
              "mode": "RW"
          }
        ],
        "docker": {
          "image": "vikrammurugesan/geolocation",
          "network": "BRIDGE",
          "portMappings": [
            {
              "containerPort": 8080,
              "hostPort": 0,
             "servicePort": 8899,
              "protocol": "tcp",
              "labels": {}
            }
          ],
          "privileged": false,
          "parameters": [],
          "forcePullImage": false
        }
      },
      .

      .

      .
  "tasksStaged": 0,
  "tasksRunning": 2,
  "tasksHealthy": 0,
  "tasksUnhealthy": 0,
  "deployments": [],
  "tasks": [
    {
      "id": "geolocation.73ad18be-838d-11e6-9e4b-
        02423267746a",
      "slaveId": "be077ff3-9864-4517-8b49-e0f8fd66d977-S0",
      "host": "192.168.99.100",
      "state": "TASK_RUNNING",
      "startedAt": "2016-09-26T02:03:44.505Z",
      "stagedAt": "2016-09-26T02:03:43.601Z",
      "ports": [
        31981
      ],
      "version": "2016-09-26T02:03:43.284Z",
      "ipAddresses": [
        {
          "ipAddress": "172.17.0.2",
          "protocol": "IPv4"
        }
```

```
      ],
        "appId": "/geolocation"
      },
      {
        "id": "geolocation.4efe1dbf-838e-11e6-9e4b-
          02423267746a",
        "slaveId": "be077ff3-9864-4517-8b49-e0f8fd66d977-S0",

          .

          .

          .

      }
    ]
  }
}
```

10. If you would like to destroy the geolocation application completely, use the DELETE method on the URL /v2/apps/geolocation. The response of the DELETE request is usually similar to that of the GET request, listing the application details and the tasks that were stopped by this DELETE request. Here's the command:

    curl -X DELETE http://192.168.99.100:8080/v2/apps/geolocation

 There are several ways of implementing continuous deployment to Marathon from tools such as Jenkins, Hudson, and other CI tools. One such option is doing the same thing we did here: use CURL. You can write shell scripts that deploy the application to Marathon using the curl command after your builds pass. The other approach is writing custom build framework plugins, such as the Maven Marathon or Gradle Marathon plugins. I'll leave that up to you to try out.

To learn how to write a Maven plugin, take a look at this page: https://maven.apache.org/guides/plugin/guide-java-plugin-development.html.

To learn how to write a Gradle plugin, take a look at this page: https://docs.gradle.org/current/userguide/custom_plugins.html.

That brings us to the end of this recipe and the chapter. You are now ready to manage your own Mesos cluster and manage your applications on a Mesos cluster using Marathon. Good luck using Mesos and Marathon!

4
Deploying Microservices on Kubernetes

In this chapter, we will learn how to deploy microservices on Kubernetes, which is an open source framework from Google for orchestrating and managing containers. We will cover the following recipes:

- Setting up a Kubernetes cluster using Docker
- Understanding the Kubernetes dashboard
- Deploying your microservice on Kubernetes
- Configuring ports in Kubernetes
- Configuring volumes in Kubernetes
- Configuring environment variables in Kubernetes
- Scaling your microservice in Kubernetes
- Destroying your microservice in Kubernetes
- Monitoring your microservice logs in Kubernetes

Introduction

Before we jump into the recipes, it is very important that you know what Kubernetes is and why we use it to deploy microservices.

If you've read the previous chapter, you will understand why we need a clustering framework like Mesos. Just as Mesos is a clustering framework from the Apache foundation, Kubernetes is a containerization platform from Google that lets you orchestrate and manage containers. It is similar to the Mesos and Marathon combo. It comes with all the features you will need to deploy containers, such as scaling, load balancing, deploying, and monitoring. One more thing Kubernetes does compared to Mesos is that it lets you deploy rkt containers. But with Mesos' recent release, they have added unified containerizer support, which will let Mesos deploy not just Docker containers, but also rkt containers. Rkt (pronounced "rock it") was initially developed with the intent of providing a much more secured containerizing framework. One thing to note here is that rkt is an implementation of appc. It is strongly recommended that you read about appc before you move on to the next section. We will not be discussing appc as it is out of the scope of this book

 To learn more about **App Container** (**appc**), visit their GitHub specifications page, which has lot of useful information, at `https://GitHub.com/appc/spec`.

With that said, you should now have understood that Kubernetes, or K8s (the *8* stands for *ubernete*) will help us deploy and manage our microservices. That's right; in this chapter, we will learn how to work with a Kubernetes cluster.

Now let's take a moment to understand the various components that make up the Kubernetes cluster. We will not be going deep into each and every component of Kubernetes as it is out of scope for this book. Instead, we will just try to understand the various components and their usage. Similar to Mesos, Kubernetes also follows a master-slave architecture. So, obviously, there is a master that is responsible for scheduling the containers on to one or more slaves. But unlike Mesos, in Kubernetes, containers are organized in smaller mortal units called **pods**. Pods (or containers in different pods, to be precise) can communicate using services. Take a look at the following diagram:

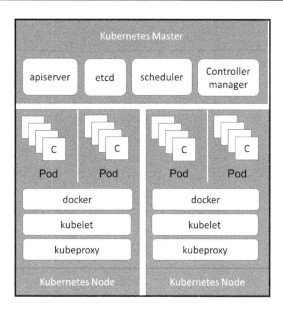

As you can see, a simple Kubernetes cluster is composed of several components. Let's break it down into multiple components and see what they are used for one by one.

Kubernetes master

The Kubernetes master consists of four major subcomponents that enable the functions of a Kubernetes cluster. In the previous diagram, we only have one master. But in an ideal production infrastructure, it is normal to have multiple masters in order to provide high availability. Now let's take a look at the four different components of the master.

API server

The master API server is responsible for handling and configuring the data for pods, services, and replication controllers. The API server holds the REST endpoints that can be used to talk to the cluster.

etcd

The etcd service is used as a persistent storage to hold the state of the master. In general, etcd is a distributed key-value store that uses the Raft protocol. It is most commonly used in cases where there are multiple nodes in a cluster trying to share configurations. Kubernetes relies heavily on etcd for storing the master's state as well as for HA configurations.

If you would like to know more about etcd, then please take a look at their website
`https://coreos.com/etcd`.

Scheduler

Simply put, the scheduler is used to bind any unbound pods to the nodes. There is a lot going on behind the binding process, such as priorities and predicates. As it is out of scope for this book, we will not be discussing them now.

 If you would like to learn more about the binding process, take a look at this GitHub readme at `https://github.com/kubernetes/community/blo b/master/contributors/devel/scheduler.md`.

Controller manager

The controller manager itself is composed of several controllers, such as a replication controller, endpoint controller, and namespace controller, which help in maintaining the state of the cluster by watching for any changes to the states in etcd. For example, the replication controller is responsible for replicating pods across nodes, also known as pod replicas.

Kubernetes node

Kubernetes nodes are similar to Mesos slaves (or agents), which are responsible for holding pods and their containers. Nodes can be either physical servers or virtual machines. Earlier, we were introduced to a new term called *Pod*. In very simple terms, a pod is just a group of containers in the same logical host. With that said, containers in the same pod share the same IP and pool of ports. In order to run a Docker container on a Kubernetes node, the node first needs Docker installed on it. That's what you see in the diagram.

In addition to Docker, a node has two other components: **kubeproxy** and **kubelet**. Let's talk about them one by one. Before we try to understand what a kubeproxy is, we have to know about Kubernetes' services. Now that we know containers reside in pods, and pods can be replicated across nodes. What if you have an application that is scaled to a factor greater than one and you would like to load-balance between the containers? That's where Kubernetes' services come in.

Kubernetes services are just abstractions of pods that define policies to access them. Services are usually identified by labels on the pods. The service and the kubeproxy together work with the DNS server to perform load balancing on requests to services (containers).

A kubelet is an agent that runs on each node. The kubelet is responsible for maintaining a YAML manifest file that describes the pods. It is also responsible for running the containers and make sure they are up and running all the time.

That was a very quick and simple illustration of a Kubernetes cluster. Of course, the functioning and internals of a Kubernetes cluster are much more complicated and sophisticated than what we've talked about here. But our goal for now is to understand the components and construction of a Kubernetes cluster. With that said, let's move on to our first recipe, where we will look at different ways to orchestrate a Kubernetes cluster.

Setting up Kubernetes cluster using Docker

We now have a basic understanding of Kubernetes and its components. Though this is sufficient to get started with our recipes, it is strongly recommended that you learn more about Kubernetes from Google's documentation at `http://kubernetes.io/docs/` before you start using Kubernetes at scale.

Getting ready

In this recipe, we will orchestrate a local Dockerized Kubernetes cluster.

1. The easiest way to create a Kubernetes cluster at scale is using Google Cloud Platform at `https://cloud.google.com/container-engine`. If you have a Google account, you should be able to use Google Cloud Platform right away. But for simplicity, in this recipe, we will be building our Kubernetes cluster on our local machines using Docker.

2. There are several ways to run a Dockerized Kubernetes cluster, including but not limited to:

   - Building our own Docker Compose file
   - Using `kid`
   - Using Minikube

3. Building our own Docker Compose file might take longer compared to using `kid` and Minikube. **Kid** stands for Kubernetes in Docker. It is a third-party script that will spin off a Kubernetes cluster using Docker. **Minikube** is Kubernetes' recommended method for creating a single-node cluster on the local machine. In this recipe, we will be using Minikube and `kubectl` to orchestrate and manage our local single-node Kubernetes cluster. `kubectl` is a CLI for managing Kubernetes clusters.

Before you start using `kubectl`, it is strongly recommended that you read its manual pages. A very descriptive overview of `kubectl` is given here at `http://kubernetes.io/docs/user-guide/kubectl-overview`.

4. One of the prerequisites for running Minikube is Oracle VirtualBox. You should already have it on your local machine if you are using `docker-machine`. If you are using native Docker, you might have to install the most recent version of VirtualBox.

You can download and find installation instructions for VirtualBox here at `https://www.virtualbox.org/wiki/Downloads`.

How to do it...

Minikube is maintained by the Kubernetes community. Installing it is as simple as running a shell script. The installation instructions for Minikube are usually included in the release page of each version. You can find the instructions for the most recent version here: `https://GitHub.com/kubernetes/minikube/releases`. At the time of writing this, the most recent version of Minikube is v0.12.0. You could install the most recent version. This page has instructions for OS X, Linux, and Windows.

In this recipe, you will find instructions for OS X. You should follow the right instructions for your operating system.

1. Open a terminal window and execute the following command,

```
curl -Lo minikube
https://storage.googleapis.com/minikube/releases/v0.12.0/minikube-darwin-am
d64 && chmod +x minikube && sudo mv minikube /usr/local/bin/
```

2. This command does three things:

   - Download the `minikube` package
   - Add execute permissions to the `minikube` binary file for all users
   - Move the `minikube` binary file to `/usr/local/bin`

3. If you are familiar with the Linux environment, you should already understand the command. The `&&` operator executes the second command only when the first is successful. The first two commands are pretty self-explanatory. The third command is required so you don't have to configure your `PATH` variable each time you open a new terminal. Upon execution, you should see something like this:

4. If you are prompted for your password, type it. It might be required to run the `mv` command as it is executed with `sudo` permissions.

5. Now let's verify that we have the `minikube` package installed successfully. Go ahead and issue the following command from the same terminal window:

```
minikube
```

6. You should see something like this:

```
Minikube is a CLI tool that provisions and manages single-node Kubernetes clusters optimized for development workflows.

Usage:
  minikube [command]

Available Commands:
  addons            Modify minikube's kubernetes addons
  config            Modify minikube config
  dashboard         Opens/displays the kubernetes dashboard URL for your local cluster
  delete            Deletes a local kubernetes cluster.
  docker-env        sets up docker env variables; similar to '$(docker-machine env)'
  get-k8s-versions  Gets the list of available kubernetes versions available for minikube.
  ip                Retrieve the IP address of the running cluster.
  logs              Gets the logs of the running localkube instance, used for debugging minikube, not user code.
  service           Gets the kubernetes URL for the specified service in your local cluster
  ssh               Log into or run a command on a machine with SSH; similar to 'docker-machine ssh'
  start             Starts a local kubernetes cluster.
  status            Gets the status of a local kubernetes cluster.
  stop              Stops a running local kubernetes cluster.
  version           Print the version of minikube.

Flags:
      --alsologtostderr value      log to standard error as well as files
  -h, --help                       help for minikube
      --log_backtrace_at value     when logging hits line file:N, emit a stack trace (default :0)
      --log_dir value              If non-empty, write log files in this directory
      --logtostderr value          log to standard error instead of files
      --show-libmachine-logs       Whether or not to show logs from libmachine.
      --stderrthreshold value      logs at or above this threshold go to stderr (default 2)
  -v, --v value                    log level for V logs
      --vmodule value              comma-separated list of pattern=N settings for file-filtered logging

Use "minikube [command] --help" for more information about a command.
```

 Take a few minutes to get familiar with the Minikube commands. If you would like to know more about Minikube, read their documentation: https://GitHub.com/kubernetes/minikube/blob/master/README.md.

If you look at the possible commands in Minikube from the screenshot, you can see that Minikube by itself is just used for orchestrating a cluster. When it comes to managing the cluster itself, you will need something like kubectl. Fortunately, minikube can work along with kubectl if you have it installed.

7. So let's install kubectl. In the same terminal window, execute the following command:

```
curl -LO
https://storage.googleapis.com/kubernetes-release/release/$(curl -s
https://storage.googleapis.com/kubernetes-release/release/stable.txt)/bin/d
arwin/amd64/kubectl && chmod +x ./kubectl && sudo mv ./kubectl
/usr/local/bin/kubectl
```

8. The preceding command is very similar to the command we used to install minikube. It has three commands executed one after the other: the first command downloads the most recent version of kubectl binary, the second command adds execute permissions to the binary file for all users, and the third command moves the kubectl file to the /usr/local/bin directory so that you don't have to configure your PATH to include the kubectl binary each time you open a new terminal.

Alternatively, if you are a Mac OS X user, you could also use Homebrew to install kubectl. This way, you don't have to worry about permissions and configuring the PATH as Homebrew takes care of that for you. To install kubectl via Homebrew, all you have to do is run this simple Homebrew command:
```
brew install kubectl
```

9. To verify that you have `kubectl` installed correct, execute the following command on the same terminal:

   kubectl

```
kubectl controls the Kubernetes cluster manager.

Find more information at https://github.com/kubernetes/kubernetes.

Usage:
  kubectl [flags]
  kubectl [command]

Available Commands:
  get             Display one or many resources
  set             Set specific features on objects
  describe        Show details of a specific resource or group of resources
  create          Create a resource by filename or stdin
  replace         Replace a resource by filename or stdin.
  patch           Update field(s) of a resource using strategic merge patch.
  delete          Delete resources by filenames, stdin, resources and names, or by resources and label selector.
  edit            Edit a resource on the server
  apply           Apply a configuration to a resource by filename or stdin
  namespace       SUPERSEDED: Set and view the current Kubernetes namespace
  logs            Print the logs for a container in a pod.
  rolling-update  Perform a rolling update of the given ReplicationController.
  scale           Set a new size for a Deployment, ReplicaSet, Replication Controller, or Job.
  cordon          Mark node as unschedulable
  drain           Drain node in preparation for maintenance
  uncordon        Mark node as schedulable
  attach          Attach to a running container.
  exec            Execute a command in a container.
  port-forward    Forward one or more local ports to a pod.
  proxy           Run a proxy to the Kubernetes API server
  run             Run a particular image on the cluster.
  expose          Take a replication controller, service, deployment or pod and expose it as a new Kubernetes Service
  autoscale       Auto-scale a Deployment, ReplicaSet, or ReplicationController
  rollout         rollout manages a deployment
  label           Update the labels on a resource
  annotate        Update the annotations on a resource
  taint           Update the taints on one or more nodes
  config          config modifies kubeconfig files
  cluster-info    Display cluster info
  api-versions    Print the supported API versions on the server, in the form of "group/version".
  version         Print the client and server version information.
  explain         Documentation of resources.
  convert         Convert config files between different API versions
  completion      Output shell completion code for the given shell (bash or zsh)
```

10. Remember to take a moment to read through the manual pages of `kubectl`. It is a very powerful CLI tool that is capable of managing your entire Kubernetes cluster. With that said, let's create our first Kubernetes cluster. Issue the following command:

    minikube start

11. It usually takes a few minutes to start your cluster because behind the scenes, Minikube tries to create a new VirtualBox VM with all necessary tools and software installed on it. You should see something like this:

```
Starting local Kubernetes cluster...
Kubectl is now configured to use the cluster.
```

12. As you can see, `kubectl` is now configured to use the cluster that was created by Minikube. Now that we have our cluster running locally, let's make sure our cluster is up and running. One way to do this is listing all the Docker containers running on the VirtualBox VM. In order to do that, you need to perform an extra step. Go ahead and run the following command:

```
eval $(minikube docker-env)
```

13. This `eval` command sets your Docker variables to work with the `minikube` VM. If you are curious about the `minikube` VM, open up VirtualBox, and you should see a newly created VM called `minikube`. Now that our environment is set, issue the following command to list all the Docker containers that are running:

```
docker ps -a
```

14. You should be able to see the containers running on the `minikube` VM:

15. As you can see, there is one container called `kube-addon-manager` and two containers for the image `pause-amd64`. The `addon-manager` container makes sure all the add-ons are update as per the Kubernetes manifest.

 To learn more about add-ons, take a look at this GitHub page `https://github.com/kubernetes/kubernetes/tree/master/cluster/add ons`.

16. The `pause` container is something special. It is responsible for storing the network information for any new pod. In our cluster, there are two `pause` containers, meaning there could potentially be two pods even before we create one. We will take a look at them in the next recipe.

17. The other components will be already installed on the `minikube` VM. If you want to be very sure about whether or not your cluster is running, you can execute the `minikube status` command. It will spit out something like this:

```
minikubeVM: Running
localkube: Running
```

18. We know that `minikubeVM` indicates the VirtualBox VM. `localkube` is nothing but the name of our Kubernetes cluster. You can stop your cluster by issuing the following command:

```
minikube stop
```

19. This will shut down the `minikube` VM in VirtualBox.

That brings us to the end of this recipe. Congratulations! You have successfully created your first Kubernetes cluster.

Understanding the Kubernetes dashboard

In the previous recipe, we learned how to start and stop our local single-node Kubernetes cluster. We call it a single-node cluster because it will just have one Kubernetes node configured. So all the containers that you deploy are going to be deployed on this single Kubernetes node. Kubernetes comes with a sophisticated web UI. The web UI acts as an administration console for your cluster. You can perform almost all operations that you can with `kubectl`, on the web UI. In fact, you could also monitor the resource utilization of your cluster from the web UI. In this recipe, we are going to get familiar with the Kubernetes dashboard so that we can easily manage our microservice on any Kubernetes cluster.

Getting ready

1. The first thing you need to know is the URL to the Kubernetes UI dashboard. One way to do that is identifying the IP of your `minikube` VM and use the default Kubernetes dashboard port, `30000`.

2. To find the IP of your `minikube` VM, run the following command on your terminal:

```
minikube ip
```

3. After you get the IP, use the port number `30000` to access the Kubernetes dashboard from your web browser.

Though this approach works most of the time, we're still making an assumption about the port number. What if the default port number changes? So let's see the other way to open our dashboard.

How to do it...

1. Fortunately, Minikube comes with an easy-to-use command that when executed in your terminal will automatically open the dashboard in your default web browser. Let's try that out:

```
minikube dashboard
```

2. If your cluster is already running, you should see the dashboard in your web browser. Sometimes, if you try to run this command right after your `minikube start` command, it might take a while to open up. Ideally, it pings the cluster status API to check the status of your Kubernetes cluster. On your browser, you should see something like this:

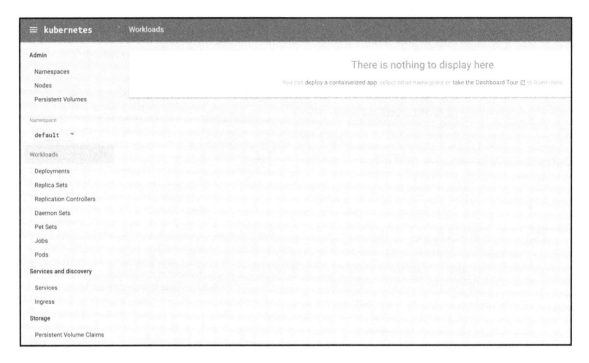

3. To better understand the interface, let's spin off a simple `echoserver` container on Kubernetes. Execute the following command on your terminal:

```
kubectl run hello-minikube --
image=gcr.io/google_containers/echoserver:1.4
```

4. For now, let's not dig deeper into how the command works. All we did was spin off a simple `echoserver` container. We are doing this only to populate the UI with some information. We will dig deeper into how to run a container in our next recipe. You should get a response similar to this:

```
deployment "hello-minikube" created
```

5. Now go to the dashboard and refresh the **Workloads** page. You should now see something like this:

6. As you can see, there are three sections:

   - **Deployments**
   - **Replica sets**
   - **Pods**

   Deployments shows all the containers that are deployed on your pod. A replica set is nothing but the next generation of replication controller. **Replica sets** sections shows the different replicas of your containers. The **Pods** section, as its name indicates, shows all the pods that are currently available in your cluster.

7. Instead of going into these individual sections on the left-hand side pane, let's go directly to the items listed in each of these sections. First, let's start with the `hello-minikube` deployment by clicking on the **hello-minikube** deployment item from the **Deployments** grid. You should see something like this:

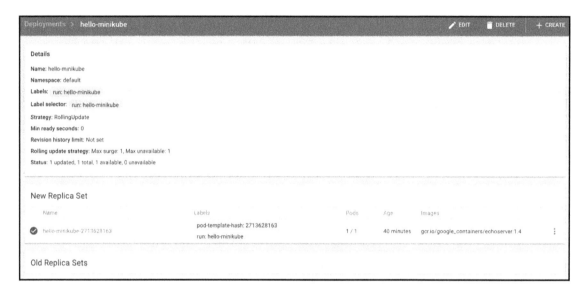

8. Some sections have been ignored in the preceding screenshot to focus just on the most important sections and the ones you will be using very often. The **Details** section is where you will find the high-level details about your Docker container deployment. Note the word "deployment" in the previous statement. If you want to see details about the Docker container itself, you will have to take a look at the **New Replica Set** section. Note the labels associated with the deployment as well as the replica set. These labels were auto-generated by Kubernetes when you deployed the container using `kubectl`.

9. You can go to the **Replica Sets** section by using the **Replica Sets** option in the left-hand side menu or by clicking on the **hello-minikube-2713628163** replica set on the **Deployments** page. Either way, you should see something like this:

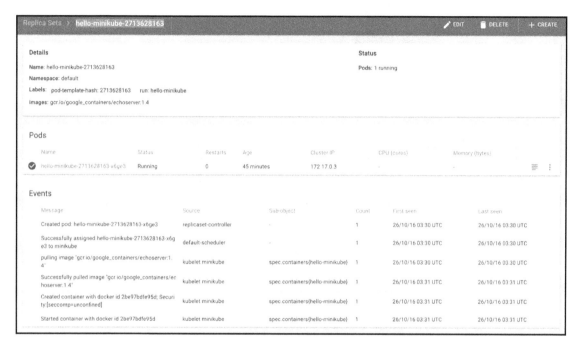

10. The **Details** section is where you will find the container information, such as image name, version, status, and replica set name. The **Pods** section lists all the pods on which this container has been deployed or replicated. It also shows the status of the pod and its own IP address. If you had the app in multiple pods, you will see all the pods listed here with their unique IPs addresses. The **Events** section shows the various events related to this container on the cluster. This is especially useful when you are debugging your application or deployment.

11. The next important section is the **Pods** section. You can go to the **Pods** section by choosing the option in the left-hand side menu or clicking on the **hello-minikube-2713628163-x6ge3** pod in the **Pods** grid of the **Replica Sets** page. Either way, you should end up on a page like this:

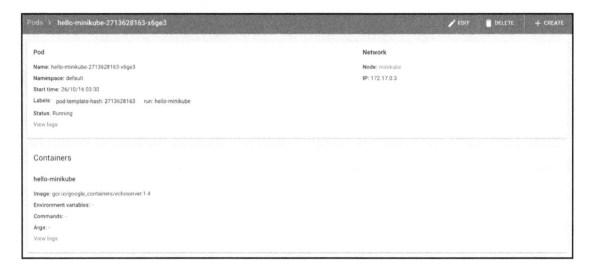

12. The top section shows the high-level details of the pod, such as name, status, labels, start time, and namespace. One important detail you will find in this section is the **Node** that this pod is running on and the IP address of the pod. The next important screen in the dashboard is the **Nodes** section. Let's get there by clicking on the node named **minikube**. You should see something like this:

13. The screenshot only shows part of the page. The rest of the page will be discussed in the next section. The **Details** and **System Info** sections give you a lot of useful information, such as OS, version information, architecture, and name. **Allocated resources** shows the resource allocation for this particular node.

14. From the screenshot, we can say that **0.005** out of **2** CPUs have been used, **50** MB out of **1.955** GB of memory has been used, and **3** out of **110** pods have been allocated. The maximum number of pods allocated per node is set to 110 due to several performance reasons. However, this can be changed with the kubelet configuration **max-pods**. The remainder of the page shows the various pods that are available on this node. For our local cluster, you should be able to see three pods:

As you can see, there are two additional pods: **kube-addon-manager-minikube** and **kubernetes-dashboard-xk3ih**. From the names of these pods, it is pretty obvious that **kube-addon-manager-minikube** has the add-on manager in it and **kubernetes-dashboard-xk3ih** has the Kubernetes dashboard itself deployed.

15. The other two important sections are **Namespaces** and **Persistent Volumes**. We will be looking at **Persistent Volumes** in later recipes in this chapter. Let's take a look at the **Namespace** section. Go ahead and click on **Namespaces** from the left-hand side menu. You should see something like this:

16. As you can see, there are two namespaces: **default** and **kube-system**. Namespaces are nothing but virtual clusters that are part of the same physical cluster. The default namespace is where the all our new deployments go, and the **kube-system** namespace is where the dashboard and add-on manager are deployed.

17. All this time, we have been looking at the default namespace. If you would like to look at the deployments, replication controllers, and pods in the **kube-system** namespace, use the **Namespace** dropdown from the left-hand side menu to choose your namespace.

That's brings us to the end of this recipe. The goal of this recipe is to get you familiar with the Kubernetes dashboard and its various sections. Kubernetes itself is a vast topic, and it is strongly recommended that you research it more before you start using it.

Deploying your microservice on Kubernetes

So far in this chapter, we have successfully orchestrated a single node Kubernetes cluster using Docker, and we have familiarized ourselves with the Kubernetes dashboard. In this recipe, we will learn how to deploy our geolocation microservice on our Kubernetes cluster.

Getting ready

Deploying a microservice in Kubernetes can be done in several ways. We can use `kubectl` to submit our deployment to the Kubernetes cluster. We can also use the dashboard to create a deployment via the UI. In the previous recipe, we used `kubectl` to create a deployment for the `echoserver` container. In this recipe, let's use the dashboard to deploy the geolocation microservice in Kubernetes.

Go ahead and open up the Kubernetes dashboard using the `minikube` command:

```
minikube dashboard
```

How to do it...

1. To create a new deployment, click on the **Create** button at the top right of the dashboard. You should see a screen similar to Marathon's **New Application** modal. Most of the properties on this screen are very similar to that of Marathon's, except maybe for the terminologies. So if you are familiar with using Marathon, you will find this really easy.

2. You will find four major fields:
    - **App name**
    - **Container name**
    - **Number of pods**
    - **Service**

3. In order to deploy our geolocation microservice, we just need the app name and container name. We will look at the number of pods and service in later recipes in this chapter. Go ahead and enter `geolocation` as the application name and `vikrammurugesan/geolocation:latest` as the container name. Please change the Docker Hub account name from mine to your account name. The `latest` tag is optional here, as it defaults to that if you don't provide one.

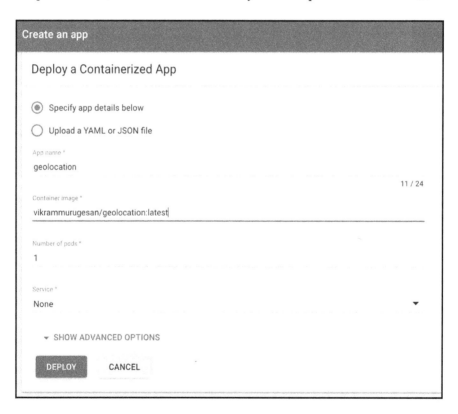

In the preceding screenshot, you can see another option for creating an application: **Upload a YAML or JSON file**. This lets you upload your app configurations in the form of a YAML or JSON file. We will look at this later in this chapter; for now, we will use the user interface to create the application.

4. Go ahead and click on the **Deploy** button when you are done. You should now see that there is one new application for geolocation and a pod associated with it:

5. It usually takes a few seconds to a few minutes to deploy your application. Once it is done, the status icons should show a green tick icon, indicating it is running. Once your pod and replication controller are up and running, you will see that a new IP has been assigned to your pod. That is the IP we will be using to access our application. In my case, the IP assigned was 172.17.0.4. So we will be using this IP in all future references to the pod.

6. Now that our geolocation application is running, let's invoke the GET API of application to make sure we get a `200` response back. Go ahead and issue the following cURL command in your terminal window:

```
curl http://172.17.0.4:8080/geolocation
curl: (7) Failed to connect to 172.17.0.4 port 8080: Operation
timed out
```

7. After a few seconds, your connection should time out. That is because the IP that we have used is an internal IP and cannot be accessed outside our host. In this case, the host is the `minikube` VirtualBox VM. Now we clearly know that we still have some work to do with respect to the ports. And that's what you will be learning in the next recipe.

But before you jump into the next recipe, if you are curious to know how the same process can be done using the YAML or JSON file approach, keep reading:

1. First, delete the replication controller and service for geolocation. Deleting the replication controller will automatically delete the pod and the containers in the pod. After they have been deleted, we now have to create a YAML file with our deployment configurations. Open your STS IDE and create a new YAML file called `kube-deployment.yml` directly under the geolocation project directory. Paste the following contents into the file:

```
apiVersion: extensions/v1beta1
kind: Deployment
metadata:
  name: geolocation
spec:
  replicas: 1
  template:
    metadata:
      labels:
        app: geolocation
    spec:
      containers:
      - name: geolocation
        image: vikrammurugesan/geolocation:latest
        ports:
        - containerPort: 8080
```

- There are a few things to talk about in this file. The `apiVersion` property identifies the version of the `extensions` API that will be used. The `extensions` API is a sophisticated API with operations related to daemon sets, deployments, jobs, and so on.

 To read more about the `extensions` API, visit `http://kubernetes.io/docs/api-reference/extensions/v1beta1/opera tions`.

- The `kind` property identifies the kind of resource we are trying to create in Kubernetes. Note that here we are creating a `Deployment`, rather than replication controller like last time.
- The `replicas` property is set to `1`, indicating that we just need one replica of this deployment. The container name is `geolocation` and the image used is `vikrammurugesan/geolocation:latest`. Please don't forget to use the image in your Docker Hub account instead of the author's. Note that we have listed the container port as `8080` in the `ports` section, which can later be exposed via a service.
- We have added a label with the key `app` and value `geolocation`. This label can be used when you create a service. We will see how to do that after we deploy the container. Save the file and close your IDE.

2. Go ahead and click on the **Create** button to create a new application. This time, choose **Upload a YAML or JSON file**. Choose the `kube-deployment.yml` file that we just created and hit **Deploy**:

3. As you can see, there is a new deployment called **geolocation**. It also created a pod, replication set, and replication controller. The same thing can be done using the following `kubectl` command:

```
kubectl create -f kube-deployment.yml
```

This command-line based approach is recommended when you are performing automated deployments using continuous integration tools such as Jenkins. One thing to note in this approach is that it will not create a service for you. You have to create the service manually, either using `kubectl` or from the dashboard. We will look at how to create a service using `kubectl` in the next recipe. The choice of whether to use the dashboard or `kubectl` depends completely on your usage. That brings us to the end of this recipe. I hope you now have a good hold on deploying your applications on Kubernetes. In the next recipe, we will look at how to configure ports and services.

Configuring ports in Kubernetes

So far in this chapter, we have created our own Kubernetes cluster and deployed our geolocation microservice on the cluster. But unfortunately, we were not able to access our microservice because we haven't exposed our ports (in the dashboard method) or created services (in the `kubectl` method). In this recipe, we will learn how to map our ports and create services.

Getting ready

When we deploy our application from the friendly form in the Kubernetes dashboard, we have some advanced settings that we could utilize to expose ports. Open the dashboard using the `minikube` command:

```
minikube dashboard
```

Delete any deployments, replication controllers, or services you already have for geolocation. You can leave the `echoserver` container that we created earlier or delete it-it shouldn't really affect us.

How to do it...

1. Go ahead and create a new application. Enter the application name `geolocation` and container image `vikrammurugesan/geolocation:latest`. This time, configure an internal service with source port `8080`, target port `8080`, and protocol TCP. The source port is the port we will use to access the service, and the target port is the port that needs to be exposed on the container.

Also expand the **Advanced Options** section to go through the other options that Kubernetes offers. Scroll down to the **CPU** section and enter `1` for **CPU requirement**. Provide the value `512` for **Memory requirement**. Once you are done, hit **Deploy**.

2. Now, let's verify that a service has been created for this port mapping. If you go to the **Services** section, you should see a new service called **geolocation**. Click on that to take a look at the service details. You should see something like this:

3. If you look at the **Connection** section, there is this field called **Cluster IP**. In the screenshot, the **Cluster IP** is 10.0.0.20. This IP is the one that we should be using to access our geolocation service on port 8080. Without further ado, let's open up a terminal. On the terminal, execute the following cURL command:

```
curl http://10.0.0.20:8080/geolocation
curl: (7) Failed to connect to 10.0.0.20 port 8080: Operation timed
out
```

4. What happened now? This time, the request timed out because although you have the service configured to perform a port mapping from port 8080 of the node to the container, we are still trying to access this host from our local computer. Since this is a Dockerized environment, we will have to run the same command from inside the minikube VM.

5. In order to run this command from inside the VM, we need to SSH into the VM. Fortunately, Minikube has the ability to SSH into the minikube VM. On the same terminal, execute the following command:

```
minikube ssh
```

6. You should get something like this:

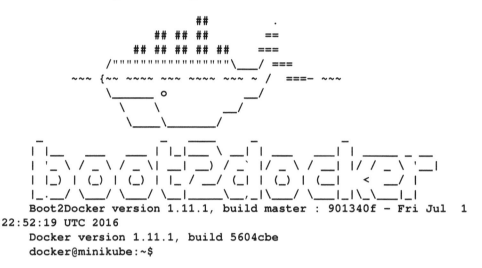

```
Boot2Docker version 1.11.1, build master : 901340f - Fri Jul 1
22:52:19 UTC 2016
Docker version 1.11.1, build 5604cbe
docker@minikube:~$
```

7. Once you are inside the VM, run the same cURL command again:

```
curl http://10.0.0.20:8080/geolocation
```

8. This time, you should get an empty array ([]) from the server, indicating that there are no geolocations available. We now know how to access our service. But wait; this is not a scalable solution because we can't log in to the VM each time we deploy one or more services. We should be able to access our services from our local computer. To do that, we need some kind of port forwarding mechanism. kubectl has port forwarding capability that forwards any request from our local machine to the pod. If we can get our request to the pod, the service will automatically take care of sending our request to the right microservice host and port. Exit from the minikube VM.

9. Before we can run the kubectl port-forward command, we need to know the name of the pod. We can either get it from the dashboard or use the following command in your terminal window:

```
kubectl get pods
```

10. You should get something like this:

```
NAME    READY   STATUS   RESTARTS   AGE
geolocation-qr86h   1/1   Running   0   27m
hello-minikube-2713628163-x6ge3   1/1
Running   0   1d
```

11. Now that we know the pod name, issue the following `kubectl` command from the same terminal window:

```
kubectl port-forward geolocation-qr86
8085:8080
Forwarding from 127.0.0.1:8085 -> 8080
Forwarding from [::1]:8085 -> 8080
```

12. In this command, the `8085` on the left-hand side of the colon indicates the port number on our local machine, and `8080` on the right-hand side of the colon indicates the port number to forward to on the pod. After you execute the command, it will go to interactive mode and keep listening for any new requests on port 8085 of your local machine. Any new requests will be forwarded to port 8080 of the pod, and the responses will be sent back to the client.

13. Now that we have our port forwarding agent and Kubernetes service set up, let's verify that our APIs are accessible from the local machine. Open a new terminal window and issue the following cURL command to create a new geolocation:

```
curl -H "Content-Type: application/json" -X POST -d '{"timestamp":
1468203975, "userId": "f1196aac-470e-11e6-beb8-9e71128cae77", "latitude":
41.803488, "longitude": -88.144040}' http://localhost:8085/geolocation
```

14. This should give you an output similar to the following (pretty-printed for readability):

```
{
    "latitude": 41.803488,
    "longitude": -88.14404,
    "userId": "f1196aac-470e-11e6-
    beb8-9e71128cae77",
    "timestamp": 1468203975
}
```

15. With that, we are able to access our geolocation microservice on the Kubernetes cluster from our local machine. The remainder of the recipe will help you create a service if you would like to use the YAML-file based `kubectl create` command to deploy your microservice on Kubernetes. If you prefer using the dashboard UI to deploy applications, feel free to skip the rest of this recipe and jump to the next recipe. If you have used the `kubectl create` command to create your microservice, it will not create a service for you. You have to manually create it using `kubectl expose` command. This is useful when you are automating deployments or automating integration tests in a continuous integration environment.

16. Creating a service using the `kubectl` command is very simple. All you need to know is your deployment name. In the `kube-deployment.yml` file, we have set the deployment name as geolocation, so we will use the same here. Open up a new terminal and issue the following command:

```
kubectl expose deployment/geolocation
service "geolocation" exposed
```

17. Now let's verify that our service has been created. Execute the following command in the same terminal window:

```
kubectl get services
NAME           CLUSTER-IP   EXTERNAL-IP   PORT(S)    AGE
geolocation    10.0.0.254   <none>        8080/TCP   1m
kubernetes     10.0.0.1     <none>        443/TCP    1d
```

18. As you can see, port 8080 has been exposed by the geolocation service. If you would like to get more information about the service without having to go to the dashboard, use the following command:

```
kubectl describe service/geolocation
Name:        geolocation
Namespace:    default
Labels:      app=geolocation
Selector:     app=geolocation
Type:        ClusterIP
IP:        10.0.0.254
Port:        <unset>   8080/TCP
Endpoints:      172.17.0.4:8080
Session Affinity:   None
No events.
```

19. From the preceding console output, we can see that the ClusterIP is `10.0.0.254`, and there is one endpoint exposed by this service at `172.17.0.4:8080`. If you are in a Dockerized environment, as we discussed earlier in this recipe, you will have to perform a port forwarding using the `kubectl port-forward` command.

That brings us to the end of this recipe. We have successfully deployed our geolocation microservice and exposed its endpoints so that it can be accessed from outside. In the following recipes, we will look at how to configure volumes and environment variables using the dashboard UI.

Configuring volumes in Kubernetes

Volumes are handled very differently in Kubernetes compared to Apache Mesos. In fact, Kubernetes persistent volumes support Azure, vCloud, and AWS. Kubernetes also supports Ceph, Flocker, Gluster FS, and even Git. This extensive support opens up opportunities for storing your data on the cloud and also enables easy backups.

 To take a look at the complete set of supported volumes, go to
`http://kubernetes.io/docs/user-guide/volumes/#types-of-volumes`.

Getting ready

In this recipe, we will learn how to map the volume where our data files are stored in the geolocation microservice.

1. First, delete any deployments, replication controllers, port forwards, or services that you already have for geolocation. You can leave the `echoserver` container that we created earlier or delete it. It shouldn't really affect us. Also, always delete the service first and the replication controller afterward. If you try to delete the pod or container, it will be recreated by the replication controller to make sure at least one replica of your pod and container is available (as our replication factor is `1`).

2. Before we jump into the recipe, you have to learn how Kubernetes handles volumes. There are two concepts: persistent volumes and persistent volume claims.

    - A persistent volume is just a storage provisioned on the cluster network by the cluster administrator. The cluster administrator can be someone in your organization responsible for the Kubernetes cluster's infrastructure and availability.

    - Unlike Mesos, where you map a volume directly from the container to the host machine, here in Kubernetes, you have to create a persistent volume first and create a persistent volume claim, which is nothing but a request made by the pod for storage on the cluster.

It is highly recommended that you read
`http://kubernetes.io/docs/user-guide/persistent-volumes` before
you start using volumes on Kubernetes, as the process is not straight-
forward.

3. In our recipe, for simplicity, we will be creating a `hostPath` volume and will be
    mapping it to the data directory of the geolocation microservice. If you remember
    from `Chapter 3`, *Deploying Microservices on Mesos*, we persisted our geolocations
    in the form of JSON files in the data directory at
    `/opt/packt/geolocation/data`. The `hostPath` volume is mostly used when
    you would like to expose something on the host machine, for example, Docker
    internals, shared folders, and config directories.

How to do it...

In this recipe, we will be deploying our microservice a little differently from the previous
methods. So far, we have created replication controllers and deployments both from the UI
and using `kubectl`. In this recipe, we will be creating a pod using `kubectl`. The reason we
are creating a pod is that we will also be creating our `hostPath` volume along with the pod.

1. Open your STS IDE and go to the `geolocation` project. Create a new YAML file
    called `kube-pod.yml`, and paste the following contents in it:

    ```
    apiVersion: v1
    kind: Pod
    metadata:
      name: geolocation
    spec:
      containers:
      - image: vikrammurugesan/geolocation:latest
        name: geolocation
        ports:
        - containerPort: 8080
        volumeMounts:
         - mountPath: /opt/packt/geolocation/data
           name: geodata
      volumes:
        - name: geodata
          hostPath:
            path: /opt/packt/geolocation/data
    ```

2. There are few things to take a look at here in the YAML file. The API version we are using is `v1`. The kind of entity we are creating is Pod. The name of the pod is `geolocation`. The pod has one container with the name `geolocation`. It uses the `vikrammurugesan/geolocation:latest` image, and the container port for this container is `8080`. The pod has one volume called `geodata`. The volume `geodata` is of type `hostPath`, and the path in the host is `/opt/packt/geolocation/data`. The geolocation container has one volume mapping for the `/opt/packt/geolocation/data` container path on the volume that matches the name `geodata` which is the `hostPath` volume.

3. Go ahead and create a new pod using the following `kubectl create` command:

```
kubectl create -f kube-pod.yml
pod "geolocation" created
```

4. Now let's make sure our pod is up and running. To verify its status, issue the following command on the terminal:

```
kubectl get pods
NAME                                 READY     STATUS           RESTARTS   AGE
geolocation                          0/1       ContainerCreating 0          5m
hello-minikube-2713628163-x6ge3 1/1    Running          1          5d
```

5. As you can see, the `geolocation` pod is in the `ContainerCreating` state, which means it is in the process of pulling and starting the container. It may take a few seconds for your pod to go into the **Running** state.

6. You can always take a look at your pod in the Kubernetes dashboard as well. Once the pod is created, look at the details of the **geolocation** pod in the dashboard. You should see something like this:

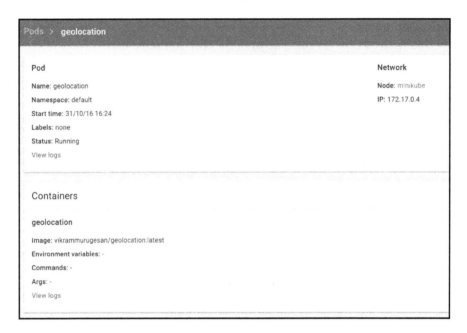

7. The next step is setting up port forwarding using `kubectl`. Use the following command to setup port forwarding:

```
kubectl port-forward geolocation 8085:8080
```

8. Now that you know your pod and container are up and running, let's send a couple of geolocations to the POST API. Use the following two `curl` commands to create geolocations:

```
curl -H "Content-Type: application/json" -X POST -d '{"timestamp":
1468203975, "userId": "f1196aac-470e-11e6-beb8-9e71128cae77", "latitude":
41.803488, "longitude": -88.144040}' http://localhost:8085/geolocation
```

9. This should give you an output similar to the following (pretty-printed for readability):

```
{
    "latitude": 41.803488,
    "longitude": -88.14404,
    "userId": "f1196aac-470e-11e6-beb8-9e71128cae77",
```

```
    "timestamp": 1468203975
}
    curl -H "Content-Type: application/json" -X POST -d '{"timestamp":
1468203976, "userId": "f1196aac-470e-11e6-beb8-9e71128cae77", "latitude":
9.568012, "longitude": 77.962444}' http://localhost:8085/geolocation
```

10. This should give you an output like this (pretty-printed for readability):

```
{
    "latitude": 9.568012,
    "longitude": 77.962444,
    "userId": "f1196aac-470e-11e6-beb8-9e71128cae77",
    "timestamp": 1468203975
}
```

11. Now let's verify whether the files we created are available on the host machine. But the question here is this: which one is the host machine? Since we are using a Dockerized environment, the host machine will be the `minikube` VirtualBox VM. To check whether the files are available in the VM, we have to SSH into the VM first. To do that, let's use the `minikubessh` command:

```
minikube ssh
```

12. You should get something like this:

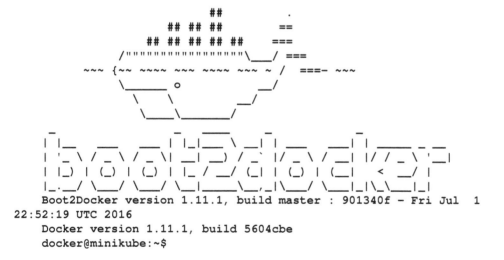

```
    Boot2Docker version 1.11.1, build master : 901340f - Fri Jul  1
22:52:19 UTC 2016
    Docker version 1.11.1, build 5604cbe
    docker@minikube:~$
```

13. Once you are inside the VM, execute the following ls command to check whether the files have been created successfully:

```
ls -ls /opt/packt/geolocation/data
```

14. You should get something like this:

```
total 8
    4 -rw-r--r--    1 root     staff         115 Oct 31 18:25 userf1196aac-470e-11e6-beb8-9e71128cae77_t1468203975
    4 -rw-r--r--    1 root     staff         114 Oct 31 18:26 userf1196aac-470e-11e6-beb8-9e71128cae77_t1468203976
```

We have successfully configured volume mappings on Kubernetes using the hostPath method. Though this is one of the simplest configurations you can achieve with Kubernetes, the idea here is to give you an introduction to the abilities of Kubernetes when it comes to Microservice deployments. In production scenarios, it is more ideal to use Azure, AWS, or vCloud, based on your stack.

Before we move on to the next recipe, let's delete our pod using the following command:

```
kubectl delete pod/geolocation
pod "geolocation" deleted
```

That brings us to the end of this recipe. In the next recipe, we will look at how to configure environment variables in Kubernetes.

Configuring environment variables in Kubernetes

In the previous chapter, we used Marathon to add an environment variable for the geolocation data directory path, which will in turn be used by the application to locate the data directory. In this recipe, we will learn how to use the Kubernetes dashboard as well as kubectl to configure the same environment variable.

Getting ready

First, delete any replication controllers, services, port forwards or pods that were created in the previous recipe. You can leave the `echoserver` up and running; it should not affect anything. There are two ways you might want to add environment variables to your container: from the dashboard UI or from the command line using `kubectl`.

We will look at the dashboard UI first. If you don't have the dashboard up and running, issue the following command to open up the Kubernetes dashboard:

```
minikube dashboard
```

How to do it...

1. Once the dashboard is up, click on the **Create** button to deploy our microservice. Let's use the friendly form to deploy the microservice. Use the following configurations:

   - **App name**: geolocation
   - **Container image**: vikrammurugesan/geolocation:latest
   - **Number of pods**: 1
   - **Service**: Internal
   - **Port**: 8080
   - **Target port**: 8080
   - **Protocol**: TCP
   - **CPU requirement** (cores): 1
   - **Memory requirement** (MiB): 512
   - **Environment Variables**
   - **Name**: GEOLOCATION_DATA_FILES_DIR
   - **Value**: /opt/packt/geolocation/data

2. Take a look at the **Environment Variables** section. We have added the
   GEOLOCATION_DATA_FILES_DIR variable with the value
   /opt/packt/geolocation/data:

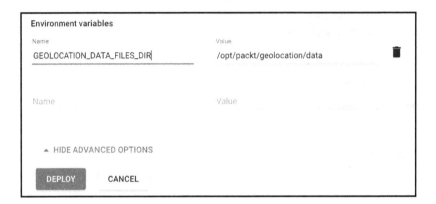

 Keep in mind that the **Environment Variables** section will be buried
under the advanced options at the bottom.

3. Once you have entered all the values, click on **Deploy** to deploy the microservice.
   It takes a few seconds for your pod and replication controller to get to the
   Running state.

4. That's it! The geolocation microservice should now use the new environment
   variable to locate the data directory inside the container. The next step is to check
   whether the **geolocation** microservice is using our newly created environment
   variable.

5. In order to verify the working of our environment variable, we have to expose
   port 8080 of the pod to our local machine. Go ahead and issue the following
   command in your terminal window:

```
kubectl port-forward geolocation-qr86 8080:8080
Forwarding from 127.0.0.1:8080 -> 8080
Forwarding from [::1]:8080 -> 8080
```

6. In this command, the name of the pod was `geolocation-qr86`. If the name of your pod is different, use that. Otherwise, you will get an error message from `kubectl` saying that a pod with the given name is not available. Now that your service is listening on port 8080 of localhost, open a new terminal window. Execute the following two `curl` commands one by one:

```
curl -H "Content-Type: application/json" -X POST -d '{"timestamp":
1468203975, "userId": "f1196aac-470e-11e6-beb8-9e71128cae77", "latitude":
41.803488, "longitude": -88.144040}' http://localhost:8080/geolocation
```

7. This should give you an output similar to the following (pretty-printed for readability):

```
{
    "latitude": 41.803488,
    "longitude": -88.14404,
    "userId": "f1196aac-470e-11e6-beb8-9e71128cae77",
    "timestamp": 1468203975
}
curl -H "Content-Type: application/json" -X POST -d '{"timestamp":
1468203976, "userId": "f1196aac-470e-11e6-beb8-9e71128cae77", "latitude":
9.568012, "longitude": 77.962444}' http://localhost:8080/geolocation
```

8. This should give you an output like the following (pretty-printed for readability):

```
{
    "latitude": 9.568012,
    "longitude": 77.962444,
    "userId": "f1196aac-470e-11e6-beb8-9e71128cae77",
    "timestamp": 1468203975
}
```

9. Now let's validate whether the files have been created using a simple `docker exec` command. You can find the ID of the geolocation container using the `docker ps` command. In the same terminal window, execute the following Docker command:

```
docker exec 9ae486e3d63a ls /opt/packt/geolocation/data
userf1196aac-470e-11e6-beb8-9e71128cae77_t1468203975
userf1196aac-470e-11e6-beb8-9e71128cae77_t1468203976
```

Yay! Our data files have been created at the location that was passed in the `GEOLOCATION_DATA_FILES_DIR` environment variable.

10. Now let's take a look at how to configure environment variables using kubectl and a YAML file. Before we move on, delete the replication controller and the services that we created.

11. Now, open the `kube-pod.yml` file that we created in the previous recipe in STS. Add the following section to the geolocation container section in the YAML file. Remember to be careful when you work with YAML files, as it does not accept tab spaces. Instead of tab spaces, use blank spaces:

    ```
    env:
    - name: GEOLOCATION_DATA_FILES_DIR
      value: "/opt/packt/geolocation/data"
    ```

12. After you have added the environment variables, your final YAML file will look like this:

    ```
    apiVersion: v1
    kind: pod
    metadata:
      name: geolocation
    spec:
      containers:
      - image: vikrammurugesan/geolocation:latest
        name: geolocation
        ports:
        - containerPort: 8080
        volumeMounts:
        - mountPath: /opt/packt/geolocation/data
          name: geodata
        env:
        - name: GEOLOCATION_DATA_FILES_DIR
          value: "/opt/packt/geolocation/data"
      volumes:
      - name: geodata
        hostPath:
          path: /opt/packt/geolocation/data
    ```

13. Spin off the pod using `kubectl` from any terminal window, using the following command:

    ```
    kubectl create -f kube-pod.yml
    pod "geolocation" created
    ```

14. Now you can verify whether the environment variable was created by posting some geolocations to the API and checking the contents of the `/opt/packt/geolocation/data` directory in the `minikube` VirtualBox VM.

Scaling your microservice in Kubernetes

If you read the previous chapter, you will know how important being able to scale microservices is. Scaling is a significant feature for any clustering framework because with the increasing usage of containers, users prefer simpler methods to scale their containers. Like Marathon, Kubernetes' dashboard can be used to easily scale containers up and down. In this recipe, we will be using the Kubernetes dashboard to scale up and scale down the geolocation microservice.

Getting ready

Open up the Kubernetes dashboard if you already have your cluster running. If not, use Minikube to start the cluster and open the dashboard. Make sure there are no instances of the geolocation container running on your Kubernetes cluster. If you have any instance of `geolocation` running, delete the replication controllers, services, and pods.

How to do it…

1. Click on the **Create** button and fill out the friendly form with the following information:
   - **App name**: `geolocation`
   - **Container image**: `vikrammurugesan/geolocation:latest`
   - **Number of pods**: `1`
   - **Service**: `Internal`
   - **Port**: `8080`
   - **Target port**: `8080`
   - **Protocol**: `TCP`
   - **CPU requirement (cores)**: `0.5`
   - **Memory requirement (MiB)**: `512`
   - **Environment Variables**
   - **Name**: `GEOLOCATION_DATA_FILES_DIR`
   - **Value**: `/opt/packt/geolocation/data`

There is one significant change in this configuration from our previous deployments. This time, we have set the CPUs to 0.5. This change is required to support the number of pods that can run in our Minikube setup. The default number of CPUs is 2, which has already been used by our first instance of geolocation, `hello-minikube`, the dashboard, and the add-on manager. You could also increase the number of CPUs used by Minikube by recreating the `minikube` VM with the `--cpu` option. Go ahead and hit **Deploy**.

For more information, read
`https://GitHub.com/kubernetes/minikube/blob/master/docs/minikube_start.md`.

2. Note that we have set the number of pods to 1. You must have guessed by now that the number of pods is what that will help us scale our microservice. Now let's say you would like to increase the number of instances of your application to 2: click on **Workloads** in the left-hand side menu. From the **Replication controllers** section, click on the three dots, and select **Scale**:

3. After you click on **Scale**, you will be prompted to enter the number of pods you would like to scale to. As you can see, you will not be scaling your application instance in the same pod; rather, Kubernetes lets you scale the number of pods itself. This is slightly different from how Apache Mesos and Marathon work. But it makes a lot of sense when it comes to scaling your applications in the Kubernetes ecosystem. In the modal, enter 2 and hit **OK**:

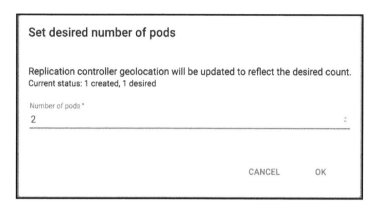

4. Now you should be able to see two pods for geolocation; they start with `geolocation-`. If you would like to learn more about your pod and the containers that are running inside it, click on the pod name:

With that, you have successfully scaled your application to a scaling factor of 2. If your cluster has sufficient resources, you will be able to easily scale your application to any number of pods.

5. Scaling down an application is very straight-forward and uses the same strategy. Now let's say you would like to down-scale the geolocation application to a scaling factor of 1. All you have to do is go to the **Workloads** page, click on the three dots next to the geolocation replication controller, and click on **Scale**. In the scaling modal, enter the scaling factor 1 and hit **OK**:

Pods				
Name	Status	Restarts	Age	Cluster IP
✓ geolocation-a2xce	Running	0	36 minutes	172.17.0.3
✓ hello-minikube-2713628163-x6ge3	Running	3	11 days	172.17.0.2

As you can see, there is only one instance of the geolocation pod, and the other one was automatically destroyed. There is no guarantee which pods will be destroyed and which ones will be retained. That decision is made by Kubernetes. So it is highly recommended that you don't write any logic that is very deployment specific. In fact, that is the whole point of building microservices.

6. There are other ways to scale your microservice, such as modifying the YAML file from inside the Kubernetes dashboard and using `kubectl` to change the `replicas` property of your deployment. We will take a very quick look at how you can do it with `kubectl`, because that is something you might want to do when automating your deployment process. From your terminal shell, execute the following `kubectl` command:

```
kubectl scale rc geolocation --replicas=2
replicationcontroller "geolocation" scaled
```

7. Here, `rc` stands for replication controller. We are requesting `kubectl` to scale the replica of the geolocation replication controller to 2. Newer versions of Kubernetes are replacing replication controllers with replica sets. Scaling them is slightly different from the preceding approach. Now to verify the number of geolocation pods running, execute the following command in the same terminal:

```
kubectl get pods
NAME                             READY   STATUS    RESTARTS   AGE
geolocation-a2xce                1/1     Running   0          42m
geolocation-150r2                1/1     Running   0          2m
hello-minikube-2713628163-x6ge3  1/1     Running   3          11d
```

8. There are 2 geolocation pods. Scaling down is as simple as using the same command with `--replicas` set to 1.

```
kubectl scale rc geolocation --replicas=1
replicationcontroller "geolocation" scaled
```

9. Now, verify that you have only one instance of the geolocation pod running, using the following command:

```
kubectl get pods
NAME                           READY   STATUS    RESTARTS   AGE
geolocation-a2xce              1/1     Running   0          44m
hello-minikube-2713628163-x6ge3  1/1   Running   3          11d
```

That brings us to the end of this recipe. In this recipe, we learned how to scale our application using `kubectl` as well as the Kubernetes dashboard.

Destroying your microservice in Kubernetes

So far in this chapter, we've learned how to deploy and scale our microservice in a Kubernetes cluster. There will be scenarios where you would want to destroy your microservice completely from your cluster, probably because you would like to perform a clean redeploy. In this recipe, we will learn how to destroy our microservice.

Getting ready

Open up the Kubernetes dashboard if you already have your cluster running. If not, use Minikube to start the cluster and open the dashboard. Make sure there are no instances of the geolocation container running on your Kubernetes cluster. If you have any instance of geolocation running, delete the replication controllers, services, and pods.

How to do it...

1. To illustrate the destroy functionality, let's deploy the geolocation microservice first. Use the friendly form and enter the following configurations to create your microservice:
   - **App name**: `geolocation`
   - **Container image**: `vikrammurugesan/geolocation:latest`

- **Number of pods**: 1
- **Service**: Internal
- **Port**: 8080
- **Target port**: 8080
- **Protocol**: TCP
- **CPU requirement (cores)**: 0.5
- **Memory requirement (MiB)**: 512
- **Environment Variables**
- **Name**: GEOLOCATION_DATA_FILES_DIR
- **Value**: /opt/packt/geolocation/data

2. Go ahead and hit **Deploy**. After your pod and replication controller are up and running, click on the three dots next to the geolocation replication controller. Then, choose **Delete** from the popup menu:

3. If you are asked for confirmation, click on **OK**. After a few seconds, you will notice that the replication controller and the pod will be destroyed successfully. At the time of writing this, I was using a version of the dashboard that needed a manual refresh to view the status of the pod and replication controller.

4. Also, if you go to the **Services** section, you will see that the geolocation service is still running. Go ahead and delete the service from the dashboard.

5. You can also do the same thing using the kubectl command when you are automating deployments using tools such as Jenkins or Hudson. Before we try our kubectl command, create the microservice again using the Kubernetes dashboard. After your service is up and running, issue the following command in a terminal window:

```
kubectl delete rc geolocation
replicationcontroller "geolocation" deleted
```

6. After a few seconds, if you refresh your dashboard page, you will see that the geolocation replication controller and pod have been successfully deleted. The geolocation service will still be up and running. In order to delete it, execute the following command from the same terminal window:

```
kubectl delete service geolocation
service "geolocation" deleted
```

Now go back to your dashboard and make sure the geolocation service has been successfully deleted.

That brings us to the end of this recipe, where we learned how to delete our replication controllers, pods, and services using the Kubernetes dashboard as well as kubectl.

 In most automation scenarios where you are trying to automate your deployments to a Kubernetes cluster, you would want to interact with Kubernetes' REST API. Fortunately, Kubernetes provides a sophisticated REST API to perform all the operations we have seen so far in this chapter. The documentation for the REST API is available here at http://kubernetes.io/docs/api.

Monitoring your microservice logs in Kubernetes

One of the most important features that will be helpful after your microservices are deployed to a cluster is being able to monitor the logs of your application. In this recipe, you will learn how to monitor the logs of your application from the Kubernetes dashboard as well as kubectl.

Getting ready

Open up the Kubernetes dashboard if you already have your cluster running. If not, use Minikube to start the cluster and open the dashboard. Make sure there are no instances of the geolocation container running on your Kubernetes cluster. If you have any instance of geolocation running, delete the replication controllers, services, and pods.

How to do it...

1. To be able to view the logs, we need our microservice deployed on Kubernetes first. Before that, let's get familiar with viewing the logs from the Kubernetes dashboard. Open it up. Use the friendly form and enter the following configurations to create your microservice:

    - **App name**: geolocation
    - **Container image**: vikrammurugesan/geolocation:latest
    - **Number of pods**: 1
    - **Service**: Internal
    - **Port**: 8080
    - **Target port**: 8080
    - **Protocol**: TCP
    - **CPU requirement (cores)**: 0.5
    - **Memory requirement (MiB)**: 512
    - **Environment Variables**
    - **Name**: GEOLOCATION_DATA_FILES_DIR
    - **Value**: /opt/packt/geolocation/data

2. Go ahead and hit Deploy. Once your application is up and running, click on the icon with four stripes next to the geolocation pod from the dashboard. This icon indicates the logs button, which will tail the logs from any container in that pod:

3. After you click on the icon, you will be shown a screen that looks very similar to your terminal shell. You should see something like this:

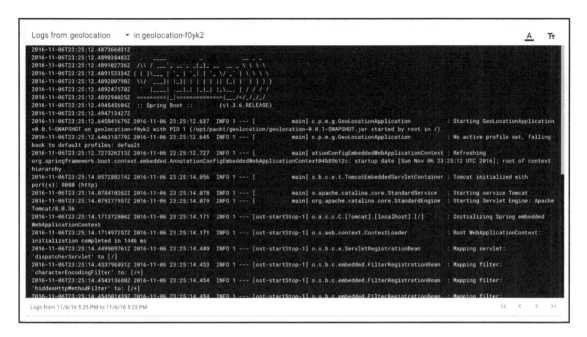

There are a few useful options in this terminal. From the dropdown in the top section, you will be able to choose the pod of your choice and view the logs for that pod. In our case, there is only one pod in the replication controller, so if you click on that dropdown, you will be able to see only one option. The icon that says **A** is used to toggle the font color and background color of your terminal. The **Tt** icon next to the **A** icon is used to toggle between two font sizes. These two options are particularly useful when you have a lot of useful logs that you would like to monitor as part of your debugging process.

4. This screenshot shows how the terminal will look like when you toggle the font color and font size:

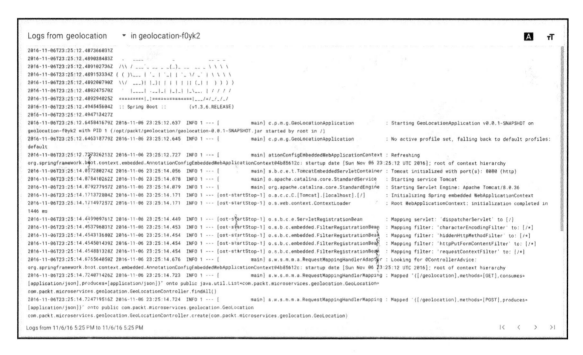

5. You will also be able to view the same logs from the **Containers** section under the pod details. Go ahead and click on the pod name and then the **View Logs** hyperlink in the **geolocation** container. This should take you to a log page like the one we saw earlier:

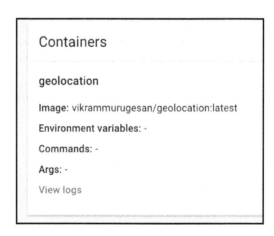

6. The next useful tip is being able to view the logs using `kubectl`. It is very simple to view the logs using `kubectl`. First, we need the pod name. Open a terminal window and execute the following command:

```
kubectl get pods
NAME                                READY      STATUS    RESTARTS    AGE
geolocation-f0yk2                    1/1       Running   0           26m
hello-minikube-2713628163-x6ge3     1/1       Running   3           11d
```

7. Now that we have our pod named `geolocation-f0yk2`, issue the following command in the same terminal:

```
kubectl logs -f geolocation-f0yk2
```

8. The `-f` option says that you want to follow the logs or, in simpler terms, it will let you tail the logs. You should see something like this:

```
 ∧∨ ⌐__.___.()._ __.  __ ¯¯¯\
( ()\    Γ |Γ|Γ | V-|\\\\
 \∨ _)|_|)| | | | | |(_| ) ) ) )
   ' |___| .__|_| |_| |_\__, | / / / /
 =========|_|==============|___/=/_/_/_/
 :: Spring Boot ::        (v1.3.6.RELEASE)

2016-11-06 23:25:12.637  INFO 1 --- [           main] c.p.m.g.GeoLocationApplication           : Starting GeoLocationApplication v0.0.1-SNAPSHOT
d by root in /)
2016-11-06 23:25:12.645  INFO 1 --- [           main] c.p.m.g.GeoLocationApplication           : No active profile set, falling back to default p
2016-11-06 23:25:12.727  INFO 1 --- [           main] ationConfigEmbeddedWebApplicationContext : Refreshing org.springframework.boot.context.embe
2 UTC 2016]; root of context hierarchy
2016-11-06 23:25:14.056  INFO 1 --- [           main] s.b.c.e.t.TomcatEmbeddedServletContainer : Tomcat initialized with port(s): 8080 (http)
2016-11-06 23:25:14.078  INFO 1 --- [           main] o.apache.catalina.core.StandardService   : Starting service Tomcat
2016-11-06 23:25:14.079  INFO 1 --- [           main] org.apache.catalina.core.StandardEngine  : Starting Servlet Engine: Apache Tomcat/8.0.36
2016-11-06 23:25:14.171  INFO 1 --- [ost-startStop-1] o.a.c.c.C.[Tomcat].[localhost].[/]       : Initializing Spring embedded WebApplicationConte
2016-11-06 23:25:14.171  INFO 1 --- [ost-startStop-1] o.s.web.context.ContextLoader            : Root WebApplicationContext: initialization compl
2016-11-06 23:25:14.449  INFO 1 --- [ost-startStop-1] o.s.b.c.e.ServletRegistrationBean        : Mapping servlet: 'dispatcherServlet' to [/]
2016-11-06 23:25:14.453  INFO 1 --- [ost-startStop-1] o.s.b.c.embedded.FilterRegistrationBean  : Mapping filter: 'characterEncodingFilter' to [/
2016-11-06 23:25:14.454  INFO 1 --- [ost-startStop-1] o.s.b.c.embedded.FilterRegistrationBean  : Mapping filter: 'hiddenHttpMethodFilter' to: [/*
2016-11-06 23:25:14.454  INFO 1 --- [ost-startStop-1] o.s.b.c.embedded.FilterRegistrationBean  : Mapping filter: 'httpPutFormContentFilter' to: [
2016-11-06 23:25:14.454  INFO 1 --- [ost-startStop-1] o.s.b.c.embedded.FilterRegistrationBean  : Mapping filter: 'requestContextFilter' to: [/*]
2016-11-06 23:25:14.676  INFO 1 --- [           main] s.w.s.m.m.a.RequestMappingHandlerAdapter : Looking for @ControllerAdvice: org.springframewo
 [Sun Nov 06 23:25:12 UTC 2016]; root of context hierarchy
2016-11-06 23:25:14.723  INFO 1 --- [           main] s.w.s.m.m.a.RequestMappingHandlerMapping : Mapped "{[/geolocation],methods=[GET],consumes=[
vices.geolocation.GeoLocation> com.packt.microservices.geolocation.GeoLocationController.findAll()
2016-11-06 23:25:14.724  INFO 1 --- [           main] s.w.s.m.m.a.RequestMappingHandlerMapping : Mapped "{[/geolocation],methods=[POST],produces=
croservices.geolocation.GeoLocationController.create(com.packt.microservices.geolocation.GeoLocation)
2016-11-06 23:25:14.726  INFO 1 --- [           main] s.w.s.m.m.a.RequestMappingHandlerMapping : Mapped "{[/error],produces=[text/html]}" onto pu
BasicErrorController.errorHtml(javax.servlet.http.HttpServletRequest,javax.servlet.http.HttpServletResponse)
2016-11-06 23:25:14.726  INFO 1 --- [           main] s.w.s.m.m.a.RequestMappingHandlerMapping : Mapped "{[/error]}" onto public org.springframew
k.boot.autoconfigure.web.BasicErrorController.error(javax.servlet.http.HttpServletRequest)
```

9. This is very similar to the `docker logs` command, right? There are a few more options that you can use with the `kubectl logs` command, for example, you can tail logs for the past few minutes or hours, and you can tail just a few lines of logs.

 To learn more about these options, read more at `http://kubernetes.io/docs/user-guide/kubectl/kubectl_logs`.

That's it! That brings us to the end of this chapter. It gave you a quick overview of the Kubernetes cluster and how to use it locally. In production deployments, there are a lot many considerations and design decisions that you might want to think about. As that is completely out of scope for our book, we will not be talking about those. However, it is strongly recommended that you read more about Kubernetes before starting to "productionalize" your deployments using Kubernetes.

5
Service Discovery and Load Balancing Microservices

In this chapter, you will learn how to implement service discovery and load balancing in microservices using Zookeeper and Consul. We will cover the following recipes:

- Setting up Zookeeper using Docker
- Load-balancing microservices using Zookeeper
- Setting up Consul using Docker
- Implementing service discovery using Spring Cloud Consul
- Load-balancing your microservice using Spring Cloud Consul
- Load-balancing your microservices using Nginx and Consul
- Load-balancing your microservice using Marathon LB

Introduction

When you break down your monolithic application to several focused microservices, you will have to find an efficient way to locate your services; moreover, services will have to communicate with each other. That is exactly what service discovery is all about. Now let's say you figured out a way to locate them: what happens to those services that are scaled to a factor greater than one? You have to efficiently load-balance them. This is another problem that this chapter intends to solve.

Setting up Zookeeper using Docker

In Chapter 3, *Deploying Microservices on Mesos*, we learned a little bit about Zookeeper. To keep it very simple, Zookeeper is a cluster-management tool that is mainly used for storing your cluster configurations. Zookeeper is used by several Apache big data projects such as Mesos, Kafka, and Bookkeeper. In this chapter, we will see how we can use Zookeeper to store our microservice configurations and later use them to perform load-balancing. This recipe will show you how to start Zookeeper and Exhibitor using Docker. Exhibitor is a management interface for Zookeeper. In addition to providing a web interface to manage Zookeeper, it also performs log file cleanups and backups. We will be using the Exhibitor web interface to verify that our service was registered on Zookeeper.

Getting ready

1. We now know that we need two components:
   - Zookeeper
   - Exhibitor

     They could either be two individual containers linked together via docker-compose or could coexist in the same container.

2. We will be using an existing image that has both Zookeeper and Exhibitor coexisting in the same image.
3. We will be creating a docker-compose.yml file just for Zookeeper and Exhibitor.
4. The reason we use Docker Compose even when there is just one container is for grouping purposes. I always like keeping my containers grouped together in Compose files so that in case you need to add a new dependent container in the future, it will be easy to add it. It also helps in versioning. On top of that, you get to use the sophisticated Docker Compose command-line features.
5. Go ahead and open your STS IDE.

How to do it...

1. Create a new file called `docker-compose-zk.yml` in the `geolocation` project. Add the following snippet to the newly created Docker compose file:

```
version: "2"
services:
  zookeeper:
    image: mbabineau/zookeeper-exhibitor:latest
    ports:
      - "8181:8181"
      - "2181:2181"
```

   As you can see, we are using the image called `mbabineau/zookeeper-exhibitor`, and we are using the `latest` tag of this image. This image comes with Zookeeper and Exhibitor by default. There are tons of other images that you can use if you prefer to use them. You can also create your own image with Zookeeper and Exhibitor in it or put Zookeeper and Exhibitor in their own images and link them using `docker-compose`. For simplicity, we are using this image as it comes out of the box with all the components we need. We have exposed two ports, `2181` and `8181`. 2181 is the port exposed by Zookeeper that we will be using in our code to connect to it. Port 8181 is where the Exhibitor web interface will be listening. So we need these two ports to be exposed from these containers. Also, as you can see, these ports are mapped to the same port number on the host.

2. Without any delay, let's spin off Zookeeper and Exhibitor. Open up a terminal shell and issue the following command:

```
docker-compose -f docker-compose-zk.yml up
```

3. As you can see, we are passing the Docker Compose YML file name as an argument as we are not using the default `docker-compose.yml` filename. It usually takes a few seconds to few minutes to start up Exhibitor and Zookeeper completely. Exhibitor may be up in a few seconds, but Zookeeper takes a few seconds to a couple of minutes. So wait for both of them to be up and running. You can verify that Zookeeper has started if you see something like this in your console:

```
zookeeper_1 | v1.5.5
zookeeper_1 | INFO  com.netflix.exhibitor.core.activity.ActivityLog  Exhibitor started [main]
zookeeper_1 | Dec 6, 2016 4:31:09 PM java.util.prefs.FileSystemPreferences$2 run
zookeeper_1 | INFO: Created user preferences directory.
zookeeper_1 | INFO  org.mortbay.log  Logging to org.slf4j.impl.Log4jLoggerAdapter(org.mortbay.log) via org.mortbay.log.Slf4jLog [main]
zookeeper_1 | INFO  org.mortbay.log  jetty-1.5.5 [main]
zookeeper_1 | Dec 6, 2016 4:31:09 PM com.sun.jersey.server.impl.application.WebApplicationImpl _initiate
zookeeper_1 | INFO: Initiating Jersey application, version 'Jersey: 1.18.3 12/01/2014 08:23 AM'
zookeeper_1 | INFO  org.mortbay.log  Started SocketConnector@0.0.0.0:8181 [main]
zookeeper_1 | Dec 6, 2016 4:31:13 PM java.util.prefs.FileSystemPreferences$7 run
zookeeper_1 | WARNING: Prefs file removed in background /root/.java/.userPrefs/prefs.xml
zookeeper_1 | INFO  com.netflix.exhibitor.core.activity.ActivityLog  State: down [ActivityQueue-0]
zookeeper_1 | INFO  com.netflix.exhibitor.core.activity.ActivityLog  Attempting to stop instance [ActivityQueue-0]
zookeeper_1 | INFO  com.netflix.exhibitor.core.activity.ActivityLog  Attempting to start/restart ZooKeeper [ActivityQueue-0]
zookeeper_1 | INFO  com.netflix.exhibitor.core.activity.ActivityLog  jps didn't find instance - assuming ZK is not running [ActivityQueue-0]
zookeeper_1 | INFO  com.netflix.exhibitor.core.activity.ActivityLog  Starting in standalone mode [ActivityQueue-0]
zookeeper_1 | ERROR com.netflix.exhibitor.core.activity.ActivityLog  ZooKeeper Server: JMX enabled by default [pool-2-thread-1]
zookeeper_1 | INFO  com.netflix.exhibitor.core.activity.ActivityLog  Process started via: /opt/zookeeper/bin/zkServer.sh [ActivityQueue-0]
zookeeper_1 | ERROR com.netflix.exhibitor.core.activity.ActivityLog  ZooKeeper Server: Using config: /opt/zookeeper/bin/../conf/zoo.cfg [pool-2-thread-1]
zookeeper_1 | INFO  com.netflix.exhibitor.core.activity.ActivityLog  ZooKeeper Server: Starting zookeeper ... STARTED [pool-2-thread-2]
```

4. After you know that both Zookeeper and Exhibitor are up and running, open up a new browser tab. Enter this URL to open the Exhibitor web interface: `http://192.168.99.100:8181/exhibitor/v1/ui/index.html`. You should see the Exhibitor home page, which shows the list of instances that are currently running:

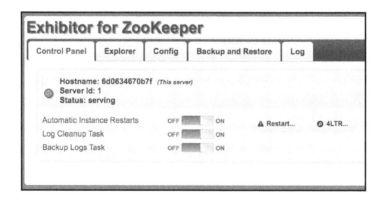

5. Now move on to the **Explorer** tab. You should see a tree that lists all the registered services. If you are able to see Zookeeper as shown in the next screenshot, Exhibitor is properly configured to work with our Zookeeper instance:

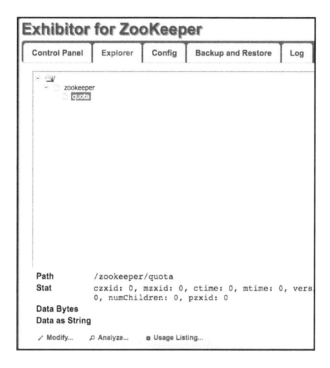

That brings us to the end of this recipe. We now have a functional Zookeeper and Exhibitor instance. In the next recipe, we will utilize these servers to load-balance the geolocation microservice.

Load balancing microservices using Zookeeper

In the previous recipe, we orchestrated a Zookeeper instance along with an Exhibitor instance. In this recipe, we will utilize these instances to load-balance the geolocation microservice. We will be spinning off two instances of the geolocation microservice and see how we can use Zookeeper and the Curator API to perform round-robin style load balancing on the HTTP endpoints exposed by the geolocation microservice.

Load-balancing HTTP-based microservices is a significant step towards onboarding your microservice to a cluster such as Mesos or Kubernetes. Scalability will not have any value unless you figure out a way to load-balance your microservices. Zookeeper is just one way to do this; with the tools currently available, there are several ways to do this: using frameworks such as Consul and Marathon LB (Mesos/Marathon specific). In fact, there are libraries that even let you perform load-balancing on the client side. We will be looking at Consul and Marathon LB later in this chapter.

Getting ready

Implementing a load balancer using Zookeeper and the Curator API involves two steps. Let's look at them one by one:

1. **Register the geolocation microservice in Zookeeper**: In this step, the geolocation microservice will be configured to register itself in Zookeeper with the host and port information of the HTTP API.
2. **Implement load balancer**: In this step, we will be creating a new load balancer microservice that will look up the geolocation configs from Zookeeper and use them to proxy the HTTP requests.

How to do it...

Let's take a look at the first step: registering the geolocation microservice in Zookeeper. This step says that as and when a new instance of the geolocation service starts, it should register itself on the Zookeeper instance. Registering the service is not just adding the service on Zookeeper, but also storing any config information about the geolocation service. In this case, it will make more sense to store the hostname and port on which the service is listening on as config information.

In this recipe, we will be relying on the Curator API to implement service discovery. Curator is a sophisticated Java library for Zookeeper that helps you work with any Zookeeper cluster. It has several libraries, such as client, framework, RPC, and discovery. In our application, we will require the framework and discovery libraries.

1. Without further ado, let's add these two dependencies to the `pom.xml` file of the geolocation project:

```
<dependency>
  <groupId>org.apache.curator</groupId>
  <artifactId>curator-framework</artifactId>
  <version>2.11.0</version>
</dependency>

<dependency>
  <groupId>org.apache.curator</groupId>
  <artifactId>curator-x-discovery</artifactId>
  <version>2.11.0</version>
</dependency>
```

> The version 2.11.0 works with the version of Zookeeper that we are using. Usually if you don't use the right version of Curator, your code will not be able to connect to Zookeeper.

2. Go ahead and perform a Maven update on the geolocation project so that Maven downloads the required dependencies. Next, let's create a new class that will register the geolocation service in Zookeeper. Create a new Java class with the name `com.packt.microservices.geolocation.Zookeeper.java`. In order to connect to Zookeeper, we need to know the host and port on which it is running. So let's define host and port as members of this class:

```
package com.packt.microservices.geolocation;

public class Zookeeper {

  private String host;
  private int port;

  public Zookeeper(String host, int port) {
    this.host = host;
    this.port = port;
  }

  public void register() {
  }
}
```

3. As you can see, we have also created a constructor to instantiate this class. If you are a Spring fan, you can create this as a Spring bean too. There is also an empty `register()` method that we will be later using to register this service in Zookeeper. Before we start implementing the `register()` method, let's decide where to invoke this method. Since our app is a Spring Boot application, it would be a good idea to invoke this method from the `main` method of the `GeolocationApplication.java` class. Go ahead and invoke the `register()` method as the last line of the `main` method in `GeolocationApplication.java`. The `GeolocationApplication.java` class will now look like this:

```java
package com.packt.microservices.geolocation;

import org.springframework.boot.SpringApplication;
import org.springframework.boot.autoconfigure.
   SpringBootApplication;

@SpringBootApplication
public class GeoLocationApplication {

    public static void main(String[] args) {
    SpringApplication.run(GeoLocationApplication.class,
       args);
     new Zookeeper("192.168.99.100", 2181).register();
    }
}
```

4. As you can see, we have hard-coded the Zookeeper host and port number as `192.168.99.100` and `2181`, respectively. To make your microservice more configurable, these two arguments can be passed as environment variables to the Docker container and I'll leave that as an exercise for you to try.

5. Now let's implement the remaining pieces in the `Zookeeper.java` class. There is one more thing we need to do before we implement the `register()` method. Yes, you are right: we need the hostname and port number on which the geolocation microservice is running, because they (at least the host) will be different for different containers. Let's first handle the hostname part of it. Go ahead and add the following method to the `Zookeeper.java` class:

```
private String getIp() {
    try {
        return InetAddress.getLocalHost().getHostAddress();
    } catch (UnknownHostException e) {
        System.err.println("Error while finding local IP. Using
            localhost for now. Details: " + e.getMessage());
        e.printStackTrace();
        return "localhost";
    }
}
```

Here, we are using the `InetAddress` class to get the local IP of the machine on which this service is running. If it throws an `UnknownHostException`, we are defaulting the hostname to `localhost`. Though this is not a great implementation, the goal of this recipe is to give you an idea of how you can use Zookeeper for load-balancing, so this implementation will work for now.

6. The next configuration we need is the port number on which the application is running. This is a little tricky because Spring Boot defaults the port number of the in-memory web server to `8080`. But if we find a way to use an environment variable, it would help us drive the port number dynamically, which can then be passed as a Docker environment variable to our geolocation container. However, if you know that you will always be using `8080`, then you don't have to change this. If you do have to change ports, fortunately, Spring Boot lets you change the port number on which the web server starts using a property in the `application.properties` file. So create a new `properties` file called `application.properties` in `src/main/resources`. In the file, drop the following line:

server.port=${GEOLOCATION_SERVICE_PORT:8080}

7. As you can see, we are deriving the port number from an environment variable called GEOLOCATION_SERVICE_PORT. If the environment variable is not defined, it is defaulted to 8080. Now let's implement a new method in the Zookeeper.java class to get this port number. Add the following method to Zookeeper.java:

```
private int getPort() {
    try {
        return Integer.valueOf(System.getenv
          ("GEOLOCATION_SERVICE_PORT"));
    } catch(Exception e) {
        System.err.println("Error while finding service port. Using
default port 8080. Details: " + e.getMessage());
        e.printStackTrace();
        return 8080;
    }
}
```

In the getPort() method, we are parsing the port number from the GEOLOCATION_SERVICE_PORT environment property. If the parsing fails, we default the port number to 8080. Again, this is not a great implementation, but it is a good start to implementing load-balancing using Zookeeper.

8. With that said, let's add implementation to the register() method. Add the following snippet to the register method:

```
public void register() {
    CuratorFramework curator =
        CuratorFrameworkFactory.newClient(host + ":" + port,
        new RetryNTimes(3, 3000));
    curator.start();

    try {
        final ServiceInstance<Object> serviceInstance =
            ServiceInstance.builder()        .uriSpec(new UriSpec("
          {scheme}://{address}:{port}"))
              .address(getIp()).port(getPort())
            .name("geolocation")
            .build();

        final ServiceDiscovery<Object> serviceDiscovery =
        ServiceDiscoveryBuilder.builder(Object.class)
            .basePath("com.packt.microservices")
            .client(curator)
            .thisInstance(serviceInstance)
```

```
      .build();

   serviceDiscovery.start();

   Runtime.getRuntime().addShutdownHook(new Thread(() -> {
      try {
   serviceDiscovery.unregisterService(serviceInstance);
      } catch (Exception e) {
        System.err.println("Error while unregistering service
          in Zookeeper. Details: " + e.getMessage());
        e.printStackTrace();
      }
   }));
   } catch (Exception e) {
   System.err.println("Error while registering service in
      Zookeeper. Details: " + e.getMessage());
   e.printStackTrace();
   }
  }
 }
```

9. There are four major things happening here. Let's take a look at them one by one:

```
CuratorFramework curator =
   CuratorFrameworkFactory.newClient(host + ":" + port, new
   RetryNTimes(3, 3000));
curator.start();
```

10. In the preceding line, we connect to Zookeeper and start the `CuratorFramework`. The `host` and `port` properties that are being used in the preceding line are the hostname and port number of Zookeeper (which were hardcoded to `192.168.99.100` and `2181`, respectively). `RetryNTimes` comes with the Curator API, and it tries three times to connect to Zookeeper with a 3-second timeout each time.

```
final ServiceInstance<Object>
   serviceInstance =
   ServiceInstance.builder().uriSpec(new
   UriSpec("{scheme}://{address}:
   {port}")).address(getIp())
   .port(getPort())
   .name("geolocation").build();
```

11. The `ServiceInstance` identifies an instance of our geolocation service in Zookeeper. As you can see, we have also passed the address and port number of our service using the `getIp()` and `getPort()` methods. The name of the service that will be used for registering and lookup is `geolocation`:

```
final ServiceDiscovery<Object>
 serviceDiscovery=ServiceDiscoveryBuilder
 .builder(Object.class)
 .basePath("com.packt.microservices")
 .client(curator)
 .thisInstance(serviceInstance)
 .build();

serviceDiscovery.start();
```

12. In the preceding snippet, we are registering the geolocation service instance in Zookeeper with the base path `com.packt.microservices`. In the future, if you would like to group multiple services, you could still use the same `basePath` but different service names.

```
Runtime.getRuntime().addShutdownHook(new Thread(() -> {
    try {
        serviceDiscovery.unregisterService(serviceInstance);
    } catch (Exception e) {
        System.err.println("Error while unregistering service in
Zookeeper. Details: " +
            e.getMessage());
        e.printStackTrace();
    }
}));
```

13. In the preceding snippet, we are adding a shutdown hook to unregister the geolocation service when the microservice shuts down. This is strongly recommended in order to clean up Zookeeper so that you don't have stale services registered in Zookeeper.

14. After these modifications, the `Zookeeper.java` class should look something like this:

```
package com.packt.microservices.geolocation;
import java.net.InetAddress;
import java.net.UnknownHostException;

import org.apache.curator.framework.CuratorFramework;
import org.apache.curator.framework.CuratorFrameworkFactory;
import org.apache.curator.retry.RetryNTimes;
import org.apache.curator.x.discovery.ServiceDiscovery;
import org.apache.curator.x.discovery.ServiceDiscoveryBuilder;
import org.apache.curator.x.discovery.ServiceInstance;
import org.apache.curator.x.discovery.UriSpec;

public class Zookeeper {

  private String host;
  private int port;

  public Zookeeper(String host, int port) {
    this.host = host;
    this.port = port;
  }

  public void register() {
    CuratorFramework curator =
CuratorFrameworkFactory.newClient(host + ":"
      + port, new RetryNTimes(3, 3000));
    curator.start();

    try {
      final ServiceInstance<Object> serviceInstance =
ServiceInstance.builder()
        .uriSpec(new UriSpec("{scheme}://{address}:{port}"))
          .address(getIp())
          .port(getPort())
          .name("geolocation")
          .build();

      final ServiceDiscovery<Object> serviceDiscovery =
        ServiceDiscoveryBuilder.builder(Object.class)
          .basePath("com.packt.microservices")
          .client(curator)
          .thisInstance(serviceInstance)
          .build();

      serviceDiscovery.start();
```

```
    Runtime.getRuntime().addShutdownHook(new
      Thread(() -> {
    try {
        serviceDiscovery.unregisterService
          (serviceInstance);
     } catch (Exception e) {
       System.err.println("Error while
         unregistering servicein Zookeeper. Details: " +
         e.getMessage());
       e.printStackTrace();
     }
    }));
   } catch (Exception e) {
   System.err.println("Error while registering
      service in Zookeeper. Details: " + e.getMessage());
   e.printStackTrace();
  }
 }

 private String getIp() {
  try {
    return InetAddress.getLocalHost().getHostAddress();
   } catch (UnknownHostException e) {
    System.err.println("Error while finding local
      IP. Using localhost for now. Details: " +
     e.getMessage());
    e.printStackTrace();
    return "localhost";
   }
 }
 private int getPort() {
   try {
     return Integer.valueOf(System.getenv
      ("GEOLOCATION_SERVICE_PORT"));
   } catch(Exception e) {
      System.err.println("Error while finding service
     port. Using default port 8080. Details: " +
        e.getMessage());
     e.printStackTrace();
    return 8080;
   }
  }
 }
```

15. Now that our microservice is ready to work with Zookeeper, let's spin off two instances of the geolocation service and verify that they register successfully on Zookeeper. But before that, let's build a new image and push it to Docker Hub.

16. Go ahead and build your project using the `mvn clean package` command. This should create a new `geolocation-0.0.1-SNAPSHOT.jar` artifact in the target directory.

17. Before we build the new image, let's remove the existing image. To do so, run the following command:

```
docker rmi vikrammurugesan/geolocation
```

18. To build our image, issue the following command on your terminal:

```
docker build -t vikrammurugesan/geolocation .
```

15. Make sure you use your account name instead of mine in the preceding commands. After your image has been built, push your Docker image to Docker Hub using the following command. You might be asked to login to your Docker Hub account if you haven't already done so.

```
docker push vikrammurugesan/geolocation
```

16. Again, make sure you use your account name instead of mine. After the image has been uploaded successfully, go to Docker Hub and verify that the **Last Updated** time of your image is something more recent. Now that our image is ready to use, open up two terminals and spin off two instances of the `geolocation` microservice:

```
docker run vikrammurugesan/geolocation
```

17. While you start the microservice, if you see a stack trace that says there is a `NullPointerException` in the `getIp()` method, it's because we did not pass the `GEOLOCATION_SERVICE_PORT` port number property to either of the containers. You can ignore as our service will use `8080` by default.

18. After both your geolocation services have started, open up the Exhibitor UI using the URL `http://192.168.99.100:8181/exhibitor/v1/ui/index.html`, and navigate to the **Explorer** tab. Now you should see a new item called `com.packt.microservices`, and you should see `geolocation` under it. If you expand `geolocation`, you should see two instances with their own unique identifiers:

19. If you want to explore further, click on any of the instances and look at its details at the bottom of the page. You should be able to see the service name, ID, host, port number, and other configurations of this service under the **Data as String** section:

Path	/com.packt.microservices/geolocation/21c0b6b2-0a1a-4fff-b5ad-50fda8adef9c
Stat	czxid: 9, mzxid: 9, ctime: 1481051430976, mtime: 1481051430976, version: 0, cversion: 0, aversion: 0, ephemeralOw 381, numChildren: 0, pzxid: 9
Data Bytes	7b 22 6e 61 6d 65 22 3a 22 67 65 6f 6c 6f 63 61 74 69 6f 6e 22 2c 22 69 64 22 3a 22 32 31 63 30 62 32 2d 30
	64 2d 35 30 66 64 61 38 61 64 65 66 39 63 22 2c 22 61 64 64 72 65 73 73 22 3a 22 31 37 32 2e 31 37 2e 30 2e 32 22
	2c 22 73 73 6c 50 6f 72 74 22 3a 6e 75 6c 6c 2c 22 70 61 79 6c 6f 61 64 22 3a 6e 75 6c 6c 2c 22 72 65 67 69 73 74
	43 22 3a 31 34 38 31 30 35 31 34 33 30 32 35 33 2c 22 73 65 72 76 69 63 65 54 79 70 65 22 3a 22 44 59 4e 41 4d 49
	3a 7b 22 70 61 72 74 73 22 3a 5b 7b 22 76 61 6c 75 65 22 3a 22 73 63 68 65 6d 65 22 2c 22 76 61 72 69 61 62 6c 65
	6c 75 65 22 3a 22 3a 2f 2f 22 2c 22 76 61 72 69 61 62 6c 65 22 3a 66 61 6c 73 65 7d 2c 7b 22 76 61 6c 75 65 22 3a
	61 72 69 61 62 6c 65 22 3a 74 72 75 65 7d 2c 7b 22 76 61 6c 75 65 22 3a 22 70 6f 72 74 22 2c 22 76 61 72 69 61 62 6c 65 22
	6c 75 65 22 3a 22 70 6f 72 74 22 2c 22 76 61 72 69 61 62 6c 65 22 3a 74 72 75 65 7d 5d 7d 7d
Data as String	{"name":"geolocation","id":"21c0b6b2-0a1a-4fff-b5ad-50fda8adef9c","address":"172.17.0.2","port":8080,"sslPort":null,"payload":null,"registrationTimeUTC":148105143025 {"parts":[{"value":"scheme","variable":true},{"value":"://","variable":false},{"value":"address","variable":true} {"value":"port","variable":true}]}}

This brings us to the end of the first part of our recipe: registering the geolocation microservice in Zookeeper.

Now let's take a look at building our Zookeeper-based load balancer. The load balancer will be another Spring Boot microservice that will proxy requests over to the geolocation microservices in a round-robin fashion. In order to achieve this behavior, we need the exact same APIs on the load balancer microservice.

1. Go ahead and create a new Maven JAR project called `geolocation-zk-lb` with the `groupId` set to `com.packt.microservices` and `artifactId` set to `geolocation-zk-lb`. As this is a Spring Boot project, add `spring-boot-starter-parent` as the `parent` module:

```
<parent>
  <groupId>org.springframework.boot</groupId>
  <artifactId>spring-boot-starter-parent</artifactId>
  <version>1.3.6.RELEASE</version>
</parent>
```

2. We will need two Maven plugins for this module: `maven-compiler-plugin` and `spring-boot-maven-plugin`. Add the snippet to your `pom.xml` file:

```
<properties>
  <start-class>com.packt.microservices.
  geolocation.lb.GeolocationZkLoadBalancer</start-class>
</properties>

<build>
    <plugins>
     <plugin>
        <groupId>org.apache.maven.plugins</groupId>
        <artifactId>maven-compiler-plugin</artifactId>
        <configuration>
         <source>1.8</source>
         <target>1.8</target>
        </configuration>
     </plugin>
     <plugin>
        <groupId>org.springframework.boot</groupId>
        <artifactId>spring-boot-maven-plugin</artifactId>
        <executions>
         <execution>
            <goals>
             <goal>repackage</goal>
            </goals>
         </execution>
        </executions>
        <configuration>
          <mainClass>${start-class}</mainClass>
        </configuration>
     </plugin>
    </plugins>
</build>
```

3. You should already be familiar with the preceding code snippet as we already created a microservice using Spring Boot in the first chapter. Now let's add the following three dependencies, which you are already familiar with:

```
<dependencies>
  <dependency>
    <groupId>org.springframework.boot</groupId>
    <artifactId>spring-boot-starter-web</artifactId>
  </dependency>
  <dependency>
    <groupId>org.apache.curator</groupId>
   <artifactId>curator-framework</artifactId>
    <version>2.11.0</version>
  </dependency>

  <dependency>
    <groupId>org.apache.curator</groupId>
    <artifactId>curator-x-discovery</artifactId>
    <version>2.11.0</version>
  </dependency>
</dependencies>
```

4. Perform a Maven update on the project to make sure all required dependencies are resolved. After the build is complete, let's create our Spring Boot application class, `com.packt.microservices.geolocation.lb.GeolocationZkLoadBalancer.java`:

```
package com.packt.microservices.geolocation.lb;

import org.springframework.boot.SpringApplication;
import
 org.springframework.boot.autoconfigure.SpringBootApplication;

@SpringBootApplication
public class GeolocationZkLoadBalancer {

  public static void main(String[] args) {
  SpringApplication.run     (GeolocationZkLoadBalancer.class,
   args);
  }
}
```

5. The next step in our load balancer microservice is writing the Zookeeper service-discovery logic that looks up the geolocation service instances from Zookeeper in a round-robin fashion. To do this, let's create a new class called `com.packt.microservices.geolocation.lb.ZookeeperServiceDiscovery.java`:

```java
package com.packt.microservices.geolocation.lb;
import java.net.URI;

import org.apache.curator.framework.CuratorFramework;
import org.apache.curator.framework.CuratorFrameworkFactory;
import org.apache.curator.retry.RetryNTimes;
import org.apache.curator.x.discovery.ServiceDiscovery;
import org.apache.curator.x.discovery.ServiceDiscoveryBuilder;
import org.apache.curator.x.discovery.ServiceProvider;

public class ZookeeperServiceDiscovery {
  private static ServiceProvider<Object>
    geolocationServiceProvider;  private static
    ServiceProvider<Object> getGeolocationServiceProvider()
    throws Exception {
    if(geolocationServiceProvider == null) {
      CuratorFramework curatorFramework =
        CuratorFrameworkFactory.newClient
        ("192.168.99.100:2181", new RetryNTimes(5, 1000));
      curatorFramework.start();
      ServiceDiscovery<Object> serviceDiscovery =
       ServiceDiscoveryBuilder.builder(Object.class)
       .basePath("com.packt.microservices")
       .client(curatorFramework)
                              .build();
      serviceDiscovery.start();
      geolocationServiceProvider =
       serviceDiscovery.serviceProviderBuilder()
                  .serviceName("geolocation")
                  .build();
      geolocationServiceProvider.start();
    }
     return geolocationServiceProvider;
  }
  public static URI getGeolocationServiceUri() throws Exception
   {
     return new
     URI(getGeolocationServiceProvider()
     .getInstance().buildUriSpec());
  }
}
```

There are a few things going on here. First, we start the Curator framework, and then, we use the `ServiceDiscovery` instance to build the `ServiceProvider` object for the geolocation microservice at the `basePath com.packt.microservices`. You can also see that the `geolocationServiceProvider` object is kept singleton so that we don't have to start the service-discovery instance each time.

6. Now that our discovery logic is ready, let's write our controller that calls proxy requests to the geolocation microservice. Go ahead and create a new controller called com.packt.microservices.geolocation.lb.GeolocationProxyController.java.

7. Let's first create the `findAll()` method, which obtains all geolocations saved by the `geolocation` microservice. Add the following snippet to the `GeolocationProxyController.java` class:

```
@RequestMapping(path = "/geolocation", method =
  RequestMethod.GET, produces = "application/json")
public @ResponseBody String findAll() throws Exception {
  URI serviceUri =
ZookeeperServiceDiscovery.getGeolocationServiceUri();

  System.out.println("Proxying GET request to service " +
    serviceUri.toString() + " at path " +
    request.getRequestURI());
  URI uri = new URI(serviceUri.getScheme(),
      null,
      serviceUri.getHost(),
      serviceUri.getPort(),
      request.getRequestURI(),
      request.getQueryString(),
      null);

  return restTemplate.getForEntity(uri,
    String.class).getBody();
}
```

In the preceding API, we are first obtaining the URI for our geolocation microservice and then using that URI to construct a new URI with the right path and headers. The newly created URI is then invoked using a `RestTemplate`.

8. We will implement a similar API for creating geolocations. Finally, a fully refactored `GeolocationProxyController.java` class will look like this:

```
package com.packt.microservices.geolocation.lb;

import java.net.URI;

import javax.servlet.http.HttpServletRequest;

import org.springframework.beans.factory.annotation.Autowired;
import org.springframework.http.HttpEntity;
import org.springframework.http.HttpHeaders;
import org.springframework.http.HttpMethod;
import org.springframework.http.MediaType;
import org.springframework.stereotype.Controller;
import org.springframework.web.bind.annotation.RequestBody;
import org.springframework.web.bind.annotation.RequestMapping;
import org.springframework.web.bind.annotation.RequestMethod;
import org.springframework.web.bind.annotation.ResponseBody;
import org.springframework.web.client.RestTemplate;
@Controller
@RequestMapping("/geolocation")
public class GeolocationProxyController {

  private RestTemplate restTemplate = new RestTemplate();
  @Autowired
   private HttpServletRequest request;
  @RequestMapping(path = "", method = RequestMethod.POST,
  produces = "application/json", consumes =
  "application/json")
  public @ResponseBody String create(@RequestBody String body)
  throws Exception {
   URI serviceUri =
   ZookeeperServiceDiscovery.getGeolocationServiceUri();
   System.out.println("Proxying POST request to service " +
    serviceUri.toString() + " at path " +
    request.getRequestURI());
   URI uri = new URI(serviceUri.getScheme(),
       null,
        serviceUri.getHost(),
        serviceUri.getPort(),
        request.getRequestURI(),
        request.getQueryString(),
        null);
   HttpHeaders headers = new HttpHeaders();
   headers.setContentType(MediaType.APPLICATION_JSON);
   HttpEntity<String> entity = new HttpEntity<String>(body,
    headers);
```

```
        return restTemplate.exchange(uri, HttpMethod.POST, entity,
          String.class).getBody();
    }
    @RequestMapping(path = "", method = RequestMethod.GET,
      produces = "application/json")
    public @ResponseBody String findAll() throws Exception {
      URI serviceUri =
        ZookeeperServiceDiscovery.getGeolocationServiceUri();
      System.out.println("Proxying GET request to service " +
        serviceUri.toString() + " at path " +
        request.getRequestURI());
      URI uri = new URI(serviceUri.getScheme(),
                null,
                serviceUri.getHost(),
                serviceUri.getPort(),
                request.getRequestURI(),
                request.getQueryString(),
                null);
      return restTemplate.getForEntity(uri,
      String.class).getBody();
    }
}
```

9. Without further delay, let's test our newly created Zookeeper-based HTTP load balancer. In order to do that, we have to follow these steps:

   1. Start Zookeeper and Exhibitor.

   2. Start two instances of geolocation (as Docker containers).

   3. Start `geolocation-zk-lb`.

10. Use the `docker-compose-zk.yml` file to start Zookeeper and Exhibitor. Open up two terminal sessions and issue the following command on both of them:

    `docker run vikrammurugesan/geolocation`

11. Once your geolocation instances are up and running (which includes registering to Zookeeper as well), verify that these services are registered in Zookeeper with the name `geolocation` under the `basePath com.packt.microservices`. You should be able to use the Exhibitor UI at `http://192.168.99.100:8181/exhibitor/v1/ui/index.html` to do this.

12. Before we can start the `geolocation-zk-lb` microservice, it needs to be Dockerized so that it can run as a Docker container. Go ahead and create a Dockerfile in the `geolocation-zk-lb` project, with the following contents:

```
FROM openjdk:8
ADD target/geolocation-zk-lb-0.0.1-SNAPSHOT.jar
/opt/packt/geolocation/
EXPOSE 8080
CMD ["java", "-jar", "/opt/packt/geolocation/geolocation-zk-lb-0.0.1-SNAPSHOT.jar"]
```

13. Build the project using the maven command: `mvn clean package`

14. Now build and start the `geolocation-zk-lb` image using the following command:

```
docker build -t vikrammurugesan/geolocation-zk-lb . && docker run
-p 8080:8080 vikrammurugesan/geolocation-zk-lb
```

15. Once the `geolocation-zk-lb` container is up and running, issue the following `curl` commands to test the load balancer:

```
curl -H "Content-Type: application/json" -X POST -d
'{"timestamp": 1468203975, "userId": "f1196aac-470e-11e6-
beb8-9e71128cae77", "latitude": 41.803488, "longitude": -88.144040}'
http://192.168.99.100:8080/geolocation
```

16. This should give you an output like the following (pretty-printed for readability):

```
{
  "latitude": 41.803488,
  "longitude": -88.14404,
  "userId": "f1196aac-470e-11e6-beb8-9e71128cae77",
  "timestamp": 1468203975
}
curl -H "Content-Type: application/json" -X POST -d
'{"timestamp": 1468203975, "userId": "f1196aac-470e-11e6-
beb8-9e71128cae77", "latitude": 9.568012, "longitude": 77.962444}'
http://192.168.99.100:8080/geolocation
```

17. This should give you an output similar to this (pretty-printed for readability):

```
{
    "latitude": 9.568012,
   "longitude": 77.962444,
    "userId": "f1196aac-470e-11e6-beb8-9e71128cae77",
  "timestamp": 1468203975
}
```

18. To check whether your entities were stored correctly, execute the following `curl` command:

```
curl http://192.168.99.100:8080/geolocation
```

19. It should give you an output similar to the following (pretty-printed for readability):

```
[
  {
    "latitude": 41.803488,
    "longitude": -88.14404,
    "userId": "f1196aac-470e-11e6-beb8-9e71128cae77",
    "timestamp": 1468203975
  }
]
```

20. But wait! We created two geolocations, so why is it showing just one? Let's try the command one more time. This time, it should give you output like this (pretty-printed for readability):

```
[
  {
    "latitude": 9.568012,
    "longitude": 77.962444,
    "userId": "f1196aac-470e-11e6-beb8-9e71128cae77",
    "timestamp": 1468203975
  }
]
```

21. Again, we get only one geolocation, but this time, it is a different one. In order to understand what is going on, we should first look at the logs of the `geolocation-zk-lb` container. You should have something like this:

```
Proxying POST request to service http://172.17.0.2:8080 at path
/geolocation
Proxying POST request to service http://172.17.0.3:8080 at path
```

```
/geolocation
        Proxying GET request to service http://172.17.0.2:8080 at path
/geolocation
        Proxying GET request to service http://172.17.0.3:8080 at path
/geolocation
```

22. If you notice the IPs in the preceding logs, they are alternating. This indicates that our service-discovery logic uses round robin and works as expected. As our geolocations are stored in memory, each geolocation instance was holding one geolocation each. That is the reason we got one as a result of the GET API each time. For simplicity, we stored our geolocations in memory, but in production scenarios, you will be storing them in databases that are shared by all these instances, so we will not have this issue.

 The `ZookeeperServiceDiscovery.java` class can be refactored to hold multiple service providers, one for each of your microservices. If your ecosystem has several microservices, you could still use this approach to load-balance them using Zookeeper. But this comes with its own merits and demerits. One of the demerits is that you have to create an API that matches the microservice's API. Any change to the microservice's API contract will require a change in the load balancer as well. So when it comes to several hundred microservices, this might not be scalable.

That brings us to the end of this recipe. Congrats! You now know how to load-balance your HTTP-based microservices using Zookeeper.

Setting up Consul using Docker

So far in this chapter, we've talked about the need for service discovery and load balancing. We also learned how to use Zookeeper to perform service discovery and load balancing. If you've tried the previous recipes in this chapter, you will have realized it requires some effort to manage your services in Zookeeper. It also requires some code to be written. In the next few recipes, we will learn to do the same thing with Consul. Consul is a service-discovery framework from HashiCorp that is multi-datacenter aware. One very useful feature Consul comes with is distributed key-value storage. This is really useful when you want to store configuration information. In this recipe, we will learn how to orchestrate Consul using Docker.

Getting ready

HashiCorp has released official images of consul and their other products. So this recipe is going to be pretty straightforward.

1. The easiest way to start Consul is by executing a `docker run` command with the image name.
2. The name of the image is pretty straightforward too: `consul`. Like we saw in the first recipe of this chapter, it is always easier to group your images into Docker Compose files.
3. So we will be creating a `docker-compose` file that has just Consul in it. We will be adding more containers to the Compose YML file in later recipes.
4. Open your STS IDE.

How to do it...

1. Create a new `docker-compose` YML file and name it `docker-compose-consul.yml`. In the `compose` file, drop the following snippet:

```
version: "2"
services:
  consul:
    image: consul:latest
    ports:
      - "8500:8500"
```

2. Now that our `docker-compose` file is complete, we are all set to start consul. Before that, let's get familiar with some basic concepts of consul. Only then will we be able to understand why we are performing the next few steps in this chapter.

Understanding the concepts of Consul

Like we already know, Consul is a service-discovery tool. It achieves this using agents. To put it in a simpler way, consul agents are long-running processes that keep track of all your services and any key-value pairs. Though this statement makes consul look as if it is a simple tool, it actually offers more than that (such as DNS), and the working of consul is more complicated than it looks. Now let's talk a little bit about agents. Agents can start either as a client or server. Ideally, in any consul cluster, there will be three to five servers and a few clients.

A client is a lightweight process responsible for registering services and performing health checks. In an ideal production scenario, there could be hundreds or even thousands of clients. One of the servers is always the **leader**, and the others are **followers**. The reason for having more servers is to ensure that if the leader goes down, there is always another server to be elected as leader. If you have a multi-datacenter infrastructure, it is recommended that you have similar clusters on each datacenter, and they all will work together. This is how an ideal consul cluster on a single datacenter looks like:

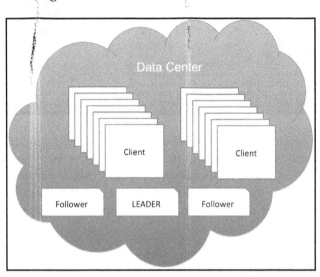

 If you would like to learn more about the architecture of consul and how all these components work together, visit consul's documentation page at `https://www.consul.io/docs/internals/architecture.html`.

With that, we now know what we need to do next. You guessed it: we need to start a consul agent. In this recipe, we will be starting an agent in development mode. Development mode starts just one server, and consul highly discourages the use of this mode in production unless used for local development and testing purposes.

1. Now, open a terminal session and issue the following command:

```
docker-compose -f docker-compose-consul.yml up
```

2. You should see something like this:

```
consul_1  | ==> Starting Consul agent...
consul_1  | ==> Starting Consul agent RPC...
consul_1  | ==> Consul agent running!
consul_1  |          Version: 'v0.7.1'
consul_1  |        Node name: 'c735ae8d5051'
consul_1  |       Datacenter: 'dc1'
consul_1  |           Server: true (bootstrap: false)
consul_1  |      Client Addr: 0.0.0.0 (HTTP: 8500, HTTPS: -1, DNS: 8600, RPC: 8400)
consul_1  |     Cluster Addr: 127.0.0.1 (LAN: 8301, WAN: 8302)
consul_1  |   Gossip encrypt: false, RPC-TLS: false, TLS-Incoming: false
consul_1  |            Atlas: <disabled>
consul_1  |
consul_1  | ==> Log data will now stream in as it occurs:
consul_1  |
consul_1  |     2016/12/09 02:22:33 [INFO] raft: Initial configuration (index=1): [{Suffrage:Voter ID:127.0.0.1:8300 Address:127.0.0.1:8300}]
consul_1  |     2016/12/09 02:22:33 [INFO] serf: EventMemberJoin: c735ae8d5051 127.0.0.1
consul_1  |     2016/12/09 02:22:33 [INFO] serf: EventMemberJoin: c735ae8d5051.dc1 127.0.0.1
consul_1  |     2016/12/09 02:22:33 [INFO] raft: Node at 127.0.0.1:8300 [Follower] entering Follower state (Leader: "")
consul_1  |     2016/12/09 02:22:33 [INFO] consul: Adding LAN server c735ae8d5051 (Addr: tcp/127.0.0.1:8300) (DC: dc1)
consul_1  |     2016/12/09 02:22:33 [INFO] consul: Adding WAN server c735ae8d5051.dc1 (Addr: tcp/127.0.0.1:8300) (DC: dc1)
```

If you look at the console logs closely, you can see that consul has started one server, and this node is part of the data center called **DC1**. The LAN and WAN servers are both running on port 8300. While the former is used for communication between nodes in the same data center, the latter is used for communication with servers on another data center.

3. Once you know that your consul agent has started successfully, open up a new browser and navigate to this URL: http://192.168.99.100:8500.

4. You will see the consul home page, and the **Services** tab will be selected by default. This is where you will see all your registered services. You should see a service called **consul**. That is because consul will have registered the server as a service:

5. The other tab you might be interested in is the **Key/Value** tab. This is where you can create, view, update, and delete your key-value pairs. At the top right, you should see a dropdown with the name of the currently selected data center. If you have multiple data centers, this dropdown will have more than one value, and you will be able to see the nodes, services, and key-value pairs in each data center. This is very useful when you have a multi-datacenter setup.

6. Though **Services** is the default tab selected when you open the UI, the **Nodes** tab is something that makes more sense to start with. Now let's click on it. On the left-hand side, you will see the list of nodes with their IDs. Click on the node. Now you will see some interesting information on the right-hand side:

As you can see, it shows the services that are currently discovered and shows the **Serf Health Status**. Serf is another product from HashiCorp that is used by consul for cluster memberships, health checks, and failure detection.

Important information to note on this page is the port number, `8300`, on the consul server widget. It tells you that the Consul server is running on port 8300. At the top right of the page, you should be able to see the **Deregister** button, which will deregister this node from the cluster. If you are interested, you can drill a little deeper to the service level.

7. Go ahead and click on the Consul service, and explore the various options that consul offers. As that is a little out of scope for our book, we will not be talking about it. However you will get a chance to understand some sections of the service page in our next recipe.

Implementing service discovery using Spring Cloud Consul

In the previous recipe, we orchestrated a consul agent in development. In this recipe, we will be using that consul agent to implement service discovery for the geolocation microservice. When we did something similar using Zookeeper, there was lot of code involved to connect to Zookeeper, identify the IP, identify the port, and finally register the service. We performed these steps using the curator API, which made our life easier. But fortunately, you don't have to do all this for consul. Spring Cloud has a library for consul, which automatically registers the service with the host and port information. All we have to provide is a couple of properties. Let's take a look at how to do that now.

Getting ready

1. In order to register the geolocation service in consul, we first have to make sure that the consul agent is up and running. If you don't have an agent running, start it using `docker-compose`.

2. Go ahead and make sure consul was properly started by accessing the web interface at `http://192.168.99.100:8500`.

3. There is one more thing we need to do before we integrate consul into our microservice. We have to comment out the line of code in the `GeolocationApplication.java` class, where it tries to connect to Zookeeper. Simply comment out that line so that the next time you start the application, it does not try to connect to Zookeeper.

4. Also, add a comment preceding it saying it has been commented out for a reason:

```
// commented out so that the service does not try to connect to zk
// new Zookeeper("192.168.99.100", 2181).register();
```

That's it! Now let's move on to the actual implementation part, where we will integrate consul with the `geolocation` microservice.

How to do it...

1. The first thing we need to do is add the required dependencies to our `pom.xml` file. The dependency that `geolocation` will need is `spring-cloud-starter-consul-all`. Let's add it to the `dependencies` section of the `pom.xml` file in the geolocation project:

```
<dependency>
  <groupId>org.springframework.cloud</groupId>
  <artifactId>spring-cloud-starter-consul-all</artifactId>
  <version>1.1.2.RELEASE</version>
</dependency>
```

> The preceding dependency packs pretty much all the dependencies that are required for our project to connect to consul and register our service. As we have added a new dependency, we have to perform a Maven update to resolve all the new dependencies.

2. When the build is complete, create a new `properties` file called `bootstrap.properties` in the `src/main/resources` directory. Add the following snippet to the file:

```
spring.application.name=geolocation
spring.cloud.consul.host=192.168.99.100
spring.cloud.consul.port=8500
```

> The `spring.application.name` property is optional, but it is highly recommended because that is the name with which this service will be registered on consul.
>
> The other two properties are required to tell Spring which Consul server to connect to. The `spring.cloud.consul.host` property indicates the host on which consul is running, and `spring.cloud.consul.port` indicates the port on which the consul is listening.

3. The next step is adding the `@EnableDiscoveryClient` annotation to the `GeolocationApplication.java` class. Go ahead and add this annotation:

```
@SpringBootApplication
@EnableDiscoveryClient
    public class GeoLocationApplication {
```

> That is all you need to register this service on consul. See how easy it was compared to doing the same thing with Zookeeper? Thanks to Spring for eliminating most of our boilerplate code.

4. Before we try to spin off an instance of `geolocation`, let's build a Docker image for the new code changes and push it to Docker Hub. Go ahead and build your project using the `mvn clean package` command. This should create a new `geolocation-0.0.1-SNAPSHOT.jar` artifact in the target directory.

5. Before we build the new image, let's remove the existing image that we already have. To do that, run the following command:

```
docker rmi vikrammurugesan/geolocation
```

6. To build our image, issue the following command on your terminal:

```
docker build -t vikrammurugesan/geolocation .
```

7. Use your account name instead of mine in the command. After your image has been built, push your Docker image to Docker Hub using the following command. You might be asked to log in to your Docker Hub account if you haven't already done so:

```
docker push vikrammurugesan/geolocation
```

8. Again, make sure you use your account name instead of mine. After the image has been uploaded successfully, go to Docker Hub and verify that the **Last Updated** time of your image shows something more recent.

9. Now that our image is ready to use, let's try to start our geolocation services. Usually, we start them using a `docker run` command, but this time, let's try starting them using `docker-compose`. Go ahead and append the following snippet to the `docker-compose-consul.yml` file:

```
geolocation-1:
image: vikrammurugesan/geolocation:latest
  ports:
    - "8080"
  environment:
```

```
GEOLOCATION_SERVICE_PORT: "8080"
  geolocation-2:
image: vikrammurugesan/geolocation:latest
    ports:
      - "8081"
    environment:
GEOLOCATION_SERVICE_PORT: "8081"
```

As you can see, we have added two instances of `geolocation`; one running on port `8080` and the other on port `8081`.

10. Now stop any running containers on your computer. Make sure there are no instances of consul or geolocation running. Start the consul agent and geolocation services using the following `docker-compose` command:

docker-compose -f docker-compose-consul.yml up

11. Usually, it takes a few minutes to register the two services on consul. In the meantime, you can open up the consul UI console at `http://192.168.99.100:8500`.

12. Keep refreshing the **Services** page and wait for both the geolocation services to be up and running. It takes at least 2-5 minutes, based on the configuration of your machine. You will know that both the services are running when you see that all four checks passed for the `geolocation` service.

13. Both the instances will have the same name `geolocation` and each of them will have two checks: Serf check and health check. We will talk more about health checks in `Chapter 6`, *Monitoring Microservices*. For now, just keep in mind that it is an endpoint exposed by Spring to provide high-level health information about the application. You will know that both the services have been registered once you see something like this:

14. Now move on to the **Nodes** tab and click on the node ID. On the right-hand side, you will see that there are two instances of geolocation services registered, one running on port `8080` and the other on port `8081`:

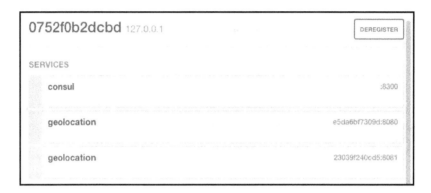

15. If you do not have access to the consul UI, you can still get the list of registered services using a simple cURL command. Consul has a good REST API that can be used to perform pretty much most of the operations that you can perform from the UI. Execute the following `curl` command in a terminal session:

    curl http://192.168.99.100:8500/v1/agent/services

16. You should have a response similar to this (pretty-printed for readability):

```
{
  "consul": {
    "ID": "consul",
    "Service": "consul",
    "Tags": [],
    "Address": "",
    "Port": 8300,
    "EnableTagOverride": false,
    "CreateIndex": 0,
    "ModifyIndex": 0
  },
  "geolocation-8080": {
    "ID": "geolocation-8080",
    "Service": "geolocation",
    "Tags": [],
    "Address": "e5da6bf7309d",
    "Port": 8080,
    "EnableTagOverride": false,
    "CreateIndex": 0,
    "ModifyIndex": 0
```

```
        },
        "geolocation-8081": {
          "ID": "geolocation-8081",
          "Service": "geolocation",
          "Tags": [],
          "Address": "23039f240cd5",
          "Port": 8081,
          "EnableTagOverride": false,
          "CreateIndex": 0,
          "ModifyIndex": 0
        }
      }
```

17. Note the address field for both the geolocation services. Those addresses will be resolved to the respective container's hostnames by Consul.

With that, we have successfully registered our services on Consul using Docker. The next step will be load-balancing our APIs using Consul, which we will learn in the next recipe.

Load balancing your microservice using Spring Cloud Consul

So far in this chapter, we've learned how to set up Consul and then learned how to implement service discovery in Consul using **Spring Cloud Consul**. Now, your other services can discover the geolocation service with the help of Consul. Earlier, we talked about how significant load balancing is and how we can do it using Zookeeper. In this recipe, we will learn how to perform load balancing using Consul with the help of Spring Cloud Consul.

Getting ready

There may be scenarios where one microservice would want to invoke another microservice's REST API. What if the target microservice is load-balanced using Consul? That is exactly what we are going to demonstrate in this recipe. We will be writing a new microservice called `geolocation-consul-lb` that will load balance against two instances of geolocation microservice in a round-robin fashion. When you move away from a monolithic application to more focused microservices, you will end up in a situation where you would want your microservices to communicate in an efficient way. This recipe along with the previous one will help you do that using Consul.

How to do it...

1. Create a new Maven JAR project with the `groupId` set to `com.packt.microservices` and `artifactId` set to `geolocation-consul-lb`. As this will be a Spring Boot project, we need to add `spring-boot-start-parent` as the parent project.

2. We'll also need the `spring-boot-maven-plugin`. Go ahead and add the following snippet to your newly created project's `pom.xml` file:

```
<parent>
  <groupId>org.springframework.boot</groupId>
  <artifactId>spring-boot-starter-parent</artifactId>
  <version>1.3.6.RELEASE</version>
</parent>

<properties>
  <start-
   class>com.packt.microservices.geolocation.lb.
   GeolocationConsulLoadBalancer</start-class>
</properties>

<build>
  <plugins>
   <plugin>
     <groupId>org.apache.maven.plugins</groupId>
     <artifactId>maven-compiler-plugin</artifactId>
     <configuration>
       <source>1.8</source>
       <target>1.8</target>
     </configuration>
    </plugin>

    <plugin>
<groupId>org.springframework.boot</groupId>
 <artifactId>spring-boot-maven-plugin</artifactId>
      <executions>
        <execution>
          <goals>
           <goal>repackage</goal>
          </goals>
        </execution>
      </executions>
       <configuration>
         <mainClass>${start-class}</mainClass>
       </configuration>
      </plugin>
```

```
    </plugins>
  </build>
```

3. We will require two dependencies for the project. One is the `spring-boot-starter-web` dependency as our project will use Spring MVC, and the other is `spring-cloud-starter-consul-all` as we will be looking up services from Consul:

```
<dependencies>
  <dependency>
    <groupId>org.springframework.boot</groupId>
    <artifactId>spring-boot-starter-web</artifactId>
  </dependency>

  <dependency>
    <groupId>org.springframework.cloud</groupId>
    <artifactId>spring-cloud-starter-Consul-all</artifactId>
    <version>1.1.2.RELEASE</version>
  </dependency>
</dependencies>
```

4. Now that the `pom.xml` file is ready, let's write our application class. Create a new class called `com.packt.microservices.geolocation.lb.GeolocationConsulLoadBalancer.java`.

5. Add the following snippet to the newly created class:

```
package com.packt.microservices.geolocation.lb;

import org.springframework.boot.SpringApplication;
import org.springframework.boot.autoconfigure.
  SpringBootApplication;
import org.springframework.cloud.client.discovery.
  EnableDiscoveryClient;
import org.springframework.cloud.client.
  loadbalancer.LoadBalanced;
import org.springframework.context.annotation.Bean;
import org.springframework.web.client.RestTemplate;

@SpringBootApplication
@EnableDiscoveryClient
public class GeolocationConsulLoadBalancer
{

  @LoadBalanced
  @Bean
```

```
public RestTemplate restTemplate() {
  return new RestTemplate();
}
public static void main(String[] args) {
  SpringApplication.run
   (GeolocationConsulLoadBalancer.class,
   args);
}
}
```

There are a couple of annotations to note here. The `@EnableDiscoveryClient` annotation is required to tell Spring that we will be connecting to Consul to look up services. The second interesting annotation is the `@LoadBalanced` annotation. This annotation says that the `RestTemplate` bean that is defined here should load-balance against the given service URL. You will understand this very clearly once we write the controller class, so hold on.

6. Let's write our controller, `com.packt.microservices.geolocation.lb.GeolocationProxyController.java`. Add the following snippet to the newly created class:

```
package com.packt.microservices.geolocation.lb;

import org.springframework.beans.factory.annotation.Autowired;
import org.springframework.http.HttpEntity;
import org.springframework.http.HttpHeaders;
import org.springframework.http.HttpMethod;
import org.springframework.http.MediaType;
import org.springframework.web.bind.annotation.RequestBody;
import org.springframework.web.bind.annotation.RequestMapping;
import org.springframework.web.bind.annotation.RequestMethod;
import org.springframework.web.bind.annotation.ResponseBody;
import org.springframework.web.bind.annotation.RestController;
import org.springframework.web.client.RestTemplate;

@RestController
@RequestMapping("/geolocation")
public class GeolocationProxyController {

  @Autowired
  private RestTemplate restTemplate;
  @RequestMapping(path = "", method = RequestMethod.GET,
    produces = "application/json")
  public @ResponseBody String findAll() throws Exception {
    return restTemplate.getForObject
```

```
      ("http://geolocation/geolocation", String.class);
  }
  @RequestMapping(path = "", method = RequestMethod.POST,
    produces = "application/json", consumes =
    "application/json")
  public @ResponseBody String create(@RequestBody String body)
    throws Exception {
    HttpHeaders headers = new HttpHeaders();
    headers.setContentType(MediaType.APPLICATION_JSON);
    HttpEntity<String> entity = new HttpEntity<String>(body,
     headers);
    return restTemplate.exchange
      ("http://geolocation/geolocation", HttpMethod.POST,
      entity, String.class).getBody();
  }
}
```

We have created two request mappings that match the APIs in `geolocation` microservice. We are actually implementing a proxy application. In each of the methods, we are using a `RestTemplate` to make calls to the `geolocation` service. See how we have autowired `RestTemplate` instead of instantiating it. That is because we would like to use the bean that was defined in the `GeolocationConsulLoadBalancer.java` class. This `restTemplate` bean will load-balance the service calls against the different instances of the target service. Note that the `restTemplate` bean makes a call to the URL `http://geolocation/geolocation`. See how the hostname is set to `geolocation`. As this `restTemplate` bean is Consul aware, it will look up services registered with the name `geolocation` and load-balance against those services in a round-robin fashion. It is as simple as that.

7. The final step we need to perform is add `application.properties` and `bootstrap.properties` to `src/main/resources`. Let's use port number `8899` as the web server port number. Add the following contents to the `application.properties` file:

server.port=8899

8. In the `bootstrap.properties` file, we will add the hostname and port number of Consul. In addition to that, we will add the `spring.application.name` property as that will be used as the service name in Consul. Add the following snippet to the `bootstrap.properties` file:

```
spring.application.name=geolocation-consul-lb
spring.cloud.consul.host=192.168.99.100
spring.cloud.consul.port=8500
```

9. Now that our load balancer is ready, let's Dockerize it. Create a new Dockerfile in the `geolocation-consul-lb` project and add the following snippet:

```
FROM openjdk:8
ADD target/geolocation-consul-lb-0.0.1-SNAPSHOT.jar
/opt/packt/geolocation/
EXPOSE 8080
CMD ["java", "-jar", "/opt/packt/geolocation/geolocation-consul-
lb-0.0.1-SNAPSHOT.jar"]
```

10. Build the project using the Maven command: `mvn clean package`

11. Now, let's build this Docker image:

```
docker build -t vikrammurugesan/geolocation-consul-lb .
```

12. Make sure you use your account name instead of mine. Earlier, we were using the `docker-compose-consul.yml` file in the geolocation project to start Consul and the geolocation services.

13. We will use the same `docker-compose` file for running the load balancer as well. Append the following snippet to `docker-compose-consul.yml`:

```
geolocation-consul-lb:
image: vikrammurugesan/geolocation-consul-lb:latest
    ports:
      - "8899:8899"
```

14. Without further ado, open a new terminal shell and start the containers using the following command:

```
docker-compose -f docker-compose-consul.yml up
```

15. It usually takes a few minutes to register all the services in Consul. You can verify that all your services have been successfully registered on Consul by viewing the services from the Consul UI at `http://192.168.99.100:8500`.

    When all the services have been registered successfully, you will see something like this when you click on your node ID in the **Nodes** tab:

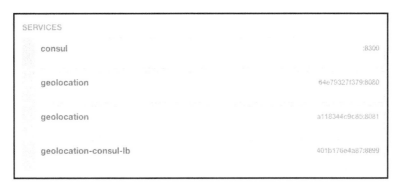

    You may find that the health check for `geolocation-consul-lb` is failing. We don't have to worry about that much as our goal is to just register the geolocation services in Consul.

16. Now that our services are registered in Consul, let's check whether our `RestTemplate` load-balances all HTTP requests. Issue the follwing `curl` commands in a new terminal window:

```
curl -H "Content-Type: application/json" -X POST -d
'{"timestamp": 1468203975, "userId": "f1196aac-470e-11e6-
beb8-9e71128cae77", "latitude": 41.803488, "longitude": -88.144040}'
http://192.168.99.100:8899/geolocation
```

17. This should give you an output similar to the following (pretty-printed for readability):

```
{
    "latitude": 41.803488,
    "longitude": -88.14404,
    "userId": "f1196aac-470e-11e6-beb8-9e71128cae77",
    "timestamp": 1468203975
}
curl -H "Content-Type: application/json" -X POST -d '{"timestamp":
1468203975, "userId": "f1196aac-470e-11e6-beb8-9e71128cae77", "latitude":
9.568012, "longitude": 77.962444}' http://192.168.99.100:8899/geolocation
```

18. This should given you an output like the following (pretty-printed for readability):

```
{
  "latitude": 9.568012,
  "longitude": 77.962444,
  "userId": "f1196aac-470e-11e6-beb8-9e71128cae77",
  "timestamp": 1468203975
}
```

19. To verify whether your entities were stored correctly, execute the following `curl` command:

```
curl http://192.168.99.100:8899/geolocation
```

20. It should give you an output that looks like the following (pretty-printed for readability):

```
[
  {
    "latitude": 41.803488,
    "longitude": -88.14404,
    "userId": "f1196aac-470e-11e6-beb8-9e71128cae77",
    "timestamp": 1468203975
  }
]
```

21. But wait; we created two geolocations, so why is it showing just one? Let's try the command one more time. This time, it should give you an output like this (pretty-printed for readability):

```
[
  {
    "latitude": 9.568012,
    "longitude": 77.962444,
    "userId": "f1196aac-470e-11e6-beb8-9e71128cae77",
    "timestamp": 1468203975
  }
]
```

Again, we get only one geolocation, but this time it is a different one. This is because our request is being sent to one geolocation service each time. Each instance has one geolocation stored in memory. As our storage mechanism uses a very simple in-memory approach, they are not grouped together in a single repo. In a real-time scenario, you will be using a database, and all instances of this microservice will connect to the same database. At least now we know why our requests were acting differently. At the same time, this proves that the load balancing works as expected.

Yay! We have learned how to use Consul and Spring Cloud Consul to load-balance HTTP-based microservices. Consul is a very powerful tool, and it offers a great many other features. What we saw is just a basic use case of Consul in microservices.

 Do spend some time going through the Consul documentation at `https://www.consul.io/docs/index.html`.

That brings us to the end of this recipe. In our next recipe, we will look at how Nginx and Consul help with load-balancing microservices.

Load balancing your microservice using Nginx and Consul

So far we have learned how to load balance our microservice using Zookeeper and Consul. Both of these approaches come with their own merits and demerits. The Zookeeper approach required us to write a lot of code, and there is still a possibility of race condition where our proxy controller could invoke a service that just went down. The Spring Cloud Consul approach required us to write the proxy controller. In fact, in both these approaches we had to write our own load balancer microservice. This might not be a scalable approach when you have hundreds of microservices and tons of APIs. That is where HTTP servers such as Apache HTTP Server and Nginx come to the rescue. Nginx is one of the most popular HTTP servers. We could potentially use Nginx as our proxy server to geolocation microservices in a round robin fashion. In this recipe we will learn how to use Nginx and Consul together to load balance our geolocation microservice.

Getting ready

In this recipe we will be using two new components: **Nginx Server** and **Consul Template**. We all know what Nginx is and how it can be used for hosting our web content. However, in our case we are very interested in Nginx's `proxy_pass` module. The `proxy_pass` module can be used to make Nginx, forward requests received from a client to another server and send back responses from the other server back to the client. In our case, we will be utilizing `proxy_pass` to proxy requests to multiple geolocation instances. Usually `proxy_pass` configurations go into the `default.conf` file of Nginx. Sounds easy? But wait, how does Nginx know where our services are located, because we will never know how many instances of geolocation are active and where they are deployed. So the easiest way is to keep updating the `default.conf` file each time a geolocation service registers or unregisters in Consul. At the same time, each time the `default.conf` file is updated, Nginx needs to be reloaded. Somehow we have to keep both Consul and Nginx in sync. That's exactly what Consul Template does. Consul Template constantly polls Consul for any changes to our geolocation service and recreates the `default.conf` file. In fact, the whole `default.conf` file will be represented as a Consul Template file. Consul template uses the `Go` template format for creating template files.

To learn more about `Go` template format, please take a look at `https://golang.org/pkg/text/template`. The overall architecture will look something like this:

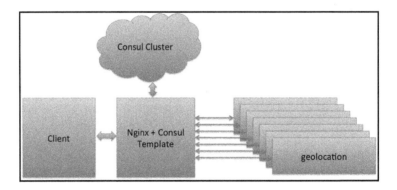

As you can see the client doesn't have to worry about the location of the geolocation microservice. All it needs to know is the location of our Nginx server.

How to do it...

The first thing that we will need is a Docker container for Nginx and Consul Template. We will be using the official Nginx Docker image and will install Consul Template inside it. Create a new directory along side the geolocation project called `geolocation-consul-nginx-lb`. Create a new Dockerfile under `geolocation-consul-nginx-lb` and add the folowing contents to it:

```
FROM nginx:latest
ENV CONSUL_URL consul:8500
RUN apt-get update && apt-get install -y unzip wget
RUN mkdir -p /opt/packt/consul-template
WORKDIR /opt/packt/consul-template
RUN wget
https://releases.hashicorp.com/consul-template/0.16.0/consul-template_0.16.
0_linux_amd64.zip && unzip consul-template_0.16.0_linux_amd64.zip
ADD default.ctmpl /opt/packt/consul-template/
ADD startup.sh /opt/packt/consul-template/
RUN chmod +777 /opt/packt/consul-template/startup.sh
RUN rm /etc/nginx/conf.d/default.conf
EXPOSE 80
ENTRYPOINT ["/opt/packt/consul-template/startup.sh"]
```

There are a lot of things going on in this file. Lets break it down into parts and try to understand it one by one. Firstly, we are basing this image off of `nginx:latest` image.

```
ENV CONSUL_URL consul:8500
```

The preceding instruction creates a new environment variable called `CONSUL_URL` with value `consul:8500`. The hostname `consul` will be resolved to the hostname of the `consul` service, if we use it in Docker compose.

```
RUN apt-get update && apt-get install -y unzip wget
```

The preceding instruction installs `unzip` and `wget`. We need them to install and unpack Consul Template.

```
RUN mkdir -p /opt/packt/consul-template
WORKDIR /opt/packt/consul-template
```

These two instructions create the `/opt/packt/consul-template` directory and set the working directory to `/opt/packt/consul-template`. We will be using this directory as the installation directory of consul template.

```
RUN wget
https://releases.hashicorp.com/consul-template/0.16.0/consul-template_0.16.
0_linux_amd64.zip && unzip consul-template_0.16.0_linux_amd64.zip
```

This instruction downloads Consul Template and unpacks the downloaded ZIP file. The content of the ZIP file is just the `consul-template` binary. As you can see we have used the version `0.16.0`, but feel free to use the most recent version found in `https://releases.hashicorp.com/consul-template`.

```
ADD default.ctmpl /opt/packt/consul-template/
ADD startup.sh /opt/packt/consul-template/
RUN chmod +x /opt/packt/consul-template/startup.sh
```

The preceding snippet does three things: adds the template file `default.ctmpl` to the installation directory at `/opt/packt/consul-template`, adds the startup script to the installation directory and provides execute privileges to the startup script. We will look at how to create the `default.ctmpl` file and `startup.sh` file later.

```
RUN rm /etc/nginx/conf.d/default.conf
```

This instruction is required to remove the default config file that comes with Nginx's installation.

```
EXPOSE 80
```

We are exposing port `80` of Nginx so that we can access it from outside (after mapping it).

```
ENTRYPOINT ["/opt/packt/consul-template/startup.sh"]
```

Finally the entry point will be the `startup.sh` script that we will be creating next. The startup script will do two things: start Nginx and start Consul Template. Create a new shell script with name `startup.sh` and add the following contents.

```
#!/bin/bash
service nginx start && /opt/packt/consul-template/consul-template -
consul=$CONSUL_URL -
template="default.ctmpl:/etc/nginx/conf.d/default.conf:service nginx
reload"
```

The preceding snippet starts the service called `nginx` and starts Consul Template with two arguments. The consul argument indicates the location of Consul. We have used the `CONSUL_URL` environment variable that was previously defined in the Dockerfile. The template argument is divided into three parts separated by a colon. The first part indicates the template file itself, the second part indicates the file that needs to be replaced after rendering the template and the third part indicates the action that needs to be performed after each update. In our case we are reloading the `nginx` service after each update.

The next file we have to create is the template file. Go ahead and create a new file called `default.ctmpl`. Add the following snippet to the newly created file:

```
upstream geolocation {
  least_conn;
  {{range service "geolocation"}}server {{.Address}}:{{.Port}}
  max_fails=3 fail_timeout=60 weight=1;
  {{else}}server 127.0.0.1:65535; # force a 502{{end}}
}

server {
  listen 80 default_server;

  charset utf-8;

  location /geolocation {
    proxy_pass http://geolocation;
    proxy_set_header X-Forwarded-For $proxy_add_x_forwarded_for;
    proxy_set_header Host $host;
    proxy_set_header X-Real-IP $remote_addr;
  }
}
```

If you are familiar with Nginx, you would already know what's going on here. All we have done is created an upstream called `geolocation`, which will be replaced with the list of geolocation servers that are registered in Consul. This rendering is what Consul Template does. Later in the server section, we have added a proxy pass to `/geolocation` URL path, which will be load balanced against the list of geolocation servers listed in `upstream geolocation`. This template file will be updated every time there is a change to the geolocation service in Consul.

That's it. We are all set to go. In order to test our setup, lets use Docker compose. Go ahead and create a new Docker compose file called `docker-compose-nginx-consul.yml`. Add the following snippet to the newly created YAML file:

```
version: "2"
services:
  consul:
    image: consul:latest
    ports:
      - "8500:8500"

  geolocation-1:
    image: vikrammurugesan/geolocation:latest
    ports:
      - "8080"
    environment:
      GEOLOCATION_SERVICE_PORT: "8080"
  geolocation-2:
    image: vikrammurugesan/geolocation:latest
    ports:
      - "8081"
    environment:
      GEOLOCATION_SERVICE_PORT: "8081"
  nginx-consul-template:
    build: .
    links:
      - consul
    depends_on:
      - consul
    ports:
      - "8900:80"
```

As you can see, we have three images that we already know: consul and 2 geolocation images. The only new image in the preceding Docker compose is the `nginx-consul-template` image. This image will be built using the Dockerfile located in the current directory. This image is linked to the consul image so that it knows where Consul is located. The `depends_on` section says that, this image has to wait for the consul image to be started. Finally port `80` of Nginx needs to be mapped to `8900` in the Docker host. Without any further ado, go ahead and start the containers using the following command:

```
docker-compose -f docker-compose-nginx-consul.yml up
```

It usually takes 2-5 minutes for the geolocation services to register to Consul depending on the configuration of your machine. So wait for them to register in Consul. You can verify if the services are registered in Consul by looking at Consul's web interface at `http://192.168.99.100:8500`. After all your services are registered, we are ready to test our load balancer. Open up a new terminal session and issue the following cURL commands:

```
curl -H "Content-Type: application/json" -X POST -d '{"timestamp":
1468203975, "userId": "f1196aac-470e-11e6-beb8-9e71128cae77", "latitude":
41.803488, "longitude": -88.144040}' http://192.168.99.100:8900/geolocation
```

This should give you an output similar to the following (pretty-printed for readability):

```
{
"latitude": 41.803488,
"longitude": -88.14404,
"userId": "f1196aac-470e-11e6-beb8-9e71128cae77",
"timestamp": 1468203975
}
curl -H "Content-Type: application/json" -X POST -d '{"timestamp":
1468203975, "userId": "f1196aac-470e-11e6-beb8-9e71128cae77", "latitude":
9.568012, "longitude": 77.962444}' http://192.168.99.100:8900/geolocation
```

This should give you an output like the following (pretty-printed for readability):

```
{
"latitude": 9.568012,
"longitude": 77.962444,
"userId": "f1196aac-470e-11e6-beb8-9e71128cae77",
"timestamp": 1468203975
}
```

To verify whether your entities were stored correctly, execute the following `curl` command:

```
curl http://192.168.99.100:8900/geolocation
```

It should give you an output that looks like the following (pretty-printed for readability):

```
[
{
"latitude": 41.803488,
    "longitude": -88.14404,
    "userId": "f1196aac-470e-11e6-beb8-9e71128cae77",
    "timestamp": 1468203975
}
]
```

But wait; we created two geolocations, so why is it showing just one? Let's try the command one more time. This time, it should give you an output like this (pretty-printed for readability):

```
[
{
"latitude": 9.568012,
    "longitude": 77.962444,
    "userId": "f1196aac-470e-11e6-beb8-9e71128cae77",
    "timestamp": 1468203975
}
]
```

Again, we get only one geolocation, but this time it is a different one. This is because our request is being sent to one geolocation service each time. Each instance has one geolocation stored in memory. As our storage mechanism uses a very simple in-memory approach, they are not grouped together in a single repo. In a real-time scenario, you will be using a database, and all instances of this microservice will connect to the same database. At least now we know that our new load balancer works as expected.

 Nginx has a paid version of their software called **Nginx Plus** which offers most of the features that you will need in any HTTP server like Monitoring, Security, Load Balancing, Caching, and so on. If you are already an Nginx user and would like to continue using it along with your microservices, it might be worth taking a look at Nginx Plus. For more information about load balancing using Nginx Plus, please take a look at https://www.nginx.com/products/application-load-balancing.

That's it. That brings us to the end of this recipe. In this recipe we not only learned how to use Consul Template and Nginx but also implemented a load balancer without having to write too much code. The real beauty of this approach is that, it configures Nginx to load balance between any number of geolocation instances that are currently registered in Consul.

Load balancing your microservice using Marathon LB

In this recipe, we will learn the concepts of Marathon LB and how it works behind the screens. At the time of writing this, Marathon LB works perfectly with DC/OS. So trying to make Marathon LB work in a non-DC/OS environment might not be the best solution in all cases. We will be learning about DC/OS in `Chapter 8`, *More Clustering Frameworks – DC/OS, Docker Swarm, and YARN*.

How it works...

Marathon LB is a Python-based tool that internally uses HAProxy to load-balance applications deployed on Marathon. HAProxy is one of the proven solutions for load-balancing HTTP-based endpoints. It has been there in the market for a while, and there are several success stories about it. When you start Marathon LB, you need to supply the base URL of Marathon as a configuration so that when Marathon LB starts, it knows where Marathon is running on your cluster. Marathon LB binds to the service ports of all the applications and routes any request that it receives to the application instances. It does three things:

- Parses the Marathon apps (using Marathon's REST API) and gets their IP and service port
- Creates a new HAProxy config and drops it in a dedicated HAProxy directory
- Reloads HAProxy (does not restart)

The working of Marathon LB is simple. It uses HAProxy as the back-end load balancer and interacts with the applications deployed on Marathon and HAProxy. The next question that you may have is how Marathon LB knows when applications in Marathon are modified: updated, removed, or created.

Marathon LB has a few strategies by which it will get notified when an application is modified on Marathon. So whenever it receives such an event, it updates HAProxy accordingly and reloads HAProxy. Not all applications will be load-balanced by Marathon LB. Marathon LB looks for applications that have the `HAPROXY_GROUP` variable set to a specific value.

If you would like to learn more about Marathon LB, visit their GitHub documentation at
`https://github.com/mesosphere/marathon-lb/blob/master/README.md`.

Like I mentioned, the easiest way to try Marathon LB is on a DC/OS cluster. And if you are so dependent on Mesos and Marathon, it is definitely worth taking a look at DC/OS.

With that, we come to the end of this chapter. You've learned a lot about service discovery and load-balancing your microservices in this chapter

6
Monitoring Microservices

In this chapter, we will learn how to setup a monitoring system for our microservice. We will cover the following recipes:

- Configuring Spring Boot Actuator metrics
- Understanding Spring Boot Actuator metrics
- Creating custom metrics using Dropwizard
- Setting up Graphite using Docker
- Using the Graphite interface
- Exporting Dropwizard metrics over to Graphite
- Exporting Spring Boot Actuator metrics over to Graphite
- Setting up Grafana using Docker
- Configuring Grafana to use Graphite
- Configuring Grafana dashboards to view metrics

Introduction

As you start scaling out to several microservices, it becomes difficult to monitor them. You might want to know when some part of your platform is not working as expected. At the same time, you want to be notified when some part of your application is not performing well. So monitoring becomes a significant aspect of microservices. At the same time, monitoring will not make sense if you don't monitor the right metrics. So exposing the right metrics for each microservices matter a lot. While you spend 60 percent of your time writing the actual functionality of the microservice, the other 40 percent should be spent on activities such as deployments, CI, monitoring, and logging. If this sounds strange to you, you will start understanding it as soon as you start writing more and more microservices.

The biggest question is where do we store these metrics. That's where Time Series Databases come into picture. There are several time series databases in the market at the moment like Graphite, Prometheus, Riak, and so on. In this chapter we will be looking at how to use Graphite to store our metrics. The next step is visualizing these metrics in form of user-friendly charts and graphs. For that purpose, we will be using one of the most popular monitoring tools called Grafana.

Configuring Spring Boot Actuator metrics

In this recipe, we will learn how to configure the geolocation project to expose some predefined metrics exposed by the Spring framework itself. Though you might not use all of them, it is always better to know that they exist so that you can find some use for them in the future. In fact, most of the metrics exposed by Spring are modifiable. On top of it, Spring adds security to them so that not everyone can view your metrics. These are some of the advantages that you get when you use Spring's metrics framework.

Getting ready

We will go through this recipe with the help of the geolocation project. We will be using the Spring Boot Actuator library to expose the metrics. So open your STS IDE. Before we jump into the actual implementation, we have to comment out a few lines of code. If you have been working on the *Setting up Consul using Docker* recipe from Chapter 5, *Service Discovery and Load Balancing Microservices*, you might still have the Zookeeper or Consul-related code in your code base. As we are not going to use either of them, let's make sure they are commented out. To comment out Zookeeper, all you have to do is comment out the line in `GeoLocationApplication.java` class file where we register our service. To comment out Consul, you have to first comment out the `@EnableDiscoveryClient` annotation from the `GeoLocationApplication.java` class and remove the unused import. The class will now look like this:

```
package com.packt.microservices.geolocation;

import org.springframework.boot.SpringApplication;
import org.springframework.boot.autoconfigure.
  SpringBootApplication;

@SpringBootApplication
// @EnableDiscoveryClient
public class GeoLocationApplication {

  public static void main(String[] args) {
```

```
        SpringApplication.run(GeoLocationApplication.class, args);
        // commented out so that the service does not try to connect
        to zk
        // new Zookeeper("192.168.99.100", 2181).register();
    }
}
```

The next step is commenting out the `spring-cloud-starter-consul-all` dependency from the `pom.xml` file:

```
    <!-- <dependency>
  <groupId>org.springframework.cloud</groupId>
        <artifactId>spring-cloud-starter-consul-all</artifactId>
        <version>1.1.2.RELEASE</version>
    </dependency> -->
```

Now that we know all the code related to Zookeeper and Consul initialization are commented out, let's work on configuring Spring Boot Actuator.

How to do it...

Before we start, let's take a minute to talk about Spring Boot Actuator and how it works. Spring Boot Actuator is just a Maven dependency that you need to add to your project. Once you add this dependency, Spring automatically injects the beans that are responsible for exposing these metrics. There are two ways to consume these metrics: HTTP or JMX. Though JMX is considered to be the standard way, HTTP is considered an easy solution, as REST is almost everywhere these days. For simplicity, in this recipe, we will be testing our metrics using the HTTP endpoints. Actuator not only exposes metrics but also some useful endpoints to manage our application. We will look at them in the next recipe.

1. Without any delay, lets' add the `spring-boot-starter-actuator` dependency to our `pom.xml` file:

```
<dependency>
    <groupId>org.springframework.boot</groupId>
    <artifactId>spring-boot-starter-actuator</artifactId>
</dependency>
```

 We have not added the version for the `spring-boot-starter-actuator` dependency. That is because it will pick up the version managed by the `spring-boot-starter-parent` POM. In our case, the version of `spring-boot-starter-actuator` that will be resolved is 1.3.6 release.

2. Now that our project is ready with Actuator, let's test it. Start the
   `GeoLocationApplication.java` class as a Spring Boot application from your
   STS IDE. If you pay close attention to the logs, this time you will see that there are
   some additional request mappings registered, such as /beans, /info,
   /configprops, /health, /autoconfig, /mappings, /metrics, /env, /trace,
   and /dump. These request mappings were added by the Spring Actuator
   dependency:

```
2016-12-14 19:31:50.730  INFO 9616 --- [     main] o.s.b.a.e.mvc.EndpointHandlerMapping   : Mapped "{[/beans || /beans.json],methods=[GET],produces=[application/
2016-12-14 19:31:50.731  INFO 9616 --- [     main] o.s.b.a.e.mvc.EndpointHandlerMapping   : Mapped "{[/info || /info.json],methods=[GET],produces=[application/jso
2016-12-14 19:31:50.732  INFO 9616 --- [     main] o.s.b.a.e.mvc.EndpointHandlerMapping   : Mapped "{[/configprops || /configprops.json],methods=[GET],produces=[a
2016-12-14 19:31:50.734  INFO 9616 --- [     main] o.s.b.a.e.mvc.EndpointHandlerMapping   : Mapped "{[/health || /health.json],produces=[application/json]}" onto
2016-12-14 19:31:50.738  INFO 9616 --- [     main] o.s.b.a.e.mvc.EndpointHandlerMapping   : Mapped "{[/autoconfig || /autoconfig.json],methods=[GET],produces=[app
2016-12-14 19:31:50.739  INFO 9616 --- [     main] o.s.b.a.e.mvc.EndpointHandlerMapping   : Mapped "{[/mappings || /mappings.json],methods=[GET],produces=[applica
2016-12-14 19:31:50.740  INFO 9616 --- [     main] o.s.b.a.e.mvc.EndpointHandlerMapping   : Mapped "{[/metrics/{name:.*}]],methods=[GET],produces=[application/jso
2016-12-14 19:31:50.741  INFO 9616 --- [     main] o.s.b.a.e.mvc.EndpointHandlerMapping   : Mapped "{[/metrics || /metrics.json],methods=[GET],produces=[applicati
2016-12-14 19:31:50.742  INFO 9616 --- [     main] o.s.b.a.e.mvc.EndpointHandlerMapping   : Mapped "{[/env/{name:.*}]],methods=[GET],produces=[application/json]}"
2016-12-14 19:31:50.742  INFO 9616 --- [     main] o.s.b.a.e.mvc.EndpointHandlerMapping   : Mapped "{[/env || /env.json],methods=[GET],produces=[application/json]
2016-12-14 19:31:50.743  INFO 9616 --- [     main] o.s.b.a.e.mvc.EndpointHandlerMapping   : Mapped "{[/trace || /trace.json],methods=[GET],produces=[application/;
2016-12-14 19:31:50.744  INFO 9616 --- [     main] o.s.b.a.e.mvc.EndpointHandlerMapping   : Mapped "{[/dump || /dump.json],methods=[GET],produces=[application/jsc
2016-12-14 19:31:50.950  INFO 9616 --- [     main] o.s.j.e.a.AnnotationMBeanExporter      : Registering beans for JMX exposure on startup
2016-12-14 19:31:50.980  INFO 9616 --- [     main] o.s.c.support.DefaultLifecycleProcessor: Starting beans in phase 0
2016-12-14 19:31:51.400  INFO 9616 --- [     main] s.b.c.e.t.TomcatEmbeddedServletContainer: Tomcat started on port(s): 8080 (http)
2016-12-14 19:31:51.406  INFO 9616 --- [     main] c.p.m.g.GeoLocationApplication         : Started GeoLocationApplication in 9.497 seconds (JVM running for 15.46
```

3. Let's test our configurations. Open a new terminal session and issue the following
   `curl` command:

   curl http://localhost:8080/metrics

   This should have returned a list of metrics that are currently being exposed
   by your microservice using Spring Boot Actuator.

4. You should see something like this (pretty-printed for readability):

```
{
  "mem": 233838,
  "mem.free": 65596,
  "processors": 4,
  "instance.uptime": 909667,
  "uptime": 924127,
  "systemload.average": 1.62548828125,
  "heap.committed": 184832,
  "heap.init": 131072,
  "heap.used": 119235,
  "heap": 1864192,
  "nonheap.committed": 49984,
  "nonheap.init": 2496,
  "nonheap.used": 49006,
  "nonheap": 0,
  "threads.peak": 29,
  "threads.daemon": 19,
  "threads.totalStarted": 36,
```

```
    "threads": 21,
    "classes": 6154,
    "classes.loaded": 6154,
    "classes.unloaded": 0,
    "gc.ps_scavenge.count": 8,
    "gc.ps_scavenge.time": 101,
    "gc.ps_marksweep.count": 1,
    "gc.ps_marksweep.time": 46,
    "httpsessions.max": -1,
    "httpsessions.active": 0,
    "gauge.response.metrics": 16,
    "gauge.response.star-star": 41,
    "counter.status.200.metrics": 1,
    "counter.status.404.star-star": 1
}
```

Ideally, you will have more metrics. As you can see, the previous metrics are more on the JVM level. You will also see some metrics that are HTTP related (such as `404` counts and `200` counts). These metrics are starter based. For example, if you have a Spring Data starter configured in your application, you will see some database-related metrics as well. If you find it difficult to read the metrics from the command line, feel free to use tools such as Postman or other browser-based plugins that can render JSON in a pretty-printed format.

5. This verifies that we have successfully configured Spring Boot Actuator in our application. These metrics may be useful on the JVM level, but they are not going to help us monitor our application-related metrics, which is what we will be learning in later recipes of this chapter.

That brings us to the end of this recipe. In this recipe, we learned how to configure Spring Boot Actuator in our application.

Understanding Spring Boot Actuator metrics

In the previous recipe, we learned how to configure Spring Boot Actuator in the geolocation application. We also verified the configuration by accessing the `/metrics` endpoint. In this recipe, we will be learning more about most of the commonly used metrics exposed by Spring Boot Actuator.

Getting ready

In order to understand the various metrics and operations exposed by the Spring Boot Actuator library, we will be invoking them one by one using cURL commands. As we will be analyzing the JSON response of our metric APIs a lot, feel free to use a tool such as Postman or another plugin for your browser to pretty-print JSON documents.

How to do it...

The next few steps in this recipe will help you go over the most important endpoints exposed by Spring Boot Actuator.

1. Some metrics exposed by Actuator depend on the API usage, so let's create some geolocations and try to query them:

```
curl -H "Content-Type: application/json" -X POST -d '{"timestamp":
1468203975, "userId": "f1196aac-470e-11e6-beb8-9e71128cae77", "latitude":
41.803488, "longitude": -88.144040}' http://localhost:8080/geolocation
```

2. This should give you an output similar to the following (pretty-printed for readability):

```
{
  "latitude": 41.803488,
  "longitude": -88.14404,
  "userId": "f1196aac-470e-11e6-beb8-9e71128cae77",
  "timestamp": 1468203975
}
```

3. To check whether our entity was stored correctly, execute the following `curl` command:

```
curl http://localhost:8080/geolocation
```

4. It should give you an output like this (pretty-printed for readability):

```
[
  {
    "latitude": 41.803488,
    "longitude": -88.14404,
    "userId": "f1196aac-470e-11e6-beb8-9e71128cae77",
    "timestamp": 1468203975
  }
]
```

5. Now let's create the second geolocation:

```
curl -H "Content-Type: application/json" -X POST -d '{"timestamp":
1468203975, "userId": "f1196aac-470e-11e6-beb8-9e71128cae77", "latitude":
9.568012, "longitude": 77.962444}' http://localhost:8080/geolocation
```

6. This should give you an output similar to the following (pretty-printed for readability):

```
{
  "latitude": 9.568012,
  "longitude": 77.962444,
  "userId": "f1196aac-470e-11e6-beb8-9e71128cae77",
  "timestamp": 1468203975
}
```

7. To verify whether your entities were stored correctly, execute the following `curl` command:

```
curl http://localhost:8080/geolocation
```

8. It should give you an output like the following (pretty-printed for readability):

```
[
  {
    "latitude": 41.803488,
    "longitude": -88.14404,
    "userId": "f1196aac-470e-11e6-beb8-9e71128cae77",
    "timestamp": 1468203975
  },
  {
    "latitude": 9.568012,
    "longitude": 77.962444,
    "userId": "f1196aac-470e-11e6-beb8-9e71128cae77",
    "timestamp": 1468203975
  }
]
```

9. Now let's invoke the `metrics` API and try to understand few of the metrics:

```
curl http://localhost:8080/metrics
```

10. You should receive a response similar to this (pretty-printed for readability):

```
{
  "mem": 254684,
  "mem.free": 112813,
```

```
"processors": 4,
"instance.uptime": 618061,
"uptime": 623669,
"systemload.average": 1.8212890625,
"heap.committed": 205312,
"heap.init": 131072,
"heap.used": 92498,
"heap": 1864192,
"nonheap.committed": 51008,
"nonheap.init": 2496,
"nonheap.used": 49372,
"nonheap": 0,
"threads.peak": 31,
"threads.daemon": 24,
"threads.totalStarted": 41,
"threads": 26,
"classes": 6262,
"classes.loaded": 6262,
"classes.unloaded": 0,
"gc.ps_scavenge.count": 7,
"gc.ps_scavenge.time": 93,
"gc.ps_marksweep.count": 1,
"gc.ps_marksweep.time": 58,
"httpsessions.max": -1,
"httpsessions.active": 0,
"gauge.response.geolocation": 5,
"gauge.response.metrics": 4,
"gauge.response.star-star.favicon.ico": 3,
"counter.status.200.star- star.favicon.ico": 3,
"counter.status.200.metrics": 4,
"counter.status.200.geolocation": 4
}
```

Here is a quick description of some of these metrics:

- `mem` and `mem.free` indicate the amount of memory used and available in KB.
- `uptime` indicates the uptime of the system whereas `instance.uptime` indicates the uptime of the application context. They are in milliseconds.
- `heap`, `heap.used`, `heap.init`, and `heap.committed` are all used to identify the current heap status. They are in KB.
- `threads`, `threads.peak`, `threads.totalStarted`, and `threads.daemon` provide the thread counts.

- `classes`, `classes.loaded`, and `classes.unloaded` provide the information about the classloader like total number of classes available, total number of classes loaded, and total number of classes unloaded.
- `httpsessions.max` and `httpsessions.active` indicate the maximum number of sessions and currently active session count, respectively.
- `gauge.response.<request_path>` indicates the response time of the last request for the given request path.
- `counter.status.<status_code>.<request_path>` indicates the number of times a particular status code was returned for the given request path.

 This list provides a quick description of the most commonly used metrics. However, there are other metrics too, such as **garbage collection**-related metrics. You might want to use them for debugging. To learn more about those metrics please visit `https://docs.spring.io/spring-boot/docs/current/reference/html/production-ready-metrics.html`.

The next useful endpoint is the `/health` endpoint. This endpoint provides a quick snapshot view of your application and its components' health. Components include any Spring module, such as Consul, Eureka, MySQL, and so on depending on whether you use them in your project. In our case, we don't have any Spring modules, so we will just see a high-level health check for our app.

1. Let's test it out:

```
curl  http://localhost:8080/health
```

2. You should receive something like this (pretty-printed for readability):

```
{
  "status": "UP",
  "diskSpace": {
    "status": "UP",
    "total": 498876809216,
    "free": 142243303424,
    "threshold": 10485760
  }
}
```

As you can see, it provides an overall health status saying it is UP and also provides the health of the disk, including some metrics. This endpoint is something that you will end up using very often, either to check whether you app is up and running or to check whether all the components of your app are working as expected.

3. The next most important endpoint is the /env endpoint. This endpoint provides useful information such as JVM arguments, system properties, and system environment variables. Let's take a quick look at it:

```
curl http://localhost:8080/env
```

4. You should receive something like this (pretty-printed for readability):

```
{
  "profiles": [],
  "server.ports": {
    "local.server.port": 8080
  },
  "commandLineArgs": {
    "spring.output.ansi.enabled": "always"
  },
  "servletContextInitParams": {
  },
  "systemProperties": {
    "com.sun.management.jmxremote.authenticate": "false",
    "java.runtime.name": "Java(TM) SE Runtime Environment",
    "java.vm.version": "25.40-b25",
    "gopherProxySet": "false",
    "java.vm.vendor": "Oracle Corporation",
    "java.vendor.url": "http://java.oracle.com/",
    "java.rmi.server.randomIDs": "true",
    "path.separator": ":",
    "java.vm.name": "Java HotSpot(TM) 64-Bit Server VM",
    "file.encoding.pkg": "sun.io",
    "user.country": "US",
    "sun.java.launcher": "SUN_STANDARD",
    "sun.os.patch.level": "unknown",
    "PID": "10883",
    "com.sun.management.jmxremote.port": "64324",
    "java.vm.specification.name": "Java Virtual Machine Specification",
    .
    .
    .
  },
  "systemEnvironment": {
    "PATH": "/usr/bin:/bin:/usr/sbin:/sbin",
```

```
      "APP_ICON_6659": "../Resources/sts.icns",
      "SHELL": "/bin/bash",
      "JAVA_MAIN_CLASS_10883":
  "com.packt.microservices.geolocation.GeoLocationApplication",
      "JAVA_STARTED_ON_FIRST_THREAD_6659": "1",
          .
          .
          .
  },
  "applicationConfig: [classpath:/application.properties]": {
    "server.port": "${GEOLOCATION_SERVICE_PORT:8080}"
  }
}
```

The most important part of this API is that it provides the JVM arguments and system environment variables with their values. This is very useful when you pass arguments to your application in the form of JVM arguments or system environment variables. In our case, we use an environment variable called GEOLOCATION_SERVICE_PORT; however, we see that it is not being supplied to the environment. This is the reason our server port is defaulted to 8080.

5. The next useful endpoint is the /dump endpoint. This endpoint performs a thread dump and provides the output as the response of the API call. Go ahead and execute the following curl command in a terminal shell:

```
curl http://localhost:8080/dump
[
    {
  "threadName": "http-nio-8080-exec-10",
        "threadId": 47,
  "blockedTime": -1,
  "blockedCount": 0,
  "waitedTime": -1,
  "waitedCount": 2,
  "lockName":
"java.util.concurrent.locks.AbstractQueuedSynchronizer$ConditionObject@3386
c54f",
  "lockOwnerId": -1,
  "lockOwnerName": null,
  "inNative": false,
  "suspended": false,
  "threadState": "WAITING",
  "stackTrace": [
  {
  "methodName": "park",
  "fileName": "Unsafe.java",
```

```
  "lineNumber": -2,
  "className": "sun.misc.Unsafe",
  "nativeMethod": true
},
```

> This response has been truncated as it was too lengthy. As you can see, the response is a JSON representation of the dump. One advantage of the JSON representation is that it can be *parsed* easily.

6. The next useful endpoint is the `/info` endpoint. This endpoint provides any information that you would like to display about your application. Some useful information could be the Git revision ID, application artifact version, and publish date time.

7. The next useful endpoint is the `/trace` endpoint. It ideally provides the trace log information of the last hundred requests made to the service. In the same terminal shell, execute the following `curl` command:

```
curl http://localhost:8080/trace
```

8. You should receive something like this (pretty-printed for readability):

```
[
  {
    "timestamp": 1481818606409,
    "info": {
      "method": "GET",
      "path": "/info",
      "headers": {
        "request": {
          "host": "localhost:8080",
          "connection": "keep-alive",
          "upgrade-insecure-requests": "1",
          "user-agent": "Mozilla/5.0 (Macintosh; Intel Mac OS X
10_11_6) AppleWebKit/537.36 (KHTML, like Gecko) Chrome/54.0.2840.98
Safari/537.36",
          "accept":
"text/html,application/xhtml+xml,application/xml;q=0.9,image/webp,*/*;q=0.8
",
          "accept-encoding": "gzip, deflate, sdch, br",
          "accept-language": "en-US,en;q=0.8,es;q=0.6"
        },
        "response": {
          "X-Application-Context": "application:8080",
          "Content-Type": "application/json;charset=UTF-8",
          "Transfer-Encoding": "chunked",
          "Date": "Thu, 15 Dec 2016 16:16:46 GMT",
```

```
        "status": "200"
      }
    }
  }
},...
```

As you can see, we have truncated the response as it was too long. The snippet shows just one request and its information. This will be particularly useful when you are debugging your API failures.

9. Oftentimes, you might want to modify these metrics. Be it exposing your own health status or exposing some information metrics, there are ways to do so using Spring.

 If you would like to invest more time on these topics, go over the descriptive documentation on Spring Boot's GitHub documentation at `https://github.com/spring-projects/spring-boot/blob/master/sprin g-boot-docs/src/main/asciidoc/production-ready-features.adoc`.

That brings us to the end of this recipe. There are other endpoints that we have not discussed in this recipe, such as `/shutdown`, `/loggers`, `/mappings`, `/configprops`, `/beans`, and `/autoconfig`. I'll leave that as an exercise for you to try out. The `/shutdown` endpoint is disabled by default. You have to enable it by setting the value of `endpoints.shutdown.enabled` to `true` in your `application.properties` file.

Creating custom metrics using Dropwizard

So far in this chapter, we've learned how to use the Spring Boot Actuator metrics. But what if your application is not Spring Boot and you still want to create metrics of your own? That is what this recipe will help you with. Not every microservice needs to be Spring Boot based. There are some microservices that could be written with other microservice frameworks. In those cases, if you would like to create your own metrics, you could use Dropwizard's Codahale library. Codahale is one of the most popular metrics libraries available for Java-based applications. In fact, Spring Boot internally uses Codahale to create some of its metrics. In this recipe, we will be using the Codahale library to create a metric for the geolocation application.

Getting ready

If you are wondering what the association between Dropwizard and Codahale is, the answer is that Codahale falls under the Dropwizard umbrella. Dropwizard is an ecosystem of libraries that can be used to build better microservices. Some of these libraries include Jetty for in-memory web servers, Jersey for building REST APIs, Jackson for working with JSON documents, and Codahale for metrics. In this recipe, we will be using just the Codahale library to expose our metrics. The great thing about this library is that it has been developed in such a way that it can be used independently as well-that means you can use Codahale even when your project does not use the other Dropwizard components. Let's create our first metric. Open your STS IDE and navigate to the `geolocation` project.

How to do it...

Before we jump in, let's decide which type of metric we are going to create. There are several metric types that Dropwizard Codahale offers:

- Gauges
- Counters
- Meters
- Timers
- Histograms

A **gauge** is a type of metric that can hold any value. It is, in fact, the most common metric type. The next type of metric is counter. **Counters**, as the name indicates, are used to maintain a counter and are usually incremented in a sequence. Any rate is usually represented as a **meter**. A **histogram** is used to measure the distribution of values. Though **timers** sound pretty straightforward, they're actually not. Timers are a combination of both histograms and meters. Understanding timers takes some time, but putting them to use will add great value. To learn more about histograms please take a look at `http://metrics.dropwizard.io/3.1.0/getting-started`. In this recipe, let's try to create two types of metrics: gauge and counter:

- `geolocationWriteRequestCount`: The number of times the POST API was invoked (`counter`)
- `geolocationLastWriteTime`: The most recent timestamp of when a geolocation was created (`gauge`)

Let's start by creating a new counter for the `geolocationWriteRequestCount` metric:

1. First add the Maven dependencies we need:

```
<dependency>
    <groupId>io.dropwizard.metrics</groupId>
    <artifactId>metrics-core</artifactId>
</dependency>
```

2. Now create a bean called
   `com.packt.microservices.geolocation.MetricSystem.java`, which will
   be responsible for instantiating and reporting our metrics. For reporting, we will
   use our basic `ConsoleReporter` until we set up our Graphite instance.

3. Create a new class called
   `com.packt.microservices.geolocation.MetricSystem.java`. Annotate
   this class with the `@Component` annotation. Also add an `init()` method with
   `@PostConstruct` annotation. This is where we will be setting up our metrics:

```
package com.packt.microservices.geolocation;

import javax.annotation.PostConstruct;

import org.springframework.beans.factory.annotation.Autowired;
import org.springframework.stereotype.Component;

import com.codahale.metrics.MetricRegistry;

@Component
public class MetricSystem {
  @Autowired
  private MetricRegistry metricRegistry;
  @PostConstruct
  public void init() {
  }
}
```

> As you can see, we have autowired a bean of type `MetricRegistry` instead
> of creating our own `MetricRegistry` instance. Spring Boot makes the
> `MetricRegistry` bean available. So any metric created with this
> `MetricRegistry` instance will be exposed by the `/metrics` endpoint as
> well. This is the reason we are autowiring the `MetricRegistry` bean.

4. Before we create the metric, let's set up a `ConsoleReporter`. Codahale provides a set of metric reporters responsible for publishing the metrics that are created to another consumption layer. Currently, there is support for Graphite, Ganglia, SLF4J, CSV, and Console. The `ConsoleReporter`, as its name indicates, reports all the metrics to `stdout`. In the next recipe, we will set up our own Graphite instance with the help of Docker. Until then, for simplicity, we will be using the `ConsoleReporter`. Add the following snippet to the `init()` method:

```
ConsoleReporter consoleReporter =
ConsoleReporter.forRegistry(metricRegistry)
        .convertRatesTo(TimeUnit.SECONDS)
        .convertDurationsTo(TimeUnit.MILLISECONDS)
        .build();

consoleReporter.start(10, TimeUnit.SECONDS);
```

There are three things to note here. The `convertRatesTo()` method says that all the rates have to be converted to seconds, and the `convertDurationsTo()` method says that all the durations should be converted to milliseconds. The `start` method, however, takes two arguments. These two arguments together tell Codahale to report metrics to the console every 10 seconds.

5. Now create a new `Counter` variable with the name `geolocationWriteRequestCount`. Let's define it in the `init()` method and put it into action:

```
package com.packt.microservices.geolocation;

import java.util.concurrent.TimeUnit;

import javax.annotation.PostConstruct;

import org.springframework.beans.factory.annotation.Autowired;
import org.springframework.stereotype.Component;

import com.codahale.metrics.ConsoleReporter;
import com.codahale.metrics.Counter;
import com.codahale.metrics.MetricRegistry;

@Component
public class MetricSystem {
  @Autowired
  private MetricRegistry metricRegistry;
  private Counter geolocationWriteRequestCount;
```

```
  @PostConstruct
  public void init() {
    ConsoleReporter consoleReporter =
ConsoleReporter.forRegistry(metricRegistry)
      .convertRatesTo(TimeUnit.SECONDS)
      .convertDurationsTo(TimeUnit.MILLISECONDS)
      .build();

    consoleReporter.start(10, TimeUnit.SECONDS);
    geolocationWriteRequestCount =
metricRegistry.counter("geolocationWriteRequestCount");
  }
  public Counter geolocationWriteRequestCount() {
    return geolocationWriteRequestCount;
  }
}
```

It is as simple as that. We have also created a method to get this counter so that it can be used from our controller.

6. Now move on to the `GeoLocationController.java` class and increment the counter using the `inc()` method as and when a new geolocation is created. Though this might not be a good practice, we are going to add it to the controller for illustration purposes only:

```
@Autowired
private MetricSystem metricSystem;

@RequestMapping(method = RequestMethod.POST, produces = "application/json",
consumes = "application/json")
public GeoLocation create(@RequestBody GeoLocation geolocation) {
  GeoLocation newGeoLocation = service.create(geolocation);

  metricSystem.geolocationWriteRequestCount().inc();

  return newGeoLocation;
}
```

As you can see, we have autowired the `MetricSystem` bean and used it to get our `geolocationWriteRequestCount` counter. We have then invoked the `inc()` method to increment the counter.

7. That's it! Now lets' test it out. Go ahead and start the
`GeoLocationApplication.java` class as a Spring Boot application from your
STS IDE. After your application has started, issue the following `curl` commands
to create two new geolocations:

```
curl -H "Content-Type: application/json" -X POST -d '{"timestamp":
1468203975, "userId": "f1196aac-470e-11e6-beb8-9e71128cae77", "latitude":
41.803488, "longitude": -88.144040}' http://localhost:8080/geolocation
curl -H "Content-Type: application/json" -X POST -d '{"timestamp":
1468203975, "userId": "f1196aac-470e-11e6-beb8-9e71128cae77", "latitude":
9.568012, "longitude": 77.962444}' http://localhost:8080/geolocation
```

This should have incremented the counter value to 2.

8. Now go back to your STS IDE, and look at the console logs of the geolocation
project. You should see something like this getting logged every 10 seconds:

```
Gauges -----------------------------------------------------
  gauge.response.geolocation
    value = 32.0
Counters ---------------------------------------------------
  counter.status.200.geolocation
    count = 2
  geolocationWriteRequestCount
    count = 2
```

We can clearly see that the value of `geolocationWriteRequestCount` is 2
now. Also note the other two metrics, `gauge.response.geolocation` and
`counter.status.200.geolocation`. These metrics are created by Spring
Boot. If you remember from the previous recipe, these metrics were
displayed on the `/metrics` endpoint.

9. Now let's quickly invoke the `/metrics` endpoint to check whether our metrics
are populated. Execute the following `curl` command on your terminal:

```
curl http://localhost:8080/metrics
{
  .
  .
  "counter.status.200.geolocation": 2,
  "gauge.response.geolocation": 32,
  "geolocationWriteRequestCount": 2,
  .
  .
}
```

This response has been trimmed as it was very long. As you can see, among other metrics, the three metrics that we saw in the console are reported.

10. Now let's create our next metric, `geolocationLastWriteTime`. This metric will be a gauge, and we will be storing the **epoch time** as the value. We can get the epoch time in Java using `System.currentTimeMillis()`. As this metric is going to store the last write timestamp, this metric needs to be updated only when a new geolocation is created. So we will need a holder variable in our `MetricSystem` bean that is updated with the time every time a new geolocation is created. The gauge is a little different from the counter for the fact that it gets calculated every time it gets reported. After adding the `geolocationLastWriteTime` gauge, the `MetricSystem` bean will look like this:

```
package com.packt.microservices.geolocation;

import java.util.concurrent.TimeUnit;

import javax.annotation.PostConstruct;

import org.springframework.beans.factory.annotation.Autowired;
import org.springframework.stereotype.Component;

import com.codahale.metrics.ConsoleReporter;
import com.codahale.metrics.Counter;
import com.codahale.metrics.Gauge;
import com.codahale.metrics.MetricRegistry;

@Component
public class MetricSystem {
  @Autowired
  private MetricRegistry metricRegistry;
  private Counter geolocationWriteRequestCount;
  private Long geolocationLastWriteTime;
  @PostConstruct
  public void init() {
    ConsoleReporter consoleReporter =
ConsoleReporter.forRegistry(metricRegistry)
        .convertRatesTo(TimeUnit.SECONDS)
        .convertDurationsTo(TimeUnit.MILLISECONDS)
        .build();

    consoleReporter.start(10, TimeUnit.SECONDS);
    geolocationWriteRequestCount =
metricRegistry.counter("geolocationWriteRequestCount");
    metricRegistry.register("geolocationLastWriteTime", new Gauge<Long>() {
      @Override
```

```
      public Long getValue() {
        return geolocationLastWriteTime;
      }
    });
  }
  public Counter geolocationWriteRequestCount() {
    return geolocationWriteRequestCount;
  }
  public void markGeolocationLastWriteTime() {
    geolocationLastWriteTime = System.currentTimeMillis();
  }
}
```

See how the gauge is registered with an inner class that has a getter method called `getValue()`. Also see how we have created the `markGeolocationLastWriteTime()` method that updates this variable with the current timestamp.

11. We are now ready to incorporate this metric into the `GeoLocationController.java`. All we need to do is add this line of code to the `create` method:

```
metricSystem.markGeolocationLastWriteTime();
```

12. That's it. Our gauge is now ready to test. Restart the `GeolocationApplication.java` class and create a couple of geolocations using the `curl` command. This time around, you should see a new gauge with the last write timestamp as its value:

```
-- Gauges --------------------------------------------------------------
--
gauge.response.geolocation
          value = 11.0
geolocationLastWriteTime
          value = 1481939509826
-- Counters ------------------------------------------------------------
--
counter.status.200.geolocation
          count = 2
geolocationWriteRequestCount
          count = 2
```

13. You can verify this by invoking the `/metrics` endpoint as well.

That's it! We now have come to the end of this recipe. In this recipe, we learned how to create custom metrics and expose them via Spring Boot's `/metrics` endpoint. We also learned how to expose them via the `ConsoleReporter`.

Setting up Graphite using Docker

In this recipe, we will learn how to set up Graphite using Docker. Before that, let's learn a few things about Graphite's architecture. Graphite consists of three major components: **Whisper**, **Carbon**, and **Graphite-Web**. Whisper is a database library that Graphite relies on. It works like a **round-robin database**. Carbon is the backend daemon that is responsible for handling client requests. The Graphite-Web interface is used to create dashboards and visualize the data stored in Graphite.

Getting ready

As usual, we will be defining our Graphite image in a `docker-compose` file. The reason we are using `docker-compose` instead of running `docker run` is that we will later be adding Grafana to this `docker-compose` file. Open up your STS IDE and navigate to the `geolocation` project.

How to do it...

The next few steps in this recipe will guide you through setting up a standalone Graphite instance using Docker.

1. Create a new `docker-compose` YAML file called `docker-compose-graphite.yml`. Add the following snippet to the newly created YAML file:

```
version: "2"

services:
  graphite:
    image: hopsoft/graphite-statsd
    ports:
      - "8100:80"
      - "2003:2003"
      - "2004:2004"
```

As you can see, we are not using an official image for Graphite. Unfortunately, there is no official version of Graphite available at the time of writing this. So we have picked this image that has both Graphite and `statsd` configured. `statsd` is a daemon developed by Etsy to consolidate application metrics and publish them over to a graphing system.

2. To learn more about `statsd`, visit their GitHub page at `https://github.com/etsy/statsd`. If you take a look at this image's documentation at `https://hub.docker.com/r/hopsoft/graphite-statsd`, there are several ports and volumes that can be mapped. We are not mapping them as we will not need them for this recipe. But feel free to use them if you need to. Port `80` is used by Nginx, where your web interface and REST endpoints reside. Port `2003` is where the Carbon receiver is listening. Port `2004` is where Carbon Pickle receiver is listening. We are not mapping port `80` on the container to port `80` on the host because port `80` is a very common port number and you might have other apps running on port `80`. So we are mapping it to port `8100` on the host machine.

 There are two types of protocols by which you can feed metrics to Carbon: Plain text and Pickle. Plain text follows the simplest format, where it sends metrics in the format of `<path> <value> <timestamp>`, where `path` indicates the path at which the metric will be stored along with the metric name. However, Pickle on the other hand is used to send a batch of metrics all at once to Carbon. It takes metrics in form of tuples: `[(path, (timestamp, value))]`. For more information, look at Graphite's descriptive documentation at `http://graphite.readthedocs.io/en/latest/feeding-carbon.html#feeding-in-your-data`.

3. Now that we have our `docker-compose` YAML file, let's spin off our first Graphite instance. Open up a new terminal window. Start `docker-machine` if it is not started already, and set up Docker using the `env` command. Change your directory to the `geolocation` project and execute the following command:

```
docker-compose -f docker-compose-graphite.yml up
```

4. You should see something like this:

```
Creating geolocation_graphite_1
Attaching to geolocation_graphite_1
graphite_1  | *** Running /etc/my_init.d/00_regen_ssh_host_keys.sh...
graphite_1  | *** Running /etc/my_init.d/01_conf_init.sh...
graphite_1  | *** Running /etc/rc.local...
graphite_1  | *** Booting runit daemon...
graphite_1  | *** Runit started as PID 13
```

5. Now that our Graphite instance is up and running, let's verify it by accessing the web interface. Open a new browser session and navigate to this URL: `http://192.168.99.100:8100`. You should see the **Graphite** dashboard page:

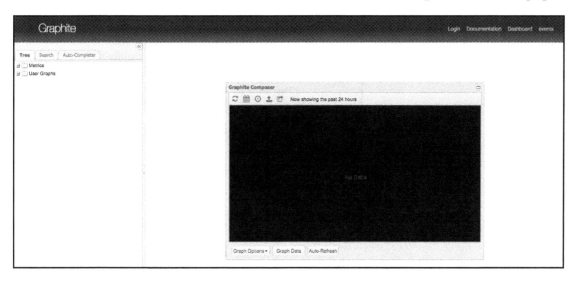

6. If you log in to the app using the credentials `root/root`, you will be able to manage the graphs that you have created. It will also enable certain features on the whole UI. Now expand the **Metrics** node and see what kind of metrics are being exposed:

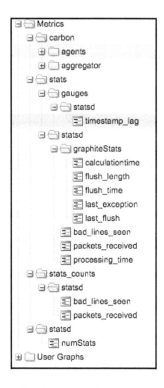

As you can see, there are some metrics ingested by `statsd`. Usually, metrics created by `statsd` start with the keyword `stats`. You can plot each of these metrics on a graph by simply clicking on them.

That brings us to the end of this recipe. Graphite by itself offers tons of features, and its true power can be experienced only when we run it in clustered mode. It is strongly recommended that you understand Graphite and its components before you start using it in production.

Fortunately, Graphite's documentation is very descriptive and has a lot of useful information. You can find it at
`http://graphite.readthedocs.io/en/latest/index.html`.

Using the Graphite interface

In this recipe, let's familiarize ourselves with the Graphite web interface. Though it looks very simple, it is packed with tons of graphing features. We will look at some of them in this recipe. For graphing, we will use the metrics that are created by `statsd`.

Getting ready

We will be picking some basic metrics from Graphite in order to demonstrate its graphing abilities. Also, let Graphite collect some metrics from `statsd`. It is recommended that you leave the Graphite container up and running for a few minutes before you try this recipe. After, say, 15 minutes, open a new browser tab and navigate to the Graphite web interface at `http://192.168.99.100:8100`.

How to do it...

The left-hand side pane of the Graphite interface is usually the metric chooser. That's where you will be able to find all the metrics that are available in Graphite. There are three tabs:

- **Tree**
- **Search**
- **Auto-Completer**

Lets start with the **Tree** view first.

Tree view

As the name indicates, you can navigate through the tree nodes and view all the metrics available under each path. Clicking on a metric will plot the metric on the graph on the right-hand side pane. In the following screenshot, we have picked the metric at `stats.statsd.processing_time`:

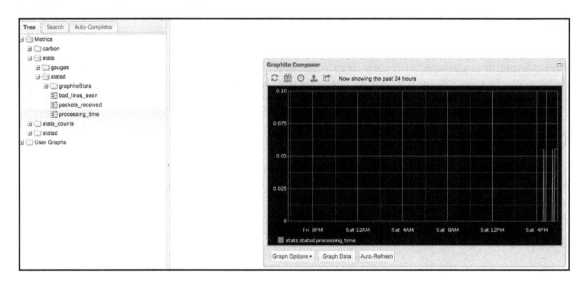

Now let's move on to the graph modal. There are some useful buttons in this modal. First off, there's the **Date Range** button that looks like a calendar. Clicking on this button gives you two calendars where you can choose the from and to dates and times. This way, you can focus on the time window that you are interested in. It looks something like this:

The next useful button in the modal is the **Select Recent Data** button, which looks like a clock. This option lets you choose the most recent time window in the measure of minutes, hours, days, weeks, months, and years. It looks something like this:

The next button that we would want to use most of the time is the **Short URL** button. This button is used to generate a short URL that we can use to render this graph from outside the Graphite web interface. It internally uses the `Render` API, and these graphs can be embedded in any web page. Sometimes, you would want to modify your graph's appearance, legend, and style. For this purpose, you can use the **Graph Options** button. It has tons of options that you can use to modify the way your graph looks:

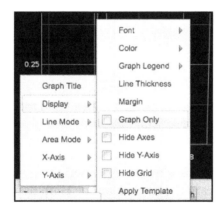

And finally, what if you want to embed multiple metrics on the same graph? You have to plot them all in a single graph. That's where the **Graph Data** button will be useful. If you click on this button, it will open up a modal from where you can choose other metrics, and it will automatically plot them in the underlying graph:

The **Auto Refresh** button is a toggle button that you can enable to automatically refresh the graph. It is useful to keep this option turned on, but keep in mind that it makes several requests frequently, and it might slow down your dashboard if you have lot of graphs that have this option enabled. By default, if this option is enabled, it refreshes every 60 seconds.

Search

Now lets move on to the next tab: **Search**. This tab might (depending on the version) be disabled if you are logged in as root user. So go ahead and logout. As the name indicates, the **Search** tab is used to search for any metrics under the given path. If you enter stats in the search bar and hit *Enter*, you should see all the matching metric names in the results section. Clicking on a metric from the result section will plot the metric on the graph in the right-side pane. Clicking on the same metric again will remove it from the plotted graph. To get more help on the **Search** feature, just click on the **Help** hyperlink. The following screenshot shows the results for the stats keyword:

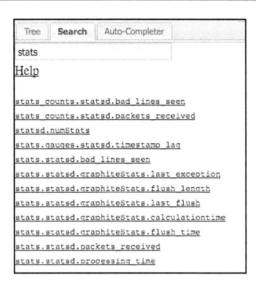

Auto-Completer

The **Auto-Completer** mode is very similar to the **Search** mode except for the fact that the search textbox has autocomplete enabled. The other difference between these two modes is that in **Auto-Completer** mode, you have to navigate to the metric in order to plot it. Use *Tab* to select a suggestion in **Auto-Completer** mode. The results pane is not very helpful in this mode. It is surprising why these two modes have been separated into two different tabs. It would make a lot of sense to merge their features and keep them together in a single tab. The following screenshot illustrates how the **Auto-Completer** mode works:

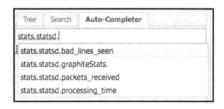

Graphite

The other important page in Graphite is the **Dashboard** page on the top right. The **Dashboard** view is used to create multiple graphs and create a dashboard. You can in fact save the graphs and dashboards and use them later. As we have not mapped the docker volume that hold the dashboards, we might not be able to recover them after we recreate the container. But in production mode, when you are running it elsewhere, keep in mind that the graphs and dashboards should be recoverable. Refer to the documentation of this container to see which volume holds what information. You can perform all the operations that we just went through on the **Dashboard** page as well. The following screenshot shows how you can create your own dashboard:

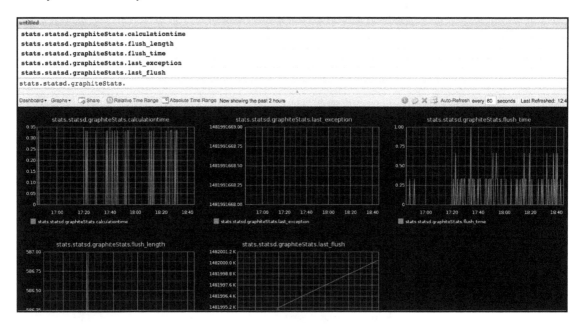

As you can see, the top section is where you choose the metrics, and the bottom section is where you customize your dashboard. There are several options that you can perform on this dashboard. I will leave it to you as an exercise to explore the **Dashboard** view. If you are wondering why you would need another tool such as Grafana when Graphite already has most of the graphing capabilities, the answer is-wait until you see the abilities of Grafana. Grafana's only focus is building monitoring systems. We will learn more about it in later recipes of this chapter.

That brings us to the end of this recipe. In this recipe, we have learned how to use the Graphite web interface. Now you know how powerful Graphite's web interface is. In fact, Graphite lets you create sophisticated graphs, save them, and share them. In the next few recipes, we will be exporting the metrics that we created in the geolocation application over to Graphite and plot them on graphs using Grafana.

Exporting Dropwizard metrics over to Graphite

In the early recipes of this chapter, we learned how to create metrics using Dropwizard's Codahale library. Later, we learned how to start Graphite using Docker and understood the basics of using the Graphite interface. In this recipe, we will be exporting the metrics we created in the geolocation application over to this Graphite instance, which will then be used by Grafana for graphing.

Getting ready

As we will be working on the geolocation application, follow these steps:

1. Open the STS IDE.
2. Navigate to the `geolocation` project, and get ready for the next step.
3. Start Graphite if you haven't done so. You can use the `docker-compose-graphite.yml` file that we created earlier to start Graphite.

How to do it...

The geolocation application currently exposes two metrics using the Codahale `MetricRegistry`: `geolocationWriteRequestCount` and `geolocationLastWriteTime`. There were two methods we used to view these metrics: using Spring's `/metrics` endpoint and using the `ConsoleReporter`.

In this recipe, we will be using a different type of report to report our metrics to Graphite. Can you guess the name of this reporter? Yes, you got it right. It is `GraphiteReporter`:

1. For the first step, let's comment out the `ConsoleReporter` as we will not need it anymore. Going forward, if we want to look at our metrics, we can always use the Graphite web interface or the `/metrics` endpoint. After you have commented out the `ConsoleReporter`, go ahead and add the below dependency to your pom.xml file:

```
<dependency>
  <groupId>io.dropwizard.metrics</groupId>
  <artifactId>metrics-graphite</artifactId>
</dependency>
```

2. Perform a maven update on the project to download the new dependency. Now add the following snippet to the `init` method right after the commented-out block:

```
Graphite graphite = new Graphite(new InetSocketAddress("192.168.99.100",
2003));
GraphiteReporter graphiteReporter =
GraphiteReporter.forRegistry(metricRegistry)
.prefixedWith("com.packt.microservices.geolocation")
.convertRatesTo(TimeUnit.SECONDS)
.convertDurationsTo(TimeUnit.MILLISECONDS)
.filter(MetricFilter.ALL)
.build(graphite);
graphiteReporter.start(60, TimeUnit.SECONDS);
```

3. There are six things to talk about here:

   - Firstly, the port on which we are connecting to Graphite. Port number 2003 is where the Carbon plaintext listener is running. If you would like to use the Pickle protocol mode, you will be using port 2004.

 To learn how to use Pickle mode, take a look at this page: `http://metrics .dropwizard.io/3.1.0/manual/graphite`.

- The `prefixedWith()` method says that any metric created on this `MetricRegistry` should be prefixed with the label `com.packt.microservices.geolocation`. This is mainly used to group our metrics together.
- We already know what the `convertRatesTo()` and `convertDurationsTo()` methods are used for.
- The `filter()` method is used to filter any metrics from being reported to Graphite. In our case, we want all our metrics to report to Graphite, so we have used `MetricFilter.ALL`, which instructs Codahale to export all metrics.

4. Finally, the interesting part is our publish interval. We have set the publish interval to 60 seconds. The reason we moved from 10 seconds to 60 is that when you are building a production-level application and your application is scaled, you will end up creating tons of metrics during each interval. Setting it to a granularity of 10 seconds might be too much. That is the reason we are going with a higher granularity of 60 seconds. But this is completely left to you to choose. It also depends on the type of metric you are reporting. If you would like to go with a different interval, feel free to do so.

5. Now, our application is completely ready to start publishing metrics over to Graphite. Go ahead and start the application as a Spring Boot application. Once your application has started, create two geolocations using the following two `curl` commands and try to get them using another `curl` command:

```
curl -H "Content-Type: application/json" -X POST -d '{"timestamp":
1468203975, "userId": "f1196aac-470e-11e6-beb8-9e71128cae77", "latitude":
41.803488, "longitude": -88.144040}' http://localhost:8080/geolocation
    curl -H "Content-Type: application/json" -X POST -d '{"timestamp":
1468203975, "userId": "f1196aac-470e-11e6-beb8-9e71128cae77", "latitude":
9.568012, "longitude": 77.962444}' http://localhost:8080/geolocation
    curl http://localhost:8080/geolocation
```

6. After executing these three CURL commands, wait *60* seconds. The reason we are waiting 60 seconds is because we have set the reporting interval to 60 seconds in our code. So by then, we can expect to see some metrics on the Graphite web interface.

7. Open a new browser tab and navigate to the Graphite web interface at `http://192.168.99.100:8100`. You should now see a new tree grouping for our metrics at `com.packt.microservices.geolocation`. The following screenshot shows how they would look like in Graphite's **Tree** view:

8. Now, there are two ways to look at your metrics stored in Graphite. The first approach is something we are already familiar with: the **Graphs** interface. The **Graphs** interface gives you a graph with all the values plotted on the graph. But this view might not be very helpful all the time.

9. Now let's look at the next approach. Graphite has a sophisticated REST API. It has two APIs: `Metrics` and `Render`. The `Metrics` API is used to search for metrics. You can use this to perhaps build a metrics discovery system. The `Render` API, however, is what we really need. As the name indicates, it is used to render metric values in various formats, such as graphs, CSV, JSON, PDF, and PNG.

To learn more about the REST APIs available in Graphite, visit their documentation page at `https://graphite-api.readthedocs.io/en/latest/api.html`.

10. Now let's look at how to use the `Render` API to query our metrics. The `Render` API requires two query parameters: `target` and `format`. The `target` parameter indicates the path at which the metrics value can be located. The `format` parameter, however, tells which format you would like your metric to be displayed in. By default, if you do not provide the format, it renders the data in PNG format. But that's not what we want; we want to see the actual data. For that, we might want to use the JSON format.

11. Open a new browser tab and paste this URL:

```
http://192.168.99.100:8100/render?target=com.packt.microservices.geolocatio
n.geolocationWriteRequestCount.count&format=json
```

12. The previous URL says that we are rendering the metric value at
    `com.packt.microservices.geolocation.geolocationWriteRequestCoun
    t.count` and the format that we have requested is JSON. See how we have
    appended `.count` to the metric name. If you want to verify, look at how the
    metric value is stored in Graphite from the tree view of the web interface. You
    will see that the leaf node is called `count` for all metrics of the counter type. This
    URL would have given you something like this:

```
[
  {
    "target":
"com.packt.microservices.geolocation.geolocationWriteRequestCount.count",
    "datapoints": [
      [
        null,
        1481917380
      ],
      [
        null,
        1481917440
      ],
      .
      .
      .
      [
        2,
        1482003720
      ]
    ]
  }
]
```

13. You will notice that there are several data points. We are particularly interested
    in the most recent data point, which will be usually populated as the last data
    point. If you scroll all the way down in your browser, you will see that the last
    data point is populated with the value 2, indicating that we have received two
    write requests for the `geolocation` API so far. Though it is difficult to work
    with such a huge JSON file, it is very useful when you are debugging. In fact, you
    can use the `from` and `until` parameters to specify a time range to query just the
    data points that were recorded during that time range.

14. The `Render` API is much more sophisticated with a lot of query parameters, such as `bgColor` and `areaMode`. Take a look at Graphite's documentation to learn more about the API before you start using it.

That brings us to the end of this recipe. We learned how to use Graphite to store metrics and also learned about the `Render` API that Graphite offers to view metrics.

Exporting Spring Boot Actuator metrics over to Graphite

In the previous recipe we learned how to export the metrics we created using Codahale over to Graphite. In this recipe, we will see how we can expose some metrics Spring Boot offers. Unfortunately, at this moment, the `MetricRegistry` does not expose all the metrics that Spring Boot offers. Only few of them are created using Codahale. If you take a look at the metrics that are available in `/metrics`, most of them are JVM related. So in this recipe, we will find another way to expose the JVM metrics via Codahale.

Getting ready

In this recipe, we will be adding a Maven dependency and some Java code to the `geolocation` project. So open up your STS IDE and navigate to the geolocation project. Make sure your Graphite instance is up and running. If not, start it using the `docker-compose-graphite.yml` file we created.

How to do it...

1. In this recipe, we are going to expose some JVM metrics using Codahale. This will be exported to Graphite automatically as we have configured the `GraphiteReporter` to expose metrics every 60 seconds. Add the following Maven dependency to the `pom.xml` file:

```
<dependency>
  <groupId>io.dropwizard.metrics</groupId>
  <artifactId>metrics-jvm</artifactId>
  <version>3.1.2</version>
</dependency>
```

2. Note that we have added a version to this dependency. That is because this is not
   the default in the parent POM, and we will have to use our own version in the
   child POM. Now, add the following snippet as the last line of the init() method
   in the MetricSystem.java bean:

```
metricRegistry.registerAll(new MetricSet() {
  @Override
  public Map<String, Metric> getMetrics() {

    Map<String, Metric> metrics = new HashMap<>();
    metrics.put("geolocationMemoryUsage", new MemoryUsageGaugeSet());
    metrics.put("geolocationClassLoading", new ClassLoadingGaugeSet());
    metrics.put("geolocationGarbageCollector", new
GarbageCollectorMetricSet());
    return metrics;
  }
});
```

> The previous snippet illustrates how you can register metric sets to the
> MetricRegistry. All the three sets-MemoryUsageGaugeSet,
> ClassLoadingGaugeSet and GarbageCollectorMetricSet come with
> the metrics-jvm dependency. There are also other sets like
> BufferPoolMericSet, CachedThreadStatesGaugeSet,
> ThreadStateGaugeSet and so on. You can try them out one by one as an
> exercise.

3. Now let's test it out. Start the application as a Spring Boot application, open a
   new browser tab, and navigate to http://localhost:8080/metrics. This
   time, you should see a bunch of JVM-related metrics that start with the keyword
   geolocation. If you navigate to the Graphite web interface after 60 seconds, you
   will see those metrics listed under the tree.

The following screenshot illustrates how it will look like in the **Tree** view of the Graphite web interface:

As you can see, we now have three new groupings: `geolocationClassLoading`, `geolocationGargbageCollector`, and `geolocationMemoryUsage`. It is recommended that you take some time to explore these three metric groups and the kind of metrics they expose.

That brings us to the end of this recipe. We learned how to configure and expose JVM metrics using Codahale over to Graphite. In the next few recipes, we will learn how to use these metrics to create valuable graphs using Grafana.

Setting up Grafana using Docker

So far in this chapter, we have learned the basics of monitoring. We laid out the foundation of our monitoring system: our metrics. We learned how to create metrics using Dropwizard's Codahale library. We then spun off a brand-new Graphite instance. Later, we exported the metrics that we created over to Graphite. In the rest of the recipes of this chapter, we will be learning more about a tool called Grafana and how it can be used in monitoring our microservices.

Getting ready

Instead of running Grafana on its own using the `docker run` command, we will be adding it to the `docker-compose` YAML file that holds Graphite. The reason we are doing this is because they are closely related to each other though they need not be linked. Before we jump in, let's take some time to understand what Grafana is. Grafana is an open source tool for metrics visualization. The Grafana interface is sophisticated enough that it be used to create several types of graphs. Very recently, Grafana came up with their notification system, where you will be alerted when a certain metric exceeds its threshold. The beauty of this feature is that it can alert you not just by e-mail but also on Slack, PagerDuty, and webhooks. Now let's open up the STS IDE.

How to do it...

The next few steps in this recipe will help you setup your first Grafana instance using Docker.

1. Open up the YAML file that already has Graphite: `docker-compose-graphite.yml`. Add the following snippet to it:

```
grafana:
  image: grafana/grafana
  ports:
    - "3000:3000"
```

That's all you need to start Grafana. Port `3000` is where the Grafana web interface will be running. We have mapped this port to port `3000` of the host machine. As you can see, there are no links to the Graphite container. The only reason we are keeping these two containers together is because they are both used to build our monitoring system.

2. Now lets stop Graphite if it is already running. Open a new terminal session, and start Grafana and Graphite together using the following command:

```
docker-compose -f docker-compose-graphite.yml up
```

3. The log messages will not be very helpful to identify whether Grafana has started or not. However, you will know that Grafana has started when your log messages stop tailing. You will see something like this:

```
grafana_1  | t=2016-12-17T20:51:27+0000 lvl=info msg="Executing migration" logger=migrator id="create alert table v1"
grafana_1  | t=2016-12-17T20:51:27+0000 lvl=info msg="Executing migration" logger=migrator id="add index alert org_id & id "
grafana_1  | t=2016-12-17T20:51:27+0000 lvl=info msg="Executing migration" logger=migrator id="add index alert state"
grafana_1  | t=2016-12-17T20:51:27+0000 lvl=info msg="Executing migration" logger=migrator id="add index alert dashboard_id"
grafana_1  | t=2016-12-17T20:51:27+0000 lvl=info msg="Executing migration" logger=migrator id="create alert_notification table
grafana_1  | t=2016-12-17T20:51:27+0000 lvl=info msg="Executing migration" logger=migrator id="Add column is_default"
grafana_1  | t=2016-12-17T20:51:27+0000 lvl=info msg="Executing migration" logger=migrator id="add index alert_notification or
grafana_1  | t=2016-12-17T20:51:27+0000 lvl=info msg="Executing migration" logger=migrator id="Drop old annotation table v4"
grafana_1  | t=2016-12-17T20:51:27+0000 lvl=info msg="Executing migration" logger=migrator id="create annotation table v5"
grafana_1  | t=2016-12-17T20:51:27+0000 lvl=info msg="Executing migration" logger=migrator id="add index annotation 0 v3"
grafana_1  | t=2016-12-17T20:51:27+0000 lvl=info msg="Executing migration" logger=migrator id="add index annotation 1 v3"
grafana_1  | t=2016-12-17T20:51:27+0000 lvl=info msg="Executing migration" logger=migrator id="add index annotation 2 v3"
grafana_1  | t=2016-12-17T20:51:27+0000 lvl=info msg="Executing migration" logger=migrator id="add index annotation 3 v3"
grafana_1  | t=2016-12-17T20:51:27+0000 lvl=info msg="Executing migration" logger=migrator id="add index annotation 4 v3"]
grafana_1  | t=2016-12-17T20:51:27+0000 lvl=info msg="Created default admin user: [admin]"
grafana_1  | t=2016-12-17T20:51:27+0000 lvl=info msg="Starting plugin search" logger=plugins
grafana_1  | t=2016-12-17T20:51:27+0000 lvl=warn msg="Plugin dir does not exist" logger=plugins dir=/var/lib/grafana/plugins
grafana_1  | t=2016-12-17T20:51:27+0000 lvl=info msg="Plugin dir created" logger=plugins dir=/var/lib/grafana/plugins
grafana_1  | t=2016-12-17T20:51:27+0000 lvl=info msg="Initializing Alerting" logger=alerting.engine
grafana_1  | t=2016-12-17T20:51:27+0000 lvl=info msg="Initializing CleanUpService" logger=cleanup
```

4. Now that your Grafana and Graphite instances are up and running, let's open the Grafana web interface. Open a new browser session and enter this URL to open Grafana: `http://192.168.99.100:3000`.

5. You will be taken to the login page. Grafana has a very good login mechanism. It even has integration with LDAP:

By default, the username and password are both set to `admin`.

6. So enter the credentials on the login page and hit **Log in**. On the home page, you will see that we do not have any dashboards, apps, panels, or data sources created:

7. The top navigation pane of Grafana is very useful. It has pretty much all the quick action buttons you will need while viewing your dashboards:

8. The first button, which has the Grafana icon, is the main menu. Clicking on that will open links to pretty much all the options and configurations.

The **Home** button acts as a quick-action bar to navigate to all the **Dashboards** you have in this instance of Grafana.

9. The next useful section in the top navigation bar is the **Refresh Range** section. Clicking on the default refresh range, **Last 6 hours**, will open a section where you can configure the time range as well as the refresh interval. This is a very sophisticated section.

That's pretty much a very high-level overview of the Grafana interface. There are still lots of features that Grafana offers. We will look at them in later recipes. With that, we've come to the end of this recipe.

Configuring Grafana to use Graphite

We now have a working version of Graphite and Grafana configured using the `docker-compose` YAML file. In this recipe, we will be configuring Grafana to use the Graphite instance we are using to export our geolocation metrics to. When we have configured Grafana to use the Graphite instance, we will soon be able to utilize the geolocation metrics to create dashboards on Grafana.

Getting ready

Before we jump into the recipe, let's understand a few concepts and terminologies used in Grafana. You will need to understand four entities:

- **Data sources**: Data sources are entities that hold the data required to plot your graphs.
- **Panels**: Panels are individual visualizations that will connect to a data source, query a certain data set, and plot them on a graph, table, single panel stat, or text.
- **Rows**: Rows are group of panels that constitute a row on the dashboard.
- **Dashboards**: Of course, we all know what a dashboard is. The dashboard comprises several rows of panels.

How to do it...

Now guess what we need to create in order to configure Grafana to use the Graphite instance that we have. Yes, you are right; we have to create a data source. Before that, make sure you have both Grafana and Graphite running. If they're not, start them using the `docker-compose` YAML file:

1. Let's start by clicking on the main menu button at the top left of the Grafana page. Then, choose **Data Sources** from the dropdown. On the next screen, click on the **Add data source** button and enter the following values in the form:

   - **Name**: `graphite`
   - **Default**: True (checked)
   - **Type**: **Graphite**
   - **Url**: `http://192.168.99.100:8100`
   - **Access**: **direct**

2. Make sure neither the **Basic Auth** nor the **With Credentials** checkbox is checked:

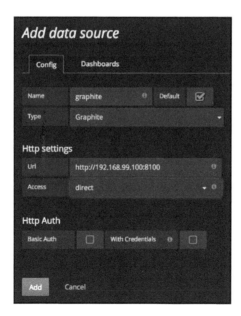

3. After entering the previous values in the form, hit the **Add** button. Right after you hit **Add**, Grafana will try to ping Graphite with the connection parameters that we provided here. If your connection is successful, you will receive a success message on the same screen:

If for some reason Grafana is not able to connect to Graphite, you will receive an error message with details. Most of the times, the error could either be that Graphite is not running or you have not mapped the Graphite ports, or that you are behind a proxy. Make sure you've set up everything right and try again.

4. Now go back to the **Data Sources** page, and you should see the newly created Graphite data source:

5. Here, you will have two types of views: the **grid view** and the **list view**. In older versions of Grafana, the grid view is the default for some reason. However, the list view is a better view as it shows the complete URL. The list view looks something like this:

This clarifies that our data source was added successfully; in other words, Grafana has been configured to use our Graphite instance.

That brings us to the end of this simple recipe.

Configuring Grafana dashboards to view metrics

So far, we've learned how to use Graphite and Grafana. In this recipe, we will learn how to create dashboards and panels using Grafana. Ideally, Grafana dashboards will be displayed on a big screen in a space where developers (or concerned people) can see them so that any odd behavior in the graphs will be clearly visible to the developers.

Getting ready

In this recipe, we will be utilizing two metrics from the `geolocation` JVM and the two metrics that we created using Codahale. These four metrics will be plotted on graphs in the dashboard.

1. First, make sure Graphite and Grafana are up and running. If they're not, start them using the `docker-compose` YAML file.
2. Next, make sure your geolocation application is up and running. If it's not, start it from your STS IDE as a Spring Boot application.

How to do it...

1. In order to generate some metrics, execute the following `curl` commands to create two geolocations:

```
curl -H "Content-Type: application/json" -X POST -d '{"timestamp":
1468203975, "userId": "f1196aac-470e-11e6-beb8-9e71128cae77", "latitude":
41.803488, "longitude": -88.144040}' http://localhost:8080/geolocation
   curl -H "Content-Type: application/json" -X POST -d '{"timestamp":
1468203975, "userId": "f1196aac-470e-11e6-beb8-9e71128cae77", "latitude":
9.568012, "longitude": 77.962444}' http://localhost:8080/geolocation
   curl http://localhost:8080/geolocation
```

2. Now, in order to generate some metrics, let the geolocation microservice, Graphite, and Grafana run for a few minutes. The reason we are doing this is to publish some metrics to Graphite. After, say, 15 minutes, go to a new browser session and navigate to the Grafana URL at `http://192.168.99.100:3000`.

3. In Grafana, change the refresh window from 6 hours to 15 minutes. Click on **Home** and then select the **Create New** button. In the next section, you will see an empty row with some panel options, such as **Graphs**, **Singlestat**, **Table**, **Text**, **Alert List**, **Dashboard list**, and **Plugin list**:

4. Before we add any new panels, let's first name our dashboard. Click on the gear button in the top navigation pane and select **Settings**. In the **Settings** section, enter the value of **Name** as `Geolocation Microservice`, and click on the **Save** button in the top navigation bar.

5. Now select **Graph** from the choice of panels. If your row was already created, hover over the three dots on the left side of the row and select **Add Panel** and then choose **Graph**. You will see an empty graph with no data. In order to edit this graph, click on the graph name **Panel Title** and select **Edit**.

6. In the **Edit** pane, navigate to the **Metrics** tab. Then, select the metric value `com.packt.microservices.geolocation.geolocationMemoryUsage.heap.used`. After you have selected the metric, you will see that the graph is plotted with some metrics. Now let's duplicate this metric and add another metric to the same graph. Click on the hamburger menu button and select **Duplicate**:

7. This time, use the metric `com.packt.microservice.geolocation.geolocationMemoryUsage.heap.committed`. Once you have added both the metrics, you will see that there are two lines, one for each metric:

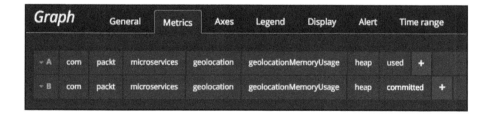

8. We now have to change the unit of our *Left Y* axis to **bytes**. Go to the **Axes** tab and select **data (Metric)** / **bytes** as the **Unit**:

9. Before you save this panel, let's give it a nice header. Go to the **General** section and change the **Title** to JVM Heap. In order to save this panel, hit the small **x** in the top-right section of this pane:

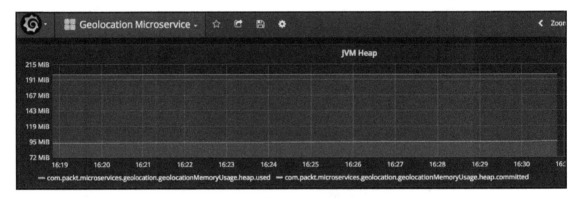

10. Now let's create panels for the other two metrics, geolocationLastWriteTime and geolocationWriteRequestCount. How about creating a new row for these two panels? Click on the **Add Row** button at the bottom of the existing row. Now add a new graph and configure it with the name geolocationWriteRequestCount and metric com.microservices.geolocation.geolocationWriteRequestCount.coun t. Let's add a new panel for geolocationLastWriteTime. Hover over the three dots on the left-hand side of this panel and choose **Add Panel**:

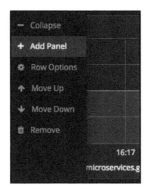

11. Configure the second panel in this row with the name
    `geolocationLastWriteTime` and metric value
    `com.microservices.geolocation.geolocationLastWriteTime`. Make sure
    you change the unit for the *Left Y* axis to **none/none**. After you have configured
    both the panels, close the configuration pane by hitting the **x** button.

12. Finally, save the dashboard by hitting the **Save** button from the top navigation
    bar. Your final dashboard will look something like this:

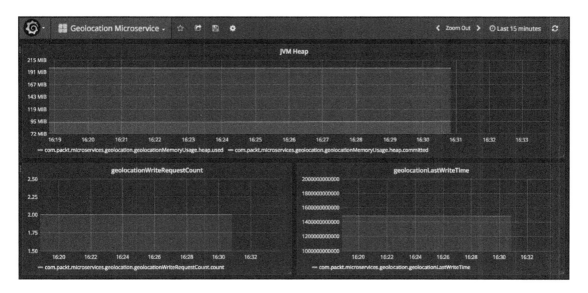

As you can see, I have added some titles to the panels in the second row. That's it! We now have our first monitoring platform for our microservice. The previous illustration might be pretty simple, but the capabilities of Grafana and Graphite are awesome if we use it in the right way. We did not go in detail into either Graphite or Grafana. But I'll leave that to you as an exercise as our goal was primarily to demonstrate the abilities of these tools. Grafana in fact gets more interesting with the use of alerts. I strongly recommend you try them before you start using it in your production environment. Good luck monitoring!

7
Building Asynchronous Streaming Systems with Kafka and Spark

In this chapter, you will learn the following recipes:

- Setting up Kafka using Docker
- Creating Kafka topics to stream data
- Writing a streaming program using Kafka Streams
- Improving the performance of the Kafka Streams program
- Writing a streaming program using Apache Spark
- Improving the performance of the Spark job
- Aggregating logs into Kafka using Log4J
- Integrating Kafka with log management systems

Introduction

Streaming has been picking up traction lately. It is one way of processing your data. In fact, there are two modes in which your data processing application can operate: batching and streaming. In batching, you work on batches of datasets at frequent intervals. However, in streaming, you process data as it gets streamed. This mode has always been a challenge. Achieving this type of streaming behavior will open up a lot of different opportunities.

You could make things happen quickly. For example, a banking application can send you relevant coupons based on your spending activity. Or a shopping application can recommend products based on your viewing activity. And all this will happen right away instead of waiting until the middle of the night for a batch job to run. Streaming has become a critical part of many businesses these days. The past couple of years have seen a tremendous improvement in streaming technologies. Frameworks such as Apex, Storm, Spark, Flink, Kafka Streams, and Samza, to name a few, are some popular streaming frameworks being used a lot these days. A streaming framework will make sense only when you have a supporting messaging system. Kafka, RabbitMQ, and Zero MQ, to name a few, are examples of popular messaging systems. In this chapter, we will focus more on Spark and Kafka.

Setting up Kafka using Docker

In order to demonstrate streaming, we first require a streaming endpoint. A streaming endpoint could be a TCP socket, messaging destination, and so on. In this chapter, we will use Kafka heavily to demonstrate its streaming abilities. In this recipe, we will learn how to set up Kafka using Docker Compose. Before we jump into the recipe and start orchestrating a Kafka instance, let's first take some time to understand how Kafka works.

Kafka

According to Kafka's documentation, it is a distributed streaming platform. It is distributed because it has clustering abilities and is fault tolerant. Achieving fault tolerance is not very easy. But Kafka's architecture makes it fault tolerant and, at the same time, simple to work with and understand. Simplicity is one of the reasons Kafka is being adopted by lot of organizations. At the same time, it is very powerful. It can handle a huge amount of data at once. Kafka utilizes Zookeeper for most of its clustering mechanism. It is a streaming platform because it has the ability to work on streams of datasets as they come through the destinations.

In the simplest terms, Kafka is a powerful pub-sub messaging system. If you come from a Java background and have experience working with JMS (Java Message Service), then you might have already guessed what Kafka could be.

There are two types of communication mechanisms possible in any messaging system:

- Point-to-point
- Pub-sub

Point-to-point mechanism

Point-to-point is where a message producer sends messages to a queue, which is then picked up by a message consumer. There can be any number of message consumers listening on the queue; however, only one consumer can consume each message.

Pub-sub mechanism

In a **pub-sub** mechanism, producers publish messages to a topic, which is then broadcasted to all the consumers subscribed to the topic. So each consumer in a pub-sub mechanism will receive one copy of all the messages. Kafka offers both of these modes with the help of topics.

Kafka terminology

There are five terminologies you have to know before you start working with Kafka:

- Brokers
- Topics
- Partitions
- Producers
- Consumers

Brokers

Brokers are nothing but Kafka servers that will host your topics and logs inside your topics.

Topics

Topics are destinations that are used in Kafka. Each topic is partitioned into multiple ordered partitions of messages.

Partitions

Partitions differentiate Kafka from other messaging systems. And they make the working of Kafka much more efficient and faster.

Producers and consumers

Producers produce messages in topics whereas **consumers** consume messages from topics.

The following diagram provides a high-level idea of how Kafka works:

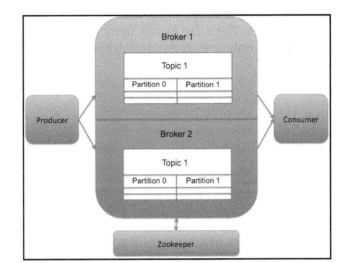

In the preceding diagram, you can see that there are two brokers in a cluster. There is one topic called **Topic 1** on both the brokers in the cluster. The topic has two partitions. Ideally, each broker will take ownership of one partition, and the other broker will have a replica of that partition. For example, if **Broker 1** owns **Partition 0** in **Topic 1**, then there will be a replica of **Partition 0** in **Broker 2** as well. In other words, **Broker 1** is the leader for **Partition 0** of **Topic 1**. I hope you are able to grasp the basics of Kafka. We will learn some advanced concepts about Kafka later in this chapter, but for now, this should give you a good head start.

Getting ready

Kafka requires Zookeeper in order to operate. It uses Zookeeper mainly for electing a controller, storing configurations of topics, storing member information of the cluster, and so on. At the time of writing this, it is not possible to run Kafka without Zookeeper. So, obviously, we will need two containers: Kafka and Zookeeper. Go ahead and open up your STS IDE and navigate to the `geolocation` project.

How to do it...

We will use Docker Compose to orchestrate Kafka. Go ahead and create a new YML file called `docker-compose-kafka.yml` directly under the `geolocation` project. Then, add the following snippet to the newly created Docker Compose file:

```
version: "2"

services:
  zookeeper:
    image: wurstmeister/zookeeper
    ports:
      - "2181:2181"
  kafka:
    image: wurstmeister/kafka:0.10.1.0-1
    ports:
      - "9092:9092"
    environment:
      KAFKA_ADVERTISED_HOST_NAME: 192.168.99.100
      KAFKA_ZOOKEEPER_CONNECT: zookeeper:2181
    volumes:
      - /var/run/docker.sock:/var/run/docker.sock
```

As you can see, we have not used any official images. At the time of writing this, there is no official image for Kafka. However, there are Kafka images listed under the Confluent organization in Docker Hub. Confluent is the company behind Kafka and the Confluent platform. It was built by a few of the early committers of Kafka back from LinkedIn. The company is primarily focused on providing streaming solutions and products to build data pipelines and platforms.

Port 2181 of Zookeeper has been mapped to the same port on the host. Similarly, port 9092 of Kafka has been mapped to the same port on the host. Port 9092 is where Kafka will be listening.

There are two required environment variables: KAFKA_ADVERTISED_HOST_NAME and KAFKA_ZOOKEEPER_CONNECT. The KAFKA_ADVERTISED_HOST_NAME property defines the hostname to which Kafka will bind to. The KAFKA_ZOOKEEPER_CONNECT property is required to specify the URL to Zookeeper. As both the images are in the same Docker Compose YML file, we have referenced the hostname of Zookeeper as zookeeper itself, which happens to be the name of the Zookeeper service.

You might be wondering why we have exposed the Docker socket file as a volume. The Docker image that we are using needs to run some Docker commands from inside the container. So it needs the Docker daemon. Once you get a hold of the socket file, you can run any operation you want. Though this doesn't sound very secure, it is still okay as it is only our local development environment.

1. Now let's spin off our first Kafka broker using Docker Compose. Open up a new terminal session and run the following docker-compose command:

   ```
   docker-compose -f docker-compose-kafka.yml up
   ```

2. You should see something like this when Kafka has started:

```
kafka_1      | [2016-12-19 23:05:08,193] INFO 1001 successfully elected as leader (kafka.server.ZookeeperLeaderElector)
kafka_1      | [2016-12-19 23:05:08,303] INFO [ExpirationReaper-1001], Starting  (kafka.server.DelayedOperationPurgatory$Expired(
kafka_1      | [2016-12-19 23:05:08,323] INFO [ExpirationReaper-1001], Starting  (kafka.server.DelayedOperationPurgatory$Expired(
kafka_1      | [2016-12-19 23:05:08,331] INFO [ExpirationReaper-1001], Starting  (kafka.server.DelayedOperationPurgatory$Expired(
kafka_1      | [2016-12-19 23:05:08,349] INFO [GroupCoordinator 1001]: Starting up. (kafka.coordinator.GroupCoordinator)
kafka_1      | [2016-12-19 23:05:08,368] INFO [GroupCoordinator 1001]: Startup complete. (kafka.coordinator.GroupCoordinator)
kafka_1      | [2016-12-19 23:05:08,371] INFO [Group Metadata Manager on Broker 1001]: Removed 0 expired offsets in 1 millisecon(
kafka_1      | [2016-12-19 23:05:08,455] INFO Will not load MX4J, mx4j-tools.jar is not in the classpath (kafka.utils.Mx4jLoader!
zookeeper_1  | 2016-12-19 23:05:08,269 [myid:] - INFO  [ProcessThread(sid:0 cport:2181)::PrepRequestProcessor@649] - Got user-le\
91954d3060000 type:delete cxid:0x35 zxid:0x18 txntype:-1 reqpath:n/a Error Path:/admin/preferred_replica_election Error:KeeperEr\
tion
zookeeper_1  | 2016-12-19 23:05:08,552 [myid:] - INFO  [ProcessThread(sid:0 cport:2181)::PrepRequestProcessor@649] - Got user-le\
91954d3060000 type:create cxid:0x40 zxid:0x19 txntype:-1 reqpath:n/a Error Path:/brokers Error:KeeperErrorCode = NodeExists for /
kafka_1      | [2016-12-19 23:05:08,538] INFO Creating /brokers/ids/1001 (is it secure? false) (kafka.utils.ZKCheckedEphemeral)
kafka_1      | [2016-12-19 23:05:08,569] INFO Result of znode creation is: OK (kafka.utils.ZKCheckedEphemeral)
kafka_1      | [2016-12-19 23:05:08,578] INFO Registered broker 1001 at path /brokers/ids/1001 with addresses: PLAINTEXT -> EndP(
kUtils)
kafka_1      | [2016-12-19 23:05:08,579] WARN No meta.properties file under dir /kafka/kafka-logs-39f32d8d150e/meta.properties (I
kafka_1      | [2016-12-19 23:05:08,609] INFO New leader is 1001 (kafka.server.ZookeeperLeaderElector$LeaderChangeListener)
kafka_1      | [2016-12-19 23:05:08,661] INFO Kafka version : 0.10.1.0 (org.apache.kafka.common.utils.AppInfoParser)
kafka_1      | [2016-12-19 23:05:08,662] INFO Kafka commitId : 3402a74efb23d1d4 (org.apache.kafka.common.utils.AppInfoParser)
```

3. Now that our Kafka broker is up and running, the next step is to verify whether it started successfully. It would be great if Kafka had a UI admin interface. Currently, there are a few third-party apps that can be used with Kafka, such as Kafka Manager and Kafka UI. For this chapter, we will not need one. So if you are interested in having one, feel free to try them out and see which one fits your needs. Throughout this chapter, we will need a client that can be used to perform operations such as creating topics, consuming messages, and producing messages. We will be making use of some of the shell scripts that come with the Kafka installation for that.

4. So download version `2-11-0.10.1.0` from the Apache Kafka website at `https://kafka.apache.org/downloads`. The version number is split into two parts. `2-11` indicates the version of Scala that was used to build this version of Kafka. `0.10.1.0` is the actual version of Kafka.

5. After your download is complete, unpack Kafka to any directory in your computer. Open a new terminal session and change the directory to the Kafka directory. Now execute the following command (Windows users, use the binary equivalent for Windows):

```
./bin/kafka-topics.sh --list --zookeeper 192.168.99.100:2181
```

6. The preceding command is used to list all the topics available in your broker. Look how we have passed the Zookeeper URL instead of Kafka's. That is because the broker is located using Zookeeper. If the command returned any errors, then you didn't install Kafka correctly, or you don't have the right Zookeeper URL. Most of the time, it is something to do with the hostname and IP of Zookeeper. If your installation was successful, you will not get any output for this command, as we do not have any topic in this broker.

That brings us to the end of this recipe. In the next few recipes, we will put Kafka into action. Go Kafka!

Creating Kafka topics to stream data

In the previous recipe, we orchestrated our Kafka broker. The next step is obviously putting Kafka to action. In order to do that, we need some topics to work with. In this recipe, we will create some topics and will also learn how to produce and consume messages. Exchanging messages can be done in two ways: scripts and Java programs. We will be learning the Java way.

Getting ready

In this recipe, we will be using the same Kafka topics script to create topics:

1. Open a new terminal shell and navigate to the directory where you have Kafka installed.
2. Let's create a new topic called `geolocations`. We will then write a basic standalone producer program that will produce geolocations for this topic. We will integrate a consumer with our geolocation application that will consume all messages produced by our standalone producer.
3. So now, our geolocation application will have two modes in which you can store geolocations: synchronous HTTP mode and asynchronous mode using Kafka. It is still possible to make your HTTP APIs work asynchronous.
4. We will not be going in depth into that topic. For illustration, we will consider our HTTP endpoint to be synchronous and our Kafka endpoint to be, obviously, asynchronous.
5. Before we jump into the actual recipe, let's comment out some unused code from the geolocation application. From the previous chapter, if you have either `ConsoleReporter` or `GraphiteReporter` configured, comment them both out.

How to do it...

The next few steps in this recipe will help you create your first Kafka Producer and Kafka Consumer programs.

1. Let's create a new topic called `geolocations`. Go ahead and execute the following command in your terminal shell:

```
./bin/kafka-topics.sh --create --zookeeper 192.168.99.100:2181 --
replication-factor 1 --partitions 2 --topic geolocations
      Created topic "geolocations".
```

There are a few things to talk about here. First, let's talk about the `replication-factor` option. The **replication factor** says how many replicas Kafka needs to maintain for each partition in the topic. It depends on the cluster size and configuration. In our case, we have set it to 1. The `partitions` option, as the name indicates, is the number of partitions this topic needs to have. The `topic` argument indicates the name of our topic. And, of course, we need the `zookeeper` argument to locate our broker:

1. Now that our topic is ready, let's create a simple Kafka producer. Add the following Maven dependency to the `pom.xml` file:

```
<dependency>
  <groupId>org.apache.kafka</groupId>
  <artifactId>kafka-clients</artifactId>
  <version>0.10.1.0</version>
</dependency>
```

2. Create a new class in the geolocation repo called `com.packt.microservices.geolocation.GeoLocationProducer.java`.

3. Add the following snippet to the newly created producer:

```
package com.packt.microservices.geolocation;

import java.util.Arrays;
import java.util.List;
import java.util.Properties;

import org.apache.kafka.clients.producer.KafkaProducer;
import org.apache.kafka.clients.producer.Producer;
import org.apache.kafka.clients.producer.ProducerRecord;
import org.apache.kafka.common.serialization.StringSerializer;

public class GeoLocationProducer {
```

```
public static void main(String[] args) {
    Properties props = new Properties();
    props.put("bootstrap.servers", "192.168.99.100:9092");
    props.put("key.serializer", StringSerializer.class.getName());
    props.put("value.serializer", StringSerializer.class.getName());
Producer<String, String> producer = new KafkaProducer<>(props);
    List<GeoLocation> geolocations = Arrays.asList(
      new GeoLocation(38.6270, 90.1994),
      new GeoLocation(93.9879, 76.9876), // invalid lat
      new GeoLocation(41.8034, -88.1440),
      new GeoLocation(40.9879, -200.9876), // invalid long
      new GeoLocation(-93.9879, 76.9876), // invalid lat
      new GeoLocation(9.5680, 77.9624),
      new GeoLocation(13.0827, 80.2707),
      new GeoLocation(40.9879, 200.9876), // invalid long
      new GeoLocation(9.9252, 78.1198));

    for(GeoLocation geolocation : geolocations) {
      System.out.println("Sending geolocaiton [" + geolocation.toString() +
"]");
      ProducerRecord<String, String> record = new ProducerRecord<>(
          "geolocations",
          geolocation.toString());
      producer.send(record);
    }

    producer.close();
  }
}
```

4. There are three things to talk about here: `producer`, `geolocations` and `ProducerRecords`. In order to instantiate `producer`, we create a `Properties` object with three properties: `bootstrap.servers`, `key.serializer`, and `value.serializer`:

- The `bootstrap.servers` property indicates the URLs to the Kafka brokers. As our cluster is a single broker cluster, we provide the URL to that broker in this property. If you have multiple brokers, you can provide comma-separated values.
- The `key.serializer` property takes the fully qualified name of the serializer that will be used to serialize the key of the message.
- Likewise, the `value.serializer` property takes the fully qualified name of the serializer that will be used to serialize the value of the message.

5. Later in the code, we create nine geolocations, out of which four are invalid (invalid geolocations have a comment right next to them). Then, for each geolocation, we create a `ProducerRecord`. The constructor of `ProducerRecord` has two arguments: the topic name and the actual message. In this recipe, the topic name is `geolocations`. Let's come back to the actual message later.

6. Also look at how the `ProducerRecord` is defined as a generic of `<String, String>`. The first generic defines the type of the key, and the second defines the type of the value. The key is usually used to assign partitions. In this recipe, the key is not significantly important, so we are going to ignore it. If you would like to use it, then you have to use the appropriate overloaded constructor for `ProducerRecord`. We then invoke the `send()` method on `producer` with the `ProducerRecord`. Finally, the `producer` instance is closed by invoking the `close()` method.

7. Now let's go back to the actual message. It is a `toString()` of the `GeoLocation` class. But wait; we haven't defined a `toString()` method in `GeoLocation`. Let's do it now. We will be converting the `GeoLocation` object to its JSON equivalent.

8. Let's use GSON to do it. GSON is a JSON library from Google and is very easy to use. Go ahead and add the following Maven dependency to the `pom.xml` file:

```
<dependency>
  <groupId>com.google.code.gson</groupId>
  <artifactId>gson</artifactId>
</dependency>
```

9. Now that our dependency is ready, add the following constructors and `toString()` method to `GeoLocation.java`:

```
public GeoLocation() {}

public GeoLocation(double latitude, double longitude) {
    this.latitude = latitude;
    this.longitude = longitude;
    this.userId = UUID.randomUUID();
    this.timestamp = System.currentTimeMillis();
}
@Override
public String toString() {
  return GSON.toJson(this);
}
```

10. GSON is defined as a constant in the same class:

```
private static final Gson GSON = new Gson();
```

11. Now all our geolocations will be sent to the Kafka topic as JSON strings.
12. The next step in this recipe is to build the Kafka consumer that will consume messages from the `geolocations` topic. Go ahead and create a new thread called `com.packt.microservices.geolocation.GeoLocationConsumer.java`.
13. Add the following snippet to the newly created consumer class:

```
package com.packt.microservices.geolocation;

import java.util.Arrays;
import java.util.Properties;

import org.apache.kafka.clients.consumer.ConsumerRecord;
import org.apache.kafka.clients.consumer.ConsumerRecords;
import org.apache.kafka.clients.consumer.KafkaConsumer;
import org.apache.kafka.common.serialization.StringDeserializer;

import com.google.gson.Gson;

public class GeoLocationConsumer implements Runnable {
  private static final Gson GSON = new Gson();
  private static final GeoLocationRepository REPO = new
GeoLocationRepository();

  public void run() {
    Properties props = new Properties();
    props.put("bootstrap.servers", "192.168.99.100:9092");
    props.put("group.id", "geolocationConsumer");
    props.put("key.deserializer", StringDeserializer.class.getName());
    props.put("value.deserializer", StringDeserializer.class.getName());

    try (KafkaConsumer<String, String> consumer = new
KafkaConsumer<>(props)) {
      consumer.subscribe(Arrays.asList("geolocations"));
      while (true) {
        ConsumerRecords<String, String> records = consumer.poll(100);
        for (ConsumerRecord<String, String> record : records) {
          System.out.printf("offset = %d, key = %s, value = %s%n",
              record.offset(),
              record.key(),
              record.value());
          REPO.addGeoLocation(GSON.fromJson(record.value(),
```

```
GeoLocation.class));
        }
    }
    } catch (Exception e) {
        System.err.println("Error while consuming geolocations. Details: " +
e.getMessage());
    }
  }
}
```

14. First, we create a new `KafkaConsumer` with four properties:
    `bootstrap.servers`, `group.id`, `key.deserializer`, and
    `value.deserializer`:

    - The `bootstrap.servers` property is the same as in the producer. We
      will talk about `group.id` later in this chapter. For now, you can keep
      in mind that it is used to group consumers.
    - The `key.deserializer` property will be the fully qualified class
      name of the deserializer that will be used to deserialize the serialized
      key of the message.
    - Likewise, `value.deserializer` is used for the value deserialization
      process. As you can see, the `consumer.subscribe()` method takes an
      argument of string arrays. So you can use the same consumer to
      consume messages from multiple topics. In this case, we have
      subscribed to the `geolocations` topic.

15. In an infinite loop, we create the `ConsumerRecord` instances for each message
    received from the topic. The messages, along with their offset in the topic, their
    key, and value, are printed out.

16. Finally, the message value is converted to `GeoLocation` using GSON and stored
    using the `GeoLocationRepository` class. As we are using an infinite loop, this
    code will run and keep listening for any new messages in the topic and store
    them as they come through.

If you are wondering why we instantiated a new repository instead of autowiring it as a bean, the reason is because Spring beans and threads do not go well with each other. Unfortunately, our consumer must be a thread. So the best way to accomplish this is to instantiate the repository as a regular Java object using the `new` keyword. The side effect of this is that the repository (and hence the in-memory collection) used by the `GeoLocationConsumer` and the `GeoLocationController` will be totally different. Ideally, in a real-time scenario, we would be using a database to store our data. So this situation will not happen. For illustrations, in this recipe, we will be verifying whether our geolocations were created by looking at the `data` directory at `/opt/packt/geolocation/data`.

17. In order to start this thread, add the following snippet to the `main` method of the `GeoLocationApplication.java` class:

```
new Thread(new GeoLocationConsumer()).start();
```

18. That's it. We have our producer and consumer ready. Let's test them out. Start the `GeoLocationApplication.java` class as a Spring Boot application. This time, along with the Spring MVC logs, you should see some Kafka consumer logs too:

```
        ssl.trustmanager.algorithm = PKIX
        ssl.truststore.location = null
        ssl.truststore.password = null
        ssl.truststore.type = JKS
        value.deserializer = class org.apache.kafka.common.serialization.StringDeserializer
2016-12-22 10:46:49.479  INFO 46265 --- [      Thread-4] o.a.kafka.common.utils.AppInfoParser     : Kafka version : 0.10.1.0
2016-12-22 10:46:49.479  INFO 46265 --- [      Thread-4] o.a.kafka.common.utils.AppInfoParser     : Kafka commitId : 3402a74efb23d1d4
2016-12-22 10:46:49.666  INFO 46265 --- [      Thread-4] o.a.k.c.c.internals.AbstractCoordinator  : Discovered coordinator 192.168.99.100:9092 (id: 2147482646 rack: null
2016-12-22 10:46:49.671  INFO 46265 --- [      Thread-4] o.a.k.c.c.internals.ConsumerCoordinator  : Revoking previously assigned partitions [] for group geolocationConsu
2016-12-22 10:46:49.671  INFO 46265 --- [      Thread-4] o.a.k.c.c.internals.AbstractCoordinator  : (Re-)joining group geolocationConsumer
2016-12-22 10:46:51.625  INFO 46265 --- [      Thread-4] o.a.k.c.c.internals.AbstractCoordinator  : Successfully joined group geolocationConsumer with generation 18
2016-12-22 10:46:51.627  INFO 46265 --- [      Thread-4] o.a.k.c.c.internals.ConsumerCoordinator  : Setting newly assigned partitions [geolocations-1, geolocations-0] fc
```

19. Now that our consumer is ready, let's execute the `GeoLocationProducer.java` class as a Java application from your STS IDE. The producer will drop all the nine geolocations into the `geolocations` topic.

20. Now look at the console of your geolocation microservice:

```
offset = 19, key = null, value = {"latitude":93.9879,"longitude":76.9876,"userId":"b6770aa1-fc01-4131-8a70-7a47d36d7602","timestamp":1482425708526}
offset = 20, key = null, value = {"latitude":40.9879,"longitude":-200.9876,"userId":"ae9dd9a7-c5e5-4358-acc7-bf5b93b5d459","timestamp":1482425708527}
offset = 21, key = null, value = {"latitude":9.568,"longitude":77.9624,"userId":"cd9167c0-afac-42eb-8219-6da9b5504e6b","timestamp":1482425708527}
offset = 22, key = null, value = {"latitude":40.9879,"longitude":200.9876,"userId":"d450c573-e61a-42da-a77b-a992bc851e68","timestamp":1482425708527}
offset = 17, key = null, value = {"latitude":38.627,"longitude":90.1994,"userId":"780f9658-cf71-4820-b3fc-95140760448d","timestamp":1482425708526}
offset = 18, key = null, value = {"latitude":41.8034,"longitude":-88.144,"userId":"5e510d39-6a4f-4d08-85b8-9fa917c8b429","timestamp":1482425708526}
offset = 19, key = null, value = {"latitude":-93.9879,"longitude":76.9876,"userId":"8a544bac-7056-41b8-bc61-03e75e2f3b5e","timestamp":1482425708527}
offset = 20, key = null, value = {"latitude":13.0827,"longitude":80.2707,"userId":"7a0bf440-5755-49d8-a4d4-4ba0d1693ab3","timestamp":1482425708527}
offset = 21, key = null, value = {"latitude":9.9252,"longitude":78.1198,"userId":"1054cb75-8839-4d6b-a29f-b70a9074ac99","timestamp":1482425708527}
```

As you can see, the consumer received nine messages that the producer produced. The offsets start from `17` instead of `0` because the producer probably produced more messages before this (I was testing it a few times before this execution).

21. Now let's verify whether our geolocations were created in the `data` directory. Run the following `ls` command from a terminal shell to view the contents of your `data` directory:

```
ls -1 /opt/packt/geolocation/data
user0e7b55ae-ae42-4fba-a0a7-09ea50f018b3_t1482426034840
user2bb53438-2650-485d-ad2c-77bf53367311_t1482426034840
user8c5334e4-8bdb-4351-af8d-20f298082a41_t1482426034840
user92e6069f-6ec8-4339-a020-10fd5fe86502_t1482426034840
usera4b88745-2b55-425f-bad5-d4ebea8c7b27_t1482426034840
userb25977d7-3770-491c-8cfd-578748148ad2_t1482426034840
userc0774179-ee5e-4bf9-92aa-03e800cf076e_t1482426034840
userca40d66f-af00-4240-8ab0-5bfe48aa1df3_t1482426034840
userce5d314a-763f-4010-812f-a07e1945d5f6_t1482426034840
```

22. The preceding command lists all the files in the given directory. If you are curious to know whether these files have the geolocations, use the `cat` command to view the contents.

That brings us to the end of this recipe. In this recipe, we wrote a simple consumer and producer to work with Kafka topics. This application can be extended to build a more sophisticated and robust application for geolocation entities. In the next recipe, we will see how to use Kafka Streams to build great streaming applications.

Writing a streaming program using Kafka Streams

In the previous recipe, we wrote a very basic Kafka producer and consumer. That might not be sufficient when you would like to work with your data. In fact, the consumer we wrote was not smart enough to filter out geolocations with invalid latitudes and longitudes. These are things you would want to do when you build a streaming application. In this recipe, we will be utilizing Kafka's Streams API to create a Kafka Streams application that will stream messages from a new topic called `geolocationStreams`, filter out bad geolocations, and forward the valid geolocations to the `geolocations` topic. This will make sure that we store only valid geolocations.

The following diagram depicts the flow of our application:

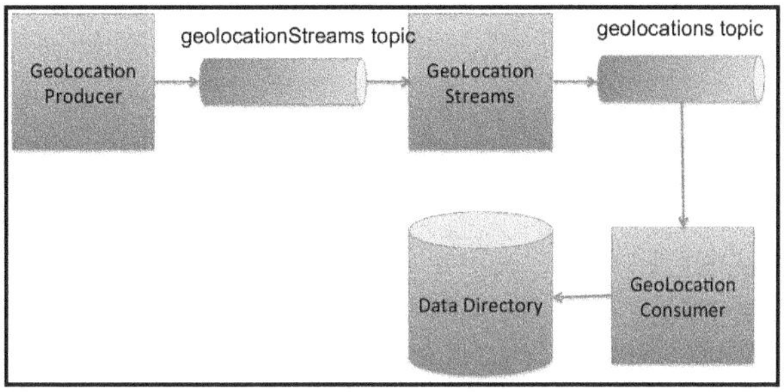

Getting ready

1. Before we write our Kafka Streams application, let's delete any existing geolocations in the `data` directory. Execute the following command in a new terminal shell:

   ```
   rm /opt/packt/geolocation/data/*
   ```

2. Now that you have cleaned up all the existing geolocations, make sure you have Kafka up and running. If it isn't running, start it using Docker Compose. If it is a fresh installation, create the `geolocations` topic.

3. The next step is creating a new topic for the streaming application. Execute the following command in the same terminal window:

   ```
   ./bin/kafka-topics.sh --create --topic geolocationStreams --
   replication-factor 1 --partitions 2 --zookeeper 192.168.99.100:2181
       Created topic "geolocationStreams".
   ```

How to do it...

1. The first step in creating the Kafka Streams application is writing the streaming logic. Add the following dependency to the geolocation project's `pom.xml` file:

   ```
   <dependency>
     <groupId>org.apache.kafka</groupId>
     <artifactId>kafka-streams</artifactId>
     <version>0.10.1.0</version>
   </dependency>
   ```

2. Create a new class called
   `com.packt.microservice.geolocation.GeoLocationStreams.java`. Add
   the following snippet to it:

```
package com.packt.microservices.geolocation;
import java.util.HashMap;
import java.util.Map;
import javax.annotation.PostConstruct;
import org.apache.kafka.common.serialization.Serdes;
import org.apache.kafka.streams.KafkaStreams;
import org.apache.kafka.streams.StreamsConfig;
import org.apache.kafka.streams.kstream.KStreamBuilder;
import org.apache.kafka.streams.kstream.Predicate;
import org.springframework.stereotype.Component;
@Component
public class GeoLocationStreams {
  @PostConstruct
  public void init() {
    Map<String, Object> props = new HashMap<>();
      props.put(StreamsConfig.APPLICATION_ID_CONFIG, "geolocation-
application");
      props.put(StreamsConfig.BOOTSTRAP_SERVERS_CONFIG,
"192.168.99.100:9092");
      props.put(StreamsConfig.KEY_SERDE_CLASS_CONFIG,
Serdes.String().getClass().getName());
      props.put(StreamsConfig.VALUE_SERDE_CLASS_CONFIG,
GeoLocationSerdes.class.getName());
      StreamsConfig config = new StreamsConfig(props);
      KStreamBuilder builder = new KStreamBuilder();
      builder.stream("geolocationStreams").filter(new Predicate<Object,
Object>() {
      @Override
      public boolean test(Object key, Object value) {
        GeoLocation geolocation = (GeoLocation) value;
        System.out.println("Stream received => " + value);
        return geolocation.getLatitude() >= -90
            && geolocation.getLatitude() < 90
            && geolocation.getLongitude() >= -180
            && geolocation.getLongitude() < 180;
      }
    }).to("geolocations");
      KafkaStreams streams = new KafkaStreams(builder, config);
      streams.start();
  }
}
```

As you can see, we first build a `StreamsConfig` instance. The `StreamsConfig` instance primarily identifies the Kafka broker URLs, SerDes for the key, and SerDes for the value. If you are wondering what **SerDes** is, it is short for **SerializerDeserializer**. See how we have used a custom SerDes for the value. We will be creating a SerDes called `GeoLocationSerdes` later in this recipe. The function of this SerDes is to serialize and deserialize the `GeoLocation` object to JSON (eventually bytes) and vice versa. We will look at how to do this later.

3. The next step is creating the `KStreamBuilder` instance. `KStreamBuilder` defines where your stream application will stream messages from, how to process the message with the help of several methods (such as `map`, `flatMap`, `filter`, and `to`), and, finally, send the messages over to a destination topic:

   - The `stream()` method tells where the messages should be streamed from. In our example, we are streaming from the `geolocationStreams` topic.
   - The `filter()` method takes a predicate that will filter geolocations that have bad latitude and longitude.
   - The `to()` method tells where the valid geolocations will be sent to.

4. In our case, we are sending them to the `geolocations` topic. If you remember, the `GeoLocationConsumer.java` class will consume these valid geolocations and store them in the `data` directory. If you would like to bypass the `GeoLocationConsumer` class, that is fine too. In fact, you can use the `map()` method to call `GeoLocationService` directly as a part of `KStreamBuilder`. Finally, we instantiate a new `KafkaStreams` instance with `KStreamsBuilder` and `StreamsConfig`. We have to invoke the `start()` method to start the streaming process.

5. Now let's see how to create our `GeoLocationSerdes.java` class. Create a new class called `com.packt.microservices.geolocation.GeoLocationSerdes.java` and add the following code to it:

```
package com.packt.microservices.geolocation;
import java.util.Map;

import org.apache.kafka.common.serialization.Deserializer;
import org.apache.kafka.common.serialization.Serde;
import org.apache.kafka.common.serialization.Serializer;
```

```java
import com.google.gson.Gson;

public class GeoLocationSerdes implements Serde<GeoLocation> {
  private static final Gson GSON = new Gson();

  public GeoLocationSerdes() {}

  @Override
  public void configure(Map<String, ?> configs, boolean isKey) {}

  @Override
  public void close() {}

  @Override
  public Serializer<GeoLocation> serializer() {
    return new Serializer<GeoLocation>() {
      @Override
      public void configure(Map<String, ?> configs, boolean isKey) {}

      @Override
      public byte[] serialize(String topic, GeoLocation data) {
        return data.toString().getBytes();
      }

      @Override
      public void close() {}
    };
  }

  @Override
  public Deserializer<GeoLocation> deserializer() {
    return new Deserializer<GeoLocation>() {
      @Override
      public void configure(Map<String, ?> configs, boolean isKey) {}

      @Override
      public GeoLocation deserialize(String topic, byte[] data) {
        return GSON.fromJson(new String(data), GeoLocation.class);
      }

      @Override
      public void close() {}
    };
  }
}
```

6. The `GeoLocationSerdes` method implements the `Serde` interface:

  - The `configure()` and `close()` methods are not very significant for this recipe, so they were not implemented in the preceding snippet
  - The `serializer()` method returns a `org.apache.kafka.common.serialization.Serializer<GeoLocation>` that has a `serialize()` method that knows how to convert the `GeoLocation` object to bytes
  - Similarly, the `deserializer()` method returns a `org.apache.kafka.common.serialization.Deserializer<GeoLocation>` that has a `deserialize()` method that knows how to convert bytes to the `GeoLocation` objects
  - That's it! Our Kafka Streams application is now ready to test. Before we start testing, we have to change the `GeoLocationProducer` class to produce messages for the `geolocationStreams` topic instead of `geolocations`.

7. So let's make that change. With that done, run the `GeoLocationApplication` class as a Spring Boot application. This time around, you should have see more log messages when you application starts, as the Streams application has started along with Spring MVC and Kafka consumer.

8. Without further ado, run `GeoLocationProducer` as a Java application. This should have produced the same nine geolocations in the `geolocationStreams` topic.

9. Now look at the console logs of the `geolocation` microservice. You should see something like this:

```
Stream received => {"latitude":38.627,"longitude":90.1994,"userId":"352752e1-f9df-4a2c-8bb5-00df1b001170","timestamp":1482431025183}
Stream received => {"latitude":41.8034,"longitude":-88.144,"userId":"cdfb7821-20c8-474e-9cc7-65b65316a78a","timestamp":1482431025183}
Stream received => {"latitude":93.9879,"longitude":76.9876,"userId":"72ce2e7e-0384-47ad-926e-e8e900876aab","timestamp":1482431025183}
Stream received => {"latitude":-93.9879,"longitude":76.9876,"userId":"03da4fde-ff8d-49f4-af2f-a0db38cdfc92","timestamp":1482431025183}
Stream received => {"latitude":40.9879,"longitude":-200.9876,"userId":"c45a6887-dd2e-4477-8d18-91c753309e70","timestamp":1482431025183}
Stream received => {"latitude":13.0827,"longitude":80.2707,"userId":"97b60125-2ef7-48df-9d31-da755ba54bc4","timestamp":1482431025183}
Stream received => {"latitude":9.568,"longitude":77.9624,"userId":"4ca44a13-f737-4bba-84b8-1ef39f5ebb60","timestamp":1482431025183}
Stream received => {"latitude":9.9252,"longitude":78.1198,"userId":"9d07e2cc-9902-4710-a311-19fc09a84f3b","timestamp":1482431025183}
Stream received => {"latitude":40.9879,"longitude":200.9876,"userId":"fa7a2421-3350-43cb-bf50-628da2759ef4","timestamp":1482431025183}
offset = 14, key = null, value = {"latitude":41.8034,"longitude":-88.144,"userId":"cdfb7821-20c8-474e-9cc7-65b65316a78a","timestamp":1482431025183}
offset = 15, key = null, value = {"latitude":9.568,"longitude":77.9624,"userId":"4ca44a13-f737-4bba-84b8-1ef39f5ebb60","timestamp":1482431025183}
offset = 13, key = null, value = {"latitude":38.627,"longitude":90.1994,"userId":"352752e1-f9df-4a2c-8bb5-00df1b001170","timestamp":1482431025183}
offset = 14, key = null, value = {"latitude":13.0827,"longitude":80.2707,"userId":"97b60125-2ef7-48df-9d31-da755ba54bc4","timestamp":1482431025183}
offset = 15, key = null, value = {"latitude":9.9252,"longitude":78.1198,"userId":"9d07e2cc-9902-4710-a311-19fc09a84f3b","timestamp":1482431025183}
```

10. As you can see, only five geolocations that had valid latitude and longitude values were sent to the `geolocations` topic. Let's verify the same by listing the contents of our `data` directory. Execute the following command on your terminal shell:

```
ls -1 /opt/packt/geolocation/data
user352752e1-f9df-4a2c-8bb5-00df1b001170_t1482431025183
user4ca44a13-f737-4bba-84b8-1ef39f5ebb60_t1482431025183
user97b60125-2ef7-48df-9d31-da755ba54bc4_t1482431025183
user9d07e2cc-9902-4710-a311-19fc09a84f3b_t1482431025183
usercdfb7821-20c8-474e-9cc7-65b65316a78a_t1482431025183
```

11. Perfect! That clarifies that our Kafka Streams application worked as expected.

With that, we come to the end of this recipe. In the next recipe, we will learn how to process more geolocations using Kafka Streams.

Improving the performance of the Kafka Streams program

Kafka claims that it is so fast that each broker can handle hundreds of megabytes of data per second from several applications. That is a bold statement. In fact, Kafka has proved to be much faster than this in several success stories. So using Kafka gives you this awesome performance by default. What if that is not sufficient? The answer to this question is *scaling*. Kafka is built in such a way that Kafka consumers or Kafka Streams applications can be scaled in such a way that they work together as a group. That's where the term "consumer group" kicks in. A **consumer group** is a group of consumers that share the same ID. Consumers in a consumer group subscribe to the same topic(s); however, each consumer group gets only one copy of each message produced in a topic. This is how Kafka achieves point-to-point behavior using topics. Internally, each consumer in the consumer group will be consuming messages from one dedicated partition. This will contribute to a parallel processing behavior.

Let's consider a situation where there is a topic with two partitions and one consumer called `consumer-01`. Now, `consumer-01` will be responsible for consuming messages from `partition-00` and `partition-01`. This is really not going to give us the performance we expect. So we have to spin off another consumer with the same group ID so that we can consume messages from both partitions in parallel. Now if we spin off `consumer -02`, `consumer-01` will consume messages from `partition-00`, and `consumer-02` will consume messages from `partition-01` (or vice versa). Now let's say you spin off another consumer called `consumer-03`. This time, it is really not going to improve your performance any further because at least one consumer is going to be idle all the time. Consumers do not share topic partitions. Keep this in mind when you build your applications using Kafka.

Getting ready

1. Before we jump into the recipe, let's delete any existing geolocations in the `data` directory. Execute the following command in a new terminal shell:

   ```
   rm /opt/packt/geolocation/data/*
   ```

2. Now that you have cleaned up all the existing geolocations, make sure you have Kafka up and running. If it is not running, start it using Docker Compose. If it is a fresh installation, create the `geolocations` and `geolocationStreams` topics.

How to do it...

1. In this recipe, we will be spinning off two instances of the `geolocation` application and will be monitoring the logs to see how the messages are distributed. Go ahead and start two instances of the `GeoLocationApplication`, one running on port 8080 and the other running on port 8081. Make sure there are no errors in your console.

2. Now run the `GeoLocationProducer` class as a Java application. This should have dropped the nine geolocations into the `geolocationStreams` topic.

3. Let's see what the console looks like for both the instances:

```
Stream received => {"latitude":38.627,"longitude":90.1994,"userId":"0337c5d9-4e4f-41c7-9388-019cb91cd91a","timestamp":1482431437277}
offset = 16, key = null, value = {"latitude":9.568,"longitude":77.9624,"userId":"633d70d7-9b5a-421c-a996-a667c4c67875","timestamp":1482431437277}
Stream received => {"latitude":41.8034,"longitude":-88.144,"userId":"a9bdd260-8fea-4a3c-a102-e6518af8c5df","timestamp":1482431437277}
Stream received => {"latitude":-93.9879,"longitude":76.9876,"userId":"91c3eddc-b939-45d6-b963-ceea820d2768","timestamp":1482431437277}
Stream received => {"latitude":13.0827,"longitude":80.2707,"userId":"23a005e7-bf9a-4235-9f02-69fa87ab9983","timestamp":1482431437277}
Stream received => {"latitude":9.9252,"longitude":78.1198,"userId":"37b92974-15fc-4fbe-8862-f456eb751023","timestamp":1482431437278}
offset = 17, key = null, value = {"latitude":38.627,"longitude":90.1994,"userId":"0337c5d9-4e4f-41c7-9388-019cb91cd91a","timestamp":1482431437277}
offset = 18, key = null, value = {"latitude":13.0827,"longitude":80.2707,"userId":"23a005e7-bf9a-4235-9f02-69fa87ab9983","timestamp":1482431437277}
```

The preceding screenshot shows the console logs from the first instance of geolocation. As you can see, the GeoLocationStreams application received five messages out of nine. And the GeoLocationConsumer application received three out of the five messages.

4. Now let's take a look at the console logs of the second instance of the geolocation microservice:

```
Stream received => {"latitude":93.9879,"longitude":76.9876,"userId":"8124c5ea-a413-49d5-91dd-68f8b5aff829","timestamp":1482431437277}
Stream received => {"latitude":40.9879,"longitude":-200.9876,"userId":"cd86cd97-666c-486d-b049-09d8e5c05d24","timestamp":1482431437277}
Stream received => {"latitude":9.568,"longitude":77.9624,"userId":"633d70d7-9b5a-421c-a996-a667c4c67875","timestamp":1482431437277}
Stream received => {"latitude":40.9879,"longitude":200.9876,"userId":"755cc1e6-1099-4e2b-ae8d-830e7fae4147","timestamp":1482431437277}
offset = 16, key = null, value = {"latitude":41.8034,"longitude":-88.144,"userId":"a9bdd260-8fea-4a3c-a102-e6518af8c5df","timestamp":1482431437277}
offset = 17, key = null, value = {"latitude":9.9252,"longitude":78.1198,"userId":"37b92974-15fc-4fbe-8862-f456eb751023","timestamp":1482431437278}
```

As you can see, four out of nine messages were received by the GeoLocationStreams application. And the GeoLocationConsumer application received two out of the five messages. This demonstrates that the KafkaStreams and KafkaConsumer instances scale as the application scales-which is obviously great news. But the real question is how? Also, we did not create any consumer groups in this recipe. In fact, we actually created a consumer group earlier.

5. Now, go back to your consumer class, and you will notice that we passed a parameter called group.id with the value geolocationConsumer. Consumers with the same group.id property will be in the same consumer group. That is the reason our GeoLocationConsumer application was scalable. Similarly, the StreamsConfig.APPLICATION_ID_CONFIG property in the GeoLocationStreams class defines the consumer group ID value. The value of this property has been set to geolocation-application. So any Kafka Streams application that has the consumer group value set to geolocation-application will be part of the same consumer group.

That brings us to the end of this recipe. In this recipe, we learned how to scale our Kafka Streams application. Kafka Streams has a lot many methods to build a complete data pipeline, such as `map`, `flatMap`, `mapValues`, `flatMapValues`, and `filter`. It is strongly recommended that you read the documentation before you start using Kafka Streams. In fact, there is a slightly different approach that you can use in Kafka Streams to build data processors. Take a look at `TopologyBuilder` and `AbstractProcessor` to try that approach. I'll leave that as an exercise for you.

Writing a streaming program using Apache Spark

You might be wondering what Apache Spark has to do with microservices. The answer is pretty simple: streaming and data processing. Not all microservices will require streaming, but most of them these days do.

There are two ways you can feed data to a microservice: via REST or message brokers. With RESTful APIs, you can achieve the performance you expect. But it has its own limitations, which is the reason companies move towards message brokers such as Kafka, RabbitMQ, and ZeroMQ. Using frameworks such as Kafka, you can achieve tremendous performance and live results. In fact, today's streaming is all about live results. Before we jump into the recipe, let's take a minute to understand Spark and some of its concepts.

Apache Spark is a fast data-processing framework. It has four major modules: Spark Streaming, Spark SQL, Spark MLlib, and Spark Graphx. Spark Streaming is used to stream data from messaging endpoints such as TCP Socket and Kafka. Spark SQL is used to execute efficient queries on huge structured datasets. Spark MLlib is Spark's machine learning library. At the time of writing this, Spark MLlib has matured so much that it can be used for any production-level use case. Spark Graphx is Spark's graph-processing API. In this recipe, we will be streaming geolocation off of a Kafka topic, filtering bad geolocations, and sending the valid geolocations to another Kafka topic. At the core of Apache Spark lies the RDD API. **RDD** stands for **Resilient Distributed Dataset**. It is resilient because when Spark jobs are executed in a cluster, even if a node goes down while processing an RDD, the RDD will be handed over to another active node in the cluster. It is distributed because RDDs are distributed across nodes in the cluster. Spark's configurations let you allocate resources such as CPU and memory for every Spark job. This makes Spark work very well with clustering framework such as Mesos and YARN.

Getting ready

Writing a Spark job is as simple as writing a Java program. With the current availability of documentation on the Internet, it just takes a few minutes to write a Spark job. The real tricky part is deploying the Spark jobs. That's where clustering frameworks such as Mesos and YARN come into the picture. But developing a Spark job shouldn't really require a huge cluster. That's the reason Spark came up with a Spark standalone mode. The standalone mode runs the Spark job in memory. In this recipe, we will be executing our Spark job in Spark standalone mode. We will perform the same logic that we did using Kafka Streams, only this time using Apache Spark. The following diagram shows the flow of our code:

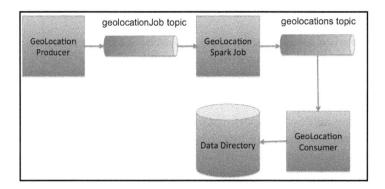

Before we jump in, let's clean up the data directory that was populated by previous recipes:

1. Execute the following command from a terminal shell:

   ```
   rm /opt/packt/geolocation/data/*
   ```

2. The next step is creating the geolocationJob topic. Execute the following script from Kafka's root directory:

```
./bin/kafka-topics.sh --create --topic geolocationJob --replication-factor
1 --partitions 2 --zookeeper 192.168.99.100:2181
```

How to do it...

1. We will need some Maven dependencies to write a Spark Streaming program. Add the following three dependencies to the pom.xml file of the geolocation project:

```
<dependency>
  <groupId>org.apache.spark</groupId>
  <artifactId>spark-core_2.11</artifactId>
  <version>2.0.2</version>
</dependency>

<dependency>
  <groupId>org.apache.spark</groupId>
  <artifactId>spark-streaming_2.11</artifactId>
  <version>2.0.2</version>
</dependency>

<dependency>
  <groupId>org.apache.spark</groupId>
  <artifactId>spark-streaming-kafka-0-10_2.11</artifactId>
  <version>2.0.2</version>
</dependency>
```

2. Let's right away create the Spark job. Create a new java class called com.packt.microservices.geolocation.GeoLocationJob.java with an empty main method:

```
package com.packt.microservices.geolocation;

public class GeoLocationJob {
  public static void main(String[] args) throws Exception {
  }
}
```

3. Writing this Spark job can be broken down into multiple logical parts:

    1. Creating a streaming context.

    2. Creating a direct stream on the geolocationJob topic.

    3. Converting string values to GeoLocation objects.

4. Filtering geolocations with invalid latitude and longitude.

5. Sending valid geolocations to the `geolocations` topic.

6. Starting the context and await termination.

4. Let's move on to the first step, where we will create the streaming context. Add the following snippet to the main method:

```
SparkConf conf = new
SparkConf().setAppName("geolocationJob").setMaster("local[1]");
JavaStreamingContext context = new JavaStreamingContext(conf, new
Duration(2000));
```

As you can see, the app name is set to `geolocationJob` and the master is set to `local[1]`. This says that we will be using standalone mode and our Spark job will use 1 thread. The `JavaStreamingContext` constructor instance takes two arguments: `SparkConf` and `Duration`. `Duration` is used to say how frequently the micro-batches should be created and processed.

5. The next step in creating our Spark job is creating a direct stream on the `geolocationJob` topic. Add the following snippet to the `main()` method:

```
Map<String, Object> kafkaParams = new HashMap<>();
kafkaParams.put("bootstrap.servers", "192.168.99.100:9092");
kafkaParams.put("key.deserializer", StringDeserializer.class);
kafkaParams.put("value.deserializer", StringDeserializer.class);
kafkaParams.put("group.id", "geolocationJob");
kafkaParams.put("auto.offset.reset", "latest");
kafkaParams.put("enable.auto.commit", false);

Collection<String> topics = Arrays.asList("geolocationJob");

final JavaInputDStream<ConsumerRecord<String, String>> dstream =
KafkaUtils.createDirectStream
    (context,
    LocationStrategies.PreferConsistent(),
      ConsumerStrategies.<String, String>Subscribe(topics, kafkaParams));
```

- You should be familiar with most of the Kafka parameters. To learn more about the properties, refer to the Kafka documentation at `https://kafka.apache.org/documentation/#newconsumerconfigs`.
- We then create a collection of topics. Here, we have used the topic name `geolocationJob`, from which we will be streaming our messages off of. Finally, we create a **direct stream** (**DStream**) from the context, topics, and Kafka parameters. The `LocationStrategy` identifies how our partitions will be distributed across executors. `ConsumerStrategy` helps Spark obtain the right consumers. The subscribe consumer strategy is used for specific topic names, like in our case. The preceding snippet will create a direct stream that will stream messages from the `geolocationJob` topic.

6. Let's move on to the next step: converting string values to the `GeoLocation` objects in `ConsumerRecord`. Add the following snippet to the `main()` method:

```
dstream.map(new Function<ConsumerRecord<String,String>, GeoLocation>() { //
map to GeoLocation
  private static final long serialVersionUID = -5289370913799710097L;

  @Override
  public GeoLocation call(ConsumerRecord<String, String> record) throws
Exception {
    return new Gson().fromJson(record.value(), GeoLocation.class);
    }
})
```

This snippet converts the string values from `ConsumerRecord` to the `GeoLocation` objects using GSON. As you can see, we have used an anonymous inner class of `org.apache.spark.api.java.function.Function`.

7. Let's move on to the next step, where we will be filtering geolocations with invalid latitude and longitude values. Append the following snippet to the previous line:

```
.filter(new Function<GeoLocation, Boolean>() { // filter out invalid
geolocations
  private static final long serialVersionUID = 6980980875802694946L;

  @Override
  public Boolean call(GeoLocation geolocation) throws Exception {
    System.out.println("Spark Job received => " + geolocation);
    return geolocation.getLatitude() >= -90
      && geolocation.getLatitude() < 90
```

```
          && geolocation.getLongitude() >= -180
          && geolocation.getLongitude() < 180;
    }
})
```

That preceding snippet makes use of `Function` that will act as a predicate to filter out geolocations with invalid latitude and longitude values.

8. The next step involves writing our valid geolocations to the `geolocations` Kafka topic. Append the following snippet to the previous line of code:

```
.foreachRDD(new VoidFunction<JavaRDD<GeoLocation>>() { //iterate over RDD
  private static final long serialVersionUID = -4161320579495422870L;

  @Override
  public void call(JavaRDD<GeoLocation> rdd) throws Exception {
    rdd.foreach(new VoidFunction<GeoLocation>() {  // send valid
geolocations to another topic
      private static final long serialVersionUID = -3282778715126743482L;

      @Override
      public void call(GeoLocation geolocation) throws Exception {
        ProducerRecord<String, String> record = new ProducerRecord<>(
          "geolocations",
          geolocation.toString());
        getProducer().send(record);
      }
    });
  }
});
```

We are using the `foreachRDD()` method to iterate over the RDDs. Then, we grab the geolocations from each RDD using the `foreach()` method. In both these cases, we have created anonymous inner classes for `org.apache.spark.api.java.function.VoidFunction`. Finally, we create a `ProducerRecord` and send it to the `geolocaitons` topic using `KafkaProducer`. We will see how the `getProducer()` method is implemented later.

 If you are wondering whether Spark supports an operation where it can drop messages onto a Kafka topic, then the answer is no. Currently, Spark does not have that support out of the box. But there are third-party libraries that can drop messages onto a Kafka topic without you having to create your own Kafka producer.

9. The final step is starting the context and awaiting termination. In this step, we will call the `start()` and `awaitTermination()` methods of the `JavaStreamingContext` instance so that we can indefinitely listen for any new messages on the `geolocationJob` topic:

```
context.start();
context.awaitTermination();
```

10. The `KafkaProducer` was earlier obtained using the `getProducer()` method. Let's see how this method looks. Add the following snippet to the `GeoLocationJob.java` class:

```
public static Producer<String, String> producer;

public static Producer<String, String> getProducer() {
if(producer == null) {
   Properties props = new Properties();
   props.put("bootstrap.servers", "192.168.99.100:9092");
   props.put("key.serializer", StringSerializer.class.getName());
   props.put("value.serializer", StringSerializer.class.getName());
   producer = new KafkaProducer<>(props);
}
   return producer;
}
```

11. That was the last step. The final `GeoLocationJob` class will look something like this:

```
package com.packt.microservices.geolocation;

import java.util.Arrays;
import java.util.Collection;
import java.util.HashMap;
import java.util.Map;
import java.util.Properties;

import org.apache.kafka.clients.consumer.ConsumerRecord;
import org.apache.kafka.clients.producer.KafkaProducer;
import org.apache.kafka.clients.producer.Producer;
import org.apache.kafka.clients.producer.ProducerRecord;
import org.apache.kafka.common.serialization.StringDeserializer;
import org.apache.kafka.common.serialization.StringSerializer;
import org.apache.spark.SparkConf;
import org.apache.spark.api.java.JavaRDD;
import org.apache.spark.api.java.function.Function;
```

```java
import org.apache.spark.api.java.function.VoidFunction;
import org.apache.spark.streaming.Duration;
import org.apache.spark.streaming.api.java.JavaInputDStream;
import org.apache.spark.streaming.api.java.JavaStreamingContext;
import org.apache.spark.streaming.kafka010.ConsumerStrategies;
import org.apache.spark.streaming.kafka010.KafkaUtils;
import org.apache.spark.streaming.kafka010.LocationStrategies;

import com.google.gson.Gson;

public class GeoLocationJob {
  public static Producer<String, String> producer;
  public static void main(String[] args) throws Exception {
    SparkConf conf = new
SparkConf().setAppName("geolocationJob").setMaster("local[1]");
    JavaStreamingContext context = new JavaStreamingContext(conf, new
Duration(2000));

    Map<String, Object> kafkaParams = new HashMap<>();
    kafkaParams.put("bootstrap.servers", "192.168.99.100:9092");
    kafkaParams.put("key.deserializer", StringDeserializer.class);
    kafkaParams.put("value.deserializer", StringDeserializer.class);
    kafkaParams.put("group.id", "geolocationJob");
    kafkaParams.put("auto.offset.reset", "latest");
    kafkaParams.put("enable.auto.commit", false);

    Collection<String> topics = Arrays.asList("geolocationJob");

    final JavaInputDStream<ConsumerRecord<String, String>> dstream =
KafkaUtils.createDirectStream
          (context,
        LocationStrategies.PreferConsistent(),
        ConsumerStrategies.<String, String>Subscribe(topics, kafkaParams));

    dstream.map(new Function<ConsumerRecord<String,String>, GeoLocation>()
{ // map to GeoLocation
      private static final long serialVersionUID = -5289370913799710097L;

      @Override
      public GeoLocation call(ConsumerRecord<String, String> record) throws
Exception {
        return new Gson().fromJson(record.value(), GeoLocation.class);
      }
    }).filter(new Function<GeoLocation, Boolean>() { // filter out invalid
geolocations
      private static final long serialVersionUID = 6980980875802694946L;

      @Override
```

```java
    public Boolean call(GeoLocation geolocation) throws Exception {
      System.out.println("Spark Job received => " + geolocation);
      return geolocation.getLatitude() >= -90
          && geolocation.getLatitude() < 90
          && geolocation.getLongitude() >= -180
          && geolocation.getLongitude() < 180;
    }
  }).foreachRDD(new VoidFunction<JavaRDD<GeoLocation>>() { //iterate over RDD
    private static final long serialVersionUID = -4161320579495422870L;

    @Override
    public void call(JavaRDD<GeoLocation> rdd) throws Exception {
      rdd.foreach(new VoidFunction<GeoLocation>() {  // send valid geolocations to another topic
        private static final long serialVersionUID = -3282778715126743482L;

        @Override
        public void call(GeoLocation geolocation) throws Exception {
          ProducerRecord<String, String> record = new ProducerRecord<>(
              "geolocations",
              geolocation.toString());
          getProducer().send(record);
        }
      });
    }
  });
  context.start();
  context.awaitTermination();
}
public static Producer<String, String> getProducer() {
  if(producer == null) {
    Properties props = new Properties();
    props.put("bootstrap.servers", "192.168.99.100:9092");
    props.put("key.serializer", StringSerializer.class.getName());
    props.put("value.serializer", StringSerializer.class.getName());
    producer = new KafkaProducer<>(props);
  }
  return producer;
}
}
```

12. Without further ado, let's test this out. Start the geolocation microservice on port 8080. This will start the `GeoLocationStreams` as well as the `GeoLocationConsumer`. Now run the `GeoLocationJob` class as a Java application. After both the geolocation microservice and the Spark job have started successfully, drop some messages on the `geolocationJob` topic. We will be utilizing the `GeoLocationProducer` class to do this. Modify the `GeoLocationProducer` class to use the `geolocationJob` topic, and execute it as a Java application. This should have created nine geolocations on the `geolocationJob` topic.

13. Let's take a look at the console logs of the Spark job first:

```
        ssl.protocol = TLS
        ssl.provider = null
        ssl.secure.random.implementation = null
        ssl.trustmanager.algorithm = PKIX
        ssl.truststore.location = null
        ssl.truststore.password = null
        ssl.truststore.type = JKS
        value.deserializer = class org.apache.kafka.common.serialization.StringDeserializer


[Stage 35:================================>                  (1 + 1) / 2]2016-12-23 11:35:16.567  INFO    --- [launch worker-0] o.a.k
2016-12-23 11:35:16.568  INFO    --- [launch worker-0] o.a.kafka.common.utils.AppInfoParser     : Kafka commitId : 3402a74efb23d1d4
Spark Job received => {"latitude":38.627,"longitude":90.1994,"userId":"6beedc41-284a-4a6a-9e9c-5434768936a0","timestamp":1482514513790}
Spark Job received => {"latitude":41.8034,"longitude":-88.144,"userId":"2288ea0c-e3e7-453c-a31c-935210195df3","timestamp":1482514513790}
Spark Job received => {"latitude":-93.9879,"longitude":76.9876,"userId":"4de7a59c-514f-467e-85a0-d1ce26d0e5fc","timestamp":1482514513790}
Spark Job received => {"latitude":13.0827,"longitude":80.2707,"userId":"45cd0dc9-df2e-4ec9-8f40-4cdd88f7e493","timestamp":1482514513790}
Spark Job received => {"latitude":9.9252,"longitude":78.1198,"userId":"caabf873-73b6-446d-a02d-c42ecce35d1b","timestamp":1482514513790}


[Stage 46:>                                                  (0 + 0) / 2]


[Stage 56:>                                                  (0 + 0) / 2]
```

As you can see, our Spark job received all the messages. The preceding screenshot does not show them all, though.

14. Now let's take a look at the log messages of the `geolocation` microservice:

```
2016-12-23 11:34:44.889  INFO 51732 --- [ StreamThread-1] o.a.k.s.p.internals.StreamThread         : stream-thread [StreamThread-1] Committing task 0.
2016-12-23 11:35:14.894  INFO 51732 --- [ StreamThread-1] o.a.k.s.p.internals.StreamThread         : stream-thread [StreamThread-1] Committing all ta
2016-12-23 11:35:14.894  INFO 51732 --- [ StreamThread-1] o.a.k.s.p.internals.StreamThread         : stream-thread [StreamThread-1] Committing task 0.
offset = 0, key = null, value = {"latitude":9.568,"longitude":77.9624,"userId":"3669998e-b114-4714-813d-f8adf9cf4a12","timestamp":1482514513790}
offset = 0, key = null, value = {"latitude":38.627,"longitude":90.1994,"userId":"6beedc41-284a-4a6a-9e9c-5434768936a0","timestamp":1482514513790}
offset = 1, key = null, value = {"latitude":13.0827,"longitude":80.2707,"userId":"45cd0dc9-df2e-4ec9-8f40-4cdd88f7e493","timestamp":1482514513790}
offset = 1, key = null, value = {"latitude":41.8034,"longitude":-88.144,"userId":"2288ea0c-e3e7-453c-a31c-935210195df3","timestamp":1482514513790}
offset = 2, key = null, value = {"latitude":9.9252,"longitude":78.1198,"userId":"caabf873-73b6-446d-a02d-c42ecce35d1b","timestamp":1482514513790}
```

As you can see, `GeoLocationConsumer` received all the geolocations with valid latitude and longitude.

15. Let's quickly verify the `data` directory. Execute the following commands to list the contents of the `data` directory:

```
ls -1 /opt/packt/geolocation/data
user2288ea0c-e3e7-453c-a31c-935210195df3_t1482514513790
user3669998e-b114-4714-813d-f8adf9cf4a12_t1482514513790
user45cd0dc9-df2e-4ec9-8f40-4cdd88f7e493_t1482514513790
user6beedc41-284a-4a6a-9e9c-5434768936a0_t1482514513790
usercaabf873-73b6-446d-a02d-c42ecce35d1b_t1482514513790
```

Awesome! We have created our first Spark job. That brings us to the end of this recipe. Spark has so much to offer that it can be applied in a lot of use cases. What we learned in this recipe was just the beginning of Spark. It is strongly recommended that your learn Spark before you try it out. In fact, Spark's official documentation is very descriptive and useful.

Improving the performance of the Spark job

In the previous recipe, we wrote a simple Spark job that filters out invalid geolocations and pushes the valid geolocations into a Kafka topic. In this recipe, we will see how we can improve the performance of our Spark job.

How to do it...

There are several ways in which you can improve the performance of your Spark job. There are a lot many configurations that Spark provides that can be tweaked to achieve desired performance. For example, based on the amount of data that your topic receives, you could change the batch duration of your stream. Also, deploying your Spark job on a Mesos or YARN cluster opens up a lot of opportunities for performance improvement. In fact, running your Spark job in local standalone mode will not help you assess the performance of your Spark job. The real test for a Spark job is when it is executed on a cluster. Each Spark job requires a certain amount of resources for execution, be it CPU or memory.

Earlier in the book, we talked about fine-grained and coarse-grained modes and how Spark utilizes the resources in both these modes. Likewise, there are several other configurations that can be tweaked to achieve the desired performance.

Now that we are talking about deployments, let's talk about whether or not the Spark job should coexist alongside the microservice. Spark jobs are best executed without other dependencies. So it is always better to run the Spark job as a separate deployment. While the `GeoLocationJob` class could run on Mesos or YARN as its own task, the geolocation microservice will run as a Docker container in Marathon or YARN. So we have two components now: API and Spark job. The Spark job sends data to the API via a Kafka topic. Now do you see the value of Kafka? Making your Spark job send data via the API will slow down your Spark job. That is the reason we chose to consume messages via Kafka topics in our geolocation microservice.

Most of the time, you can look at how your job is performing using the Spark web console at `http://localhost:4040`. You should see something like this:

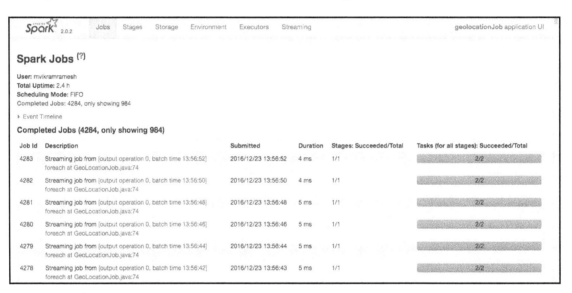

As you can see, the **Spark Jobs** page shows a high-level metric for each operation in our Spark job. In the preceding screenshot, it shows metrics for the `foreach` operations in our Spark job. Clicking on each `foreach` job will show more details about it, such as **Event Timeline** and DAG visualization. Now let's take a quick look at the **Streaming** tab:

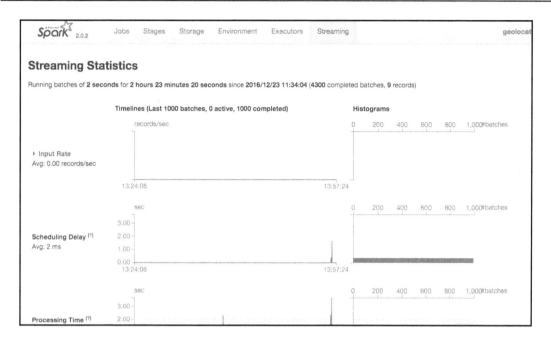

The **Streaming** tab provides better insights into the streaming framework. The current version of Spark provides metrics such as **Input Rate**, **Scheduling Delay**, **Processing Time**, and **Total Delay**. Though there is not much data to make sense out of these charts and histograms in our use case, when you are dealing with huge datasets, these monitoring tools will be very useful.

That brings us to the end of this recipe. As already mentioned, Apache Spark is a huge library and it takes time to master it. I strongly recommend that you read about it from their documentation before using it.

Aggregating logs into Kafka using Log4J

Log management is a critical part of any microservice deployment. When it comes to debugging your application, the two things that matter a lot are logs and metrics. We've already learned how to use metrics to monitor our application, and in this recipe, we will learn how to consolidate our logs. Logs can be stored in plenty of stores. In this recipe, we will look at how to store our logs in a Kafka topic. Once we get our log messages in a Kafka topic, we can use Log Management tools to make some sense out of it.

Getting ready

In this recipe, we will be configuring the geolocation microservice to send log messages over to a Kafka topic called `geolocationLogs`.

Let's get ready by creating the topic in Kafka. If you don't have Kafka up and running, run it using Docker Compose.

Open a new terminal shell and navigate to the `home` directory of Kafka. Execute the following command:

```
./bin/kafka-topics.sh --create --topic geolocationLogs --
replication-factor 1 --partitions 1 --zookeeper 192.168.99.100:2181
```

How to do it...

The easiest way to send our log messages to Kafka is using a log appender. A **log appender** is a utility in any logging framework that knows how to send messages to a specific destination. Similarly, a Kafka appender knows how to send log messages to a Kafka topic. To make it simpler, let's try to use the underlying logging framework of Spring Boot. By default, Spring Boot uses logback. At the time of writing this, it is not very easy to configure logback with a Kafka appender. But Log4J2 comes with a Kafka appender out of the box. Let's see how to use Kafka appender with Log4J2 in our Spring Boot app. If you are not using a Spring Boot app, then it is real simple. All you have to do is add the `log4j2` dependency and start configuring the Kafka appender. However, in this recipe, we will be learning how to do it on a Spring Boot app as it is a little tricky.

1. The first thing we need to do is configure our app to use Log4J2 instead of Logback. Add the following two dependencies to the `pom.xml` file of the `geolocation` project:

```
<dependency>
  <groupId>org.springframework.boot</groupId>
  <artifactId>spring-boot-starter</artifactId>
  <exclusions>
    <exclusion>
      <groupId>org.springframework.boot</groupId>
      <artifactId>spring-boot-starter-logging</artifactId>
    </exclusion>
  </exclusions>
</dependency>

<dependency>
```

```
        <groupId>org.springframework.boot</groupId>
        <artifactId>spring-boot-starter-log4j2</artifactId>
</dependency>
```

As you can see, we have excluded the basic `spring-boot-starter-logging` dependency and added the `spring-boot-starter-log4j2` dependency. This will introduce `log4j2` into the project.

2. The Spark dependencies usually have `slf4j-log4j12` bindings. In order to use log4j2 we need to remove the `slf4j-log4j12` bindings. Go ahead and exclude this artifact from `kafka-streams`, `spark-core_2.11` and `spark-streaming-kafka-0-10_2.11`:

```
<dependency>
    <groupId>org.apache.kafka</groupId>
    <artifactId>kafka-streams</artifactId>
    <version>0.10.1.0</version>
    <exclusions>
        <exclusion>
            <groupId>org.slf4j</groupId>
            <artifactId>slf4j-log4j12</artifactId>
        </exclusion>
    </exclusions>
</dependency>

<dependency>
    <groupId>org.apache.spark</groupId>
    <artifactId>spark-core_2.11</artifactId>
    <version>2.0.2</version>
    <exclusions>
        <exclusion>
            <groupId>org.slf4j</groupId>
            <artifactId>slf4j-log4j12</artifactId>
        </exclusion>
    </exclusions>
</dependency>
<dependency>
    <groupId>org.apache.spark</groupId>
    <artifactId>spark-streaming-kafka-0-10_2.11</artifactId>
    <version>2.0.2</version>
    <exclusions>
        <exclusion>
            <groupId>org.slf4j</groupId>
            <artifactId>slf4j-log4j12</artifactId>
        </exclusion>
    </exclusions>
</dependency>
```

3. Now let's add the `log4j2.xml` config file to the `src/main/resources` directory. Add the following snippet to the `log4j2.xml` file:

```xml
<?xml version="1.0" encoding="UTF-8"?>
<Configuration status="INFO">
  <Appenders>
    <Console name="Console" target="SYSTEM_OUT">
      <PatternLayout pattern="%d{HH:mm:ss.SSS} [%t] %-5level %logger{36} -
%msg%n" />
    </Console>
    <Kafka name="Kafka" topic="geolocationLogs">
      <PatternLayout pattern="%date %message" />
      <Property name="bootstrap.servers">192.168.99.100:9092</Property>
    </Kafka>
  </Appenders>

  <Loggers>
    <Root level="INFO">
      <AppenderRef ref="Console" />
      <AppenderRef ref="Kafka" />
    </Root>
    <Logger name="org.apache.kafka" level="ERROR" /> <!-- avoid recursive
logging -->
  </Loggers>
</Configuration>
```

4. The configuration is pretty straightforward. All we have to do is add the Kafka appender and define the `bootstrap.servers` property with the Kafka broker URL. The logger for the `org.apache.kafka` package is set to `ERROR` to make sure we avoid recursive logging.

That's it! We have configured a Kafka appender for Log4J2 to send our log messages to the `geolocationLogs` Kafka topic. We are now ready to test this out. In order to do so, we need a Kafka consumer that can consume messages from the `geolocationLogs` topic. Let's utilize the command-line console consumer to perform this task. Open up a new terminal window and navigate to the `home` folder of your Kafka installation. Execute the following command:

```
./bin/kafka-console-consumer.sh --topic geolocationLogs --zookeeper
192.168.99.100:2181
```

Now that our consumer is ready, let's start the `geolocation` microservice as a Spring Boot application and keep an eye on the consumer logs:

```
2016-12-23 14:49:38,462 Registering beans for JMX exposure on startup
2016-12-23 14:49:38,473 Registering beans for JMX exposure on startup
2016-12-23 14:49:38,486 Starting beans in phase 0
2016-12-23 14:49:38,498 Located managed bean 'requestMappingEndpoint': registering with JMX server as MBean [org.springframework.boot:type=Endpo
2016-12-23 14:49:38,547 Located managed bean 'environmentEndpoint': registering with JMX server as MBean [org.springframework.boot:type=Endpoint
2016-12-23 14:49:38,561 Located managed bean 'healthEndpoint': registering with JMX server as MBean [org.springframework.boot:type=Endpoint,name
2016-12-23 14:49:38,572 Located managed bean 'beansEndpoint': registering with JMX server as MBean [org.springframework.boot:type=Endpoint,name=
2016-12-23 14:49:38,587 Located managed bean 'infoEndpoint': registering with JMX server as MBean [org.springframework.boot:type=Endpoint,name=i
2016-12-23 14:49:38,605 Located managed bean 'metricsEndpoint': registering with JMX server as MBean [org.springframework.boot:type=Endpoint,nam
2016-12-23 14:49:38,614 Located managed bean 'traceEndpoint': registering with JMX server as MBean [org.springframework.boot:type=Endpoint,name=
2016-12-23 14:49:38,627 Located managed bean 'dumpEndpoint': registering with JMX server as MBean [org.springframework.boot:type=Endpoint,name=d
2016-12-23 14:49:38,647 Located managed bean 'autoConfigurationReportEndpoint': registering with JMX server as MBean [org.springframework.boot:t
nReportEndpoint]
2016-12-23 14:49:38,658 Located managed bean 'configurationPropertiesReportEndpoint': registering with JMX server as MBean [org.springframework.
ionPropertiesReportEndpoint]
2016-12-23 14:49:38,738 Initializing ProtocolHandler ["http-nio-8080"]
2016-12-23 14:49:38,752 Starting ProtocolHandler ["http-nio-8080"]
2016-12-23 14:49:38,760 Using a shared selector for servlet write/read
2016-12-23 14:49:38,783 Tomcat started on port(s): 8080 (http)
2016-12-23 14:49:38,795 Started GeoLocationApplication in 6.045 seconds (JVM running for 7.449)
```

As you can see, all our log messages are now directed to the `geolocationLogs` topic in addition to the console. Now, it is up to us to use these log messages in the tool of our choice.

That brings us to the end of this recipe. Good luck logging with Kafka!

Integrating Kafka with log management systems

In the previous recipe, we learned how to consolidate log messages from microservices into a Kafka topic using Log4J2 and Kafka. In this recipe, we will look at various options that we have to visualize our logs. There are several log-management systems available in the market at the moment. We will talk about few of them in this recipe.

How it works…

There are several log-management tools, such as Splunk, Graylog2, and Loggly. Most of them nowadays come with a Kafka listener. However, at the time of writing this, Splunk does not have an official Kafka consumer. There are several third-partly plugins that you can install with Splunk to consume messages from Kafka topics.

Graylog2 is another popular log-management tool that has picked up traction lately mostly because it is open source. It comes packed with tons of features. Though the interface is not very sophisticated, it gets the job done well. Graylog came with their own log format called **Graylog Extended Log Format (GELF)** to address the pain points in regular log formats. Graylog has official support to consume messages from a Kafka topic. For more information on how to configure Graylog with Kafka, look at their documentation page at `http://docs.graylog.org`.

The other way of implementing your own log-management system is using the ELK stack. **ELK** stands for **Elasticsearch, Log Stash, and Kibana**. You can write your own microservice to bridge messages from the Kafka topic over to Log Stash. There are several tutorials out there to set up the ELK stack. We will not be covering them as it is out of scope for this book.

That brings us to the end of this recipe. In this chapter, we learned how to use Kafka in a microservice ecosystem. Later, we looked at how Apache Spark can be used so stream messages from Kafka. Finally, we had a look at log management. Good luck streaming!

8
More Clustering Frameworks - DC/OS, Docker Swarm, and YARN

In this chapter, we will look at the following recipes:

- Deploying infrastructure with DC/OS
- Deploying containers with Docker Swarm
- Deploying containers on YARN

Introduction

In the previous chapters of this book, we learned how to use frameworks such as Mesos and Kubernetes to perform deployments. There are many such frameworks like Hashicorp Nomad, Lightbend Lagom, Mesosphere DC/OS, Docker Swarm, and YARN that can be utilized to deploy and manage microservices. In this chapter, you will be introduced to three of these frameworks. The goal of this chapter is to give you a heads-up of these frameworks and their capabilities. I will also help you by listing down some tools that will be handy when deploying your microservices on these frameworks. Of course, there are other similar frameworks in the market that help with managing microservices. Please feel free to choose a framework that fits your needs and go from there.

Deploying infrastructure with DC/OS

DC/OS stands for **Datacenter Operating System**. DC/OS is built and maintained by Mesosphere. Mesosphere offers an open source version of DC/OS, as well as an enterprise version. You can think of DC/OS as an enterprise-ready version of Mesos with sophisticated features and a collection of installable tools and frameworks. One of the trickiest parts of managing your own Mesos cluster is orchestrating the frameworks. DC/OS has made this task much easier with its command-line interface. You could potentially install the DC/OS CLI on your local computer and manage any remote DC/OS cluster. Using the CLI, you can install Marathon, submit Docker containers, and so on. In this recipe, we will be going over the DC/OS interface to understand its features and capabilities.

Getting ready

In this recipe, we will be orchestrating a DC/OS cluster on AWS and then we will go over the basics of DC/OS. There are several ways you can orchestrate a DC/OS cluster: using Vagrant, using AWS, and so on. Using Vagrant, you can spin off a minimal cluster that you can use for local development testing. In this recipe, we have orchestrated a real DC/OS cluster on AWS. The instructions on the DC/OS website for orchestrating DC/OS on AWS is very easy because it uses AWS CloudFormation. AWS CloudFormation is nothing but Infrastructure as Code. You will be describing your infrastructure using CloudFormation templates, which can later be used for orchestration on AWS. You can learn more about CloudFormation at `http://docs.aws.amazon.com/AWSCloudFormation/latest/UserGuide/GettingStarted.html`. Fortunately, Mesosphere was kind enough to create these CloudFormation scripts for us. So spinning off a DC/OS cluster using CloudFormation just takes a button click and will be done in minutes. For more information, take a look at `https://dcos.io`.

How to do it...

If you follow the installation instructions on the DC/OS website for installing DC/OS on AWS, you will be able to land on the DC/OS web interface. In this recipe, we have orchestrated the single master and five slave cluster. If you would like to pick a different configuration, please feel free to do so. Once the orchestration is done, you should see something like this:

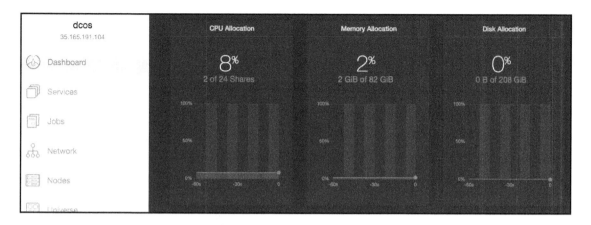

As you can see, it provides high-level resource allocation and usage details of the cluster. The cluster in the screenshot says that, out of 24 CPUs only two of them are used. The two of them are used by the Marathon package that was installed on this cluster. By default, the cluster will not have any packages or services running. You can install them from the universe of packages available for installation. They can also be installed from the DC/OS command-line interface. Our cluster has 82 GB of memory, out of which 2 GB is being allocated to Marathon. Similarly, our total disk space of 208 GB remains unused. The dashboard page provides more metrics, such as node count and task count. As I've already mentioned, this cluster has one master and five slaves, so you should see that there are six nodes in total. If you navigate to the **Nodes** tab, then you will see the list of all nodes and their resource utilization. There are two views that you can utilize in the **Nodes** tab: **Grid** and **List**. The **List** view is a traditional list-based view. However, the **Grid** view is interesting because it displays the nodes in the form of circles with the CPU utilization percent in them. The most amazing part about these widgets is that they get updated real-time. Also, the circles are color-coded based on the service that utilizes the resources on that node:

The preceding figure illustrates the grid view of the nodes. You can see that the last node uses 50 percent of its CPU, which is being utilized by Marathon. The **List** view looks something like this:

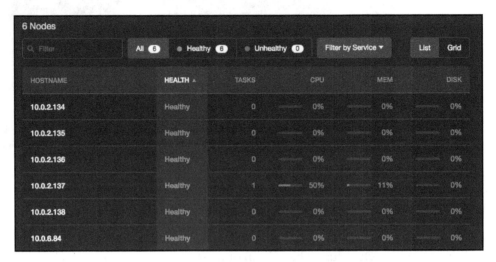

As you can see, in the **List** view, you can see the actual IPs of the slave nodes and their health status, task count, CPU utilization, memory utilization, and disk space utilization.

TASKS are nothing but Mesos tasks. DC/OS is backed by a Mesos cluster. So any task that is being submitted to this DC/OS cluster is actually submitted to the backing Mesos cluster. The services and packages that can be installed on DC/OS can be viewed from the **Universe** tab. The Universe is a package manager for DC/OS, where you can find all the packages and services that you can install on DC/OS. Kafka, Cassandra, Marathon, and ArangoDB are a few of the packages that you can install on DC/OS:

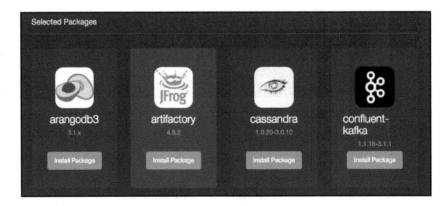

All it takes to install a package is to hit the **Install Package** button, or if you would like to use the DC/OS CLI, then it just takes one command to install packages. The newer version of DC/OS has the ability to spin off tasks from the UI. Previously, in order to spin off tasks, you had to use a CLI command. The true power of DC/OS is the ability to view a cluster of six nodes as one single machine and being able to utilize resources in a very granular manner.

Now let's come to the real usage of DC/OS in our context: microservices. We know that microservices by themselves cannot work alone; they need to work together with other tools such as Spark, Kafka, Consul, and Zookeeper. One good reason for using DC/OS is being able to manage them all under one roof: Marathon, load balancer, databases, middleware, and so on. There are several packages in the DC/OS Universe that can help us, including databases, middleware, and even microservice-management tools such as VAMP. If you would like to go with DC/OS, take some time to go over the list of packages and services that are available in the Universe. That way, you will know whether your architecture can be managed with DC/OS or not. One scenario where you might not be able to get the most out of DC/OS is when you are on the Hadoop Ecosystem. At the time of writing this, DC/OS has minimal support for using Hadoop. DC/OS has a framework for HDFS. But if you are already on the Hadoop Platform and use lot of its components, you might not be able to migrate them all over to DC/OS.

By now, you will either be very excited to learn more about DC/OS or you will have more questions about DC/OS. Either ways, it is strongly recommended that you go over DC/OS and its documentation before using it in production. With that said, we come to the end of this recipe. So far in this recipe, we've seen that DC/OS is a sophisticated cluster-management platform that not only helps us with microservice deployments but also manages our whole infrastructure. In the next recipe, you will learn more about Docker's clustering framework, called **Docker Swarm**.

Deploying containers with Docker Swarm

Docker Swarm is Docker's solution to clustering multiple Docker engines into one cluster. If your organization is heavily reliant on Docker and Docker containers, it might be worth looking at Docker Swarm. When you have several Docker installations that you maintain on separate Docker hosts, then these Docker hosts will be grouped together as a cluster using Docker Swarm. Docker Swarm brings in a whole lot of features that will help manage your apps on a Swarm cluster. Another great advantage of using Docker Swarm is that since it uses the Docker API, working with a Swarm cluster is no different than working with a Docker daemon. So tools such as Shipyard still continue to work with Docker Swarm. We will look at Shipyard later in this recipe.

Getting ready

At this moment, the easiest way to orchestrate a Docker Swarm cluster locally is by using `docker-machine` instances. Before you start the Docker Swarm cluster, let's familiarize ourselves with some concepts of Docker Swarm.

Docker Swarm comprises two types of nodes: manager and agent. A manager is responsible for scheduling containers and managing the cluster. An agent is the node where the containers are run. There can be several managers and agents, depending on the type of architecture you require. In our recipe, we will create a Docker Swarm cluster with one manager and one agent. So start two terminal sessions: one for the manager and the other for the agent.

How to do it...

1. The first step toward creating the Swarm cluster is creating `docker-machine` instances for the nodes themselves. Let's create our manager first. In the terminal session dedicated for the manager, issue the following command:

   ```
   docker-machine create --driver virtualbox manager && eval $(docker-machine env manager)
   ```

   > This command starts the new VM and sets the environment variables. Also stop any `docker-machine` instances that are not being used, in order to free up some resources.

2. Once your terminal session is ready, go ahead and SSH into the VM using the following command:

   ```
   docker-machine ssh manager
   ```

   > You should now be logged in to the VM as the `docker` user. Hereafter, we will be using some `docker swarm` commands.

3. First, we need to initiate a new cluster. For that we will need the IP of this Docker machine instance. Use the `docker-machine ip manager` command to find the IP of this instance. In my case the IP was `192.168.99.100`. Now go ahead and issue the following command on the same terminal:

   ```
   docker@manager:~$ docker swarm init --advertise-addr 192.168.99.100
   Swarm initialized: current node (93h99zo91q7o8cvc0s3pvlwvu) is now a manager
   ```

```
To add a worker to this swarm, run the following command:
     docker swarm join \
       --token
SWMTKN-1-1xd50ogywv31v4dmcg70tu15xqt7opsqds3qhe0zu8dp856krl-
arslqq0p4qhd85uj2qze4ei5q \
       192.168.99.100:2377

To add a manager to this swarm, run docker swarm join-token manager and
follow the instructions.
```

4. We have successfully set up our manager and initiated a new Swarm cluster. The result of the previous command actually gave us the command that we need to execute from the agent node to join this cluster. Before we move on, let's quickly verify whether our manager was created correctly by listing all the nodes participating in this cluster:

```
docker@manager:~$ docker node ls
    ID                    HOSTNAME   STATUS   AVAILABILITY   MANAGER STATUS
93h99zo91q7o8cvc0s3pvlwvu *   manager     Ready      Active       Leader
```

5. There is just one node in our cluster that acts as the Leader. The next step is to add a new agent node to this cluster. Now move on to the next terminal window that was dedicated for our agent. We are going to call this node worker. Go ahead and create this new VM first:

```
docker-machine create --driver virtualbox worker && eval $(docker-
machine env worker)
```

This command starts the new VM and sets the environment variables.

6. Once your terminal session is ready, go ahead and SSH into the VM using the following command:

```
docker-machine ssh worker
```

7. Let's issue the docker swarm join command that we received as output when we initiated the cluster on the manager:

```
docker@worker:~$ docker swarm join \
  >      --token
SWMTKN-1-1xd50ogywv31v4dmcg70tu15xqt7opsqds3qhe0zu8dp856krl-
arslqq0p4qhd85uj2qze4ei5q \
  >      192.168.99.100:2377
  This node joined a swarm as a worker.
```

8. We have successfully set up our agent. Now go back to the manager terminal session and execute `docker node ls` to verify whether there are two nodes in the cluster now. You should receive something like this:

```
ID                          HOSTNAME  STATUS  AVAILABILITY  MANAGER STATUS
3i78zp35bxmioy3dvdfmui3gv    worker    Ready   Ready         Active
93h99zo91q7o8cvc0s3pvlwvu *  manager   Ready   Ready         Active   Leader
```

That's it! You have successfully orchestrated a minimal `docker swarm` cluster.

9. Our next step would be spinning off our geolocation service on this cluster. Without any further delay, execute the following command to start the geolocation service on the cluster:

```
docker service create --replicas 2 --name geolocation
vikrammurugesan/geolocation
```

This command says that we would like to start two containers for the image `vikrammurugesan/geolocation` with the service name `geolocation`.

10. To list down all the services running in the cluster, execute the following `docker service` command:

```
docker service ps geolocation
ID              NAME IMAGE NODE    DESIRED STATE CURRENT STATE   ERROR
46zzwpszqfqvmmmqz0tx8rgo3   geolocation.1   vikrammurugesan/geolocation
manager   Running         Preparing about a minute ago
9ppgez120vme1p6fi4ko7mui1   geolocation.2   vikrammurugesan/geolocation
worker    Running         Preparing about a minute ago
```

11. If you would like to know more about your service, you could use the `inspect` command to do so:

```
docker service inspect --pretty geolocation
ID:     68jy7i3vwe88c2a797jri6anv
Name:    geolocation
Mode:    Replicated
Replicas:  2
Placement:
UpdateConfig:
Parallelism:  1
On failure:pause
ContainerSpec:
Image:    vikrammurugesan/geolocation
```

[354]

Resources:

> This console output has been truncated as it is lengthy. If you would like to view the output in JSON format, just omit the `--pretty` argument from the `inspect` command.

12. Now wait for the containers to start up. Before the containers try to start up, Docker will pull the image from Docker Hub first. So for the first time, it might take a few minutes depending on the size of your image. Great! Now the next thing that you might want to do is scale your microservice. Fortunately, Docker Swarm comes with a command to scale our services. Let's try to scale down our geolocation service to a factor of 1.

```
docker service scale geolocation=1
geolocation scaled to 1
```

13. Easy, isn't it? Now let's say you would like to delete this service; you would use the `docker service rm` command:

```
docker service rm geolocation
```

These are some of the basic operations you would want to do with your Swarm cluster. Of course, there are tons of other things you could do with Docker Swarm. But that is a little out of scope for our book, so we won't go any deeper. However, one of the most common things that you would want to do is being able to manage a Swarm cluster with ease. Command-line management will get a little trickier if your cluster is huge. That's where tools such as Shipyard, Rancher, and cAdvisor come into picture. Shipyard is a tool used for managing Docker containers and images. It also has the ability to work with private registries. Similarly, Rancher is a sophisticated tool for managing containers. cAdvisor is a little different as it is a monitoring tool for containers. You might also want to look at Docker's remote API, if you would like to automate deployments to Docker Swarm: `https://docs.docker.com/engine/api/`.

That brings us to the end of this recipe. In this recipe, we learned how Docker Swarm could be used to deploy our microservices. Of course, this is just an introduction. If you are interested in investing more time in Docker Swarm, read their documentation; it usually has everything you would need.

Deploying containers on YARN

In this recipe, you will learn how YARN can be used as a cluster to deploy applications. The framework used to deploy applications to YARN is called Apache Slider. At the time of writing this, Apache Slider is still in Apache's Incubator status. In order to learn Apache Slider, you will need a YARN cluster. For those of you who are not familiar with **YARN**, it stands for **Yet Another Resource Navigator**, and it is the cluster on which most of your Hadoop ecosystem operates. The goal of the Slider project is to provide the ability to run applications on the YARN cluster, scale them, and monitor them. In this recipe, I will only be able give you an overview of Slider as it is still nascent.

Getting ready

The first thing that you need is a YARN cluster. There are several ways to orchestrate a YARN cluster. You could orchestrate your own vanilla Hadoop cluster, or you could use platforms such as Hortonworks or Cloudera to make it much more easier. Using platforms such as Hortonworks or Cloudera comes with its own advantages. Read through their documentation and pick what is right for you.

How it works...

There are three main components in a YARN cluster: **Resource Manager**, **Node Manager** and **Application Master**. The **Resource Manager** is the core component of the cluster and is responsible for any resource allocation to applications. The **Resource Manager** performs this with the help of a **Scheduler** that allocates resources to applications based on the offer and priority. Resources are nothing but CPU, memory and disk space. The **Node Manager** is available on each node of the cluster and is responsible for spinning of tasks, monitoring resource usage and so on. Lastly, the **Application Master** is a framework specific component that is responsible for running the tasks on the nodes. The following diagram shows the components of a YARN cluster:

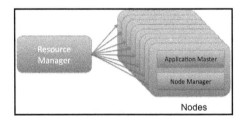

Slider is a command-line tool. At the core of Slider lies the YARN **Application Master** (**AM**), the Slider AM, and a client that communicates between YARN and Slider AM using APIs. The client is the command line interface that can be used to talk to Slider. To learn more about the working of Slider AM, please take a look at `https://slider.incubator.apache.org/design/architecture.html#am-architecture`. The Slider deployment requests indicate the resources required for the application as well as the details of the application. The deployment requests are usually in the form of JSON that looks very similar to Marathon's JSON request. There are two JSON documents that you need to provide in order to deploy applications using Slider: `resources.json` and `appConfig.json`.

The `resources.json` file is used to tell Slider how much resources (memory and CPU) should be allocated for that particular application. Some resource config options are `yarn.memory`, `yarn.vcores`, `yarn.container.failure.threshold`, `yarn.component.instances`, and `yarn.role.priority`.

While most of these properties are self-explanatory, `yarn.role.priority` might deserve an explanation. It is mainly used when you have multiple components. Components with the highest priority (`1`) will be orchestrated first.

The `yarn.container.failure.threshold` option indicates the number of times a component may fail within the given time window. The failure time window is usually indicated using three properties:`yarn.container.failure.window.days`, `yarn.container.failure.window.hours`, and `yarn.container.failure.minutes`.

The next JSON file that you will need is `appConfig.json`. While `resources.json` was more of a config file to Slider (or YARN), `appConfig.json` is mostly for the application. Two of the most important properties are `application.def` and `java_home`. In addition to this, you could add your own properties as well, such as JVM size. The `application.def` property indicates the location of the application package itself on HDFS. Usually, the application is packaged as a ZIP file.

Slider is currently CLI driven. Though Slider needs more features to become more sophisticated like other schedulers, it is currently the only available solution for YARN. If you are using YARN already, it is worth checking out.

To learn more about Slider, visit their *Getting Started* page: `http://slider.incubator.apache.org/docs/getting_started.html`. At the time of writing this, the link still lives in Apache's incubator domain. If this link is broken, feel free to visit Slider's website and navigate to their *Getting Started* page.

With that said, we come to the end of the recipe, the chapter, and the book. In this book, I have introduced you to a lot of technologies, tools, and frameworks. While it takes more than a book to make you an expert on each of them, my goal was to give you a head start and show you how to proceed and solve the most common challenges. Throughout the book, we have learned recipes to address most of the challenges that you will face when you move toward a microservice-based architecture, including *development, containerization, deployments, service discovery, load balancing, monitoring, logging,* and *streaming*. Of course, there will be more challenges as you start scaling out to hundreds and hundreds of microservices in your organization. But there are always tools and frameworks out there to solve them. I hope this book will help you out on your microservice journey. Happy microservicing!

Index

www.ingramcontent.com/pod-product-compliance
Lightning Source LLC
Chambersburg PA
CBHW062048050326
40690CB00016B/3022